Policing Pu

Policing Public Disorder
Theory and Practice

David P. Waddington

WILLAN
PUBLISHING

Published by

Willan Publishing
Culmcott House
Mill Street, Uffculme
Cullompton, Devon
EX15 3AT, UK
Tel: +44(0)1884 840337
Fax: +44(0)1884 840251
e-mail: info@willanpublishing.co.uk
website: www.willanpublishing.co.uk

Published simultaneously in the USA and Canada by

Willan Publishing
c/o ISBS, 920 NE 58th Ave, Suite 300,
Portland, Oregon 97213-3786, USA
Tel: +001(0)503 287 3093, USA
Fax: +001(0)503 280 8832
e-mail: info@isbs.com
website: www.isbs.com

First published 2007

Hardback
ISBN: 978-1-84392-234-6

Paperback
ISBN: 978-1-84392-233-9

British Library Cataloguing-in-Publication Data

A catalogue record for this book is available from the British Library

Project managed by Deer Park Productions, Tavistock, Devon
Typeset by Kestrel Data, Exeter, Devon
Printed and bound by T.J. International Ltd, Padstow, Cornwall

Contents

List of figures and tables

Acknowledgements

This book would never have been written were it not for the invaluable help and encouragement of numerous friends, colleagues, outside agencies and members of my family.

In March 2005, I underwent heart surgery at Sheffield's Northern General Hospital. The operation proved so successful that, within three months, I was able to participate in and observe a series of protests against the meeting of the G8 Justice and Home Affairs Ministers in Sheffield city centre. I will forever be indebted to the fabulous surgical team led by Mr Peter Braidley and the dedicated staff of the Chesterman wings of the hospital. I have them to thank for prolonging my life and making it possible for me to continue to work on the type of project you are holding in your hands.

Chapter 6 of this book comprises a case study of the Sheffield G8 protests. As on previous occasions, I am extremely grateful for the co-operation of local institutions like South Yorkshire Police, Sheffield City Council, BBC *Look North* and BBC Radio Sheffield, as well as those demonstrators who also consented to be interviewed.

The encouragement and support of colleagues in the Department of Communication Studies at Sheffield Hallam University have also been vital to the completion of this work. My good friends, Mike Beaken, Karen Grainger, Peter Jones and Martin Jordin, all acted as participant observers on my behalf during the G8 demonstrations. Others, like Chas Critcher and Noel Williams were kind enough to comment on draft chapters, while all of the above, with the addition of Brian Tweedale, ensured that my spirits seldom sagged while I was in the process of writing up these pages. Chas was also instrumental, alongside Simeon Yates (Head of the Communication and Computing Research Centre) and Olivia Baguste (Head of Human Resources), in ensuring that I was given sufficient study leave in which to complete the book. I am grateful to all three of them for their generosity and kindness.

Other people have also assisted me immensely. I have good reason to be thankful to my close friend and colleague, Professor Mike King of the University of Central England in Birmingham. Mike and I have worked on several projects together in recent years and, as ever, I occasionally turned to him for advice and reassurance. It was Mike who set up the meeting between me and Brian Willan (at an Indian restaurant in Philadelphia) that eventually resulted in our book contract. I am greatly indebted to Brian – and three anonymous reviewers of my book proposal – for having shown the requisite faith in my ability. Another good friend to whom I am most grateful is Phil Roddis of *People and Planet Communications* who kindly drew the map for me which appears in Chapter 6.

Finally, and most of all, I want to thank my wife, Joanna, my children (Jon-Paul, Laura and Joseph) and stepdaughters (Taraneh, Parissa and Yasamin) for all the goodwill they showed and all the sacrifices they made while I was in the process of writing up this work. Joanna helped me to design and produce the figures and tables appearing in the book but her overall contribution hardly ended there. Hers was the first face I saw when I came round after my operation – looking out for me as usual and making me feel extra glad to be alive, as she continued to do for the duration of this project.

David Waddington
Sheffield, England

Introduction

A very familiar ring

At approximately 3.45 p.m. on Wednesday, 6 July 2005, the United States President, George W. Bush, arrived at the Gleneagles Hotel Auchterarder, just outside of Edinburgh, for the annual G8 (Group of 8) summit meeting of the political leaders of America, Canada, France, Germany, Great Britain, Italy, Russia and Spain. It was also around this time that the leading section of a 10-thousand-strong anti-G8 protest march came to within touching distance of a section of the 6-foot-high, 5.5-mile-wide perimeter fence (a much-publicised 'ring of steel') standing between the G8 delegates and the outside world (Alexander 2005). Five rows of police in riot gear were stationed behind the fence, with a further row of mounted officers positioned at their backs. The overriding mood of the march had so far been peaceful, with its police escort showing commendable patience and good humour. Suddenly, though, a small section of marchers set about dismantling the fence and angrily confronted the police (*ibid.*).

March organisers frantically appealed to those involved to refrain from further violence, while stewards urgently exhorted other participants to continue on their way. Most people heeded the latter directive but the violent minority continued to throw objects and try to breach the barricade. Fifty metres to the right of this fierce encounter, the security fencing stretched out across an open field with only token signs of police protection. The only thing preventing access to this vast expanse of land was a 1-foot-high barbed wire fence, skirting the 'official' route of the march (*ibid.*).

Emerging from the centre of this mayhem, an African man carrying a cardboard coffin (in protest against the alleged genocide of

5 million Congolese in Rwanda) gracefully stepped over the barbed wire and walked, unopposed, up to the unguarded perimeter fencing. He was soon joined by some 1,500 other people. Members of this breakaway contingent then started pulling at a section of fencing adjacent to a plywood-covered watchtower. At first, the police were strangely unresponsive.

> Within ten minutes, however, the field resembled a battle zone and there were cries of disbelief that this was happening on Scottish soil. As the police horses on the far side of the cordon mysteriously retreated at 4.30 pm, an RAF Chinook helicopter appeared. It executed two circuits before touching down on the field on the far side of the cordon, yards from demonstrators. The doors flew open and out poured riot police who ran to the section of the fence where the demonstrators were. Two minutes later, police and dogs began running along inside the fence towards the demonstrators. Another Chinook screamed in and offloaded troops, just as an Army Lynx helicopter screamed past, in an atmosphere more like Bosnia than Scotland. The police horses re-appeared and charged towards protesters. It emerged that part of the security fence had been breached by protesters and, while none seemed to have got inside, riot police had run through the breach and were engaged in running battles, with hundreds of protesters running back across the fields. (*ibid.*)

After a brief period of confrontation, police equipped with batons and round, perspex riot shields succeeded in forming a restrictive arc around the protesters. Mounted police were then deployed to nudge the protesters back onto the official route of the march. A few stones, placards and sods of grass were defiantly thrown in the police's direction, though not sufficiently to prevent them from re-establishing complete control (Black *et al.* 2005).

The elaborate police fortification measures used to protect and isolate the G8 visitors to Scotland will have a very familiar ring to those of us with knowledge of preceding international summit meetings. Such people are also unlikely to be shocked by the un-compromising nature of the police tactics used to organise and disperse the crowd, since these, too, were reminiscent of methods applied at previous international events (della Porta *et al.* 2006). However, whilst it is inarguable that, in the course of the last two to three decades, public order policing in Western societies has become considerably more militarised (P. A. J. Waddington 2003), there is an obvious danger of characterising it too stereotypically. This possibility is illustrated by the fact that conspicuous variations were apparent, not only in the policing of subsidiary G8 meetings occurring prior to Gleneagles in the major English cities of Derby and Sheffield, but also in Edinburgh itself in the week containing the Scottish meeting of heads of government.

At the Derby meeting of G8 Environmental Ministers in March 2005, police drew a similar 'ring of steel' around the golf course location where the ministers were meeting and invoked public order legislation to restrict protesters to a small area of the city centre, miles out of reach of the summit venue. In Sheffield, in June 2005, police allowed a 1,000-strong march, days before the meeting of G8 Justice and Home Affairs Ministers, to proceed, without obvious restriction, through the city centre. During the actual meeting, though, police enforced a two-mile exclusion zone around the suburban hotel in which formal discussions were held. South Yorkshire Police then invoked public order legislation to severely restrict the size and location of two further protests coinciding with civic receptions for the delegates and their entourages. Though the policing of both these events was generally tolerant, police used batons, corralling techniques and snatch-squads to disable unscheduled marches.

The 2005 Scottish G8 summit meeting entailed a number of qualitatively different policing strategies. Prior to the actual summit period of 6–8 July, the city of Edinburgh hosted a 'Make Poverty History' (MPH) march by 225,000 people from families, faith groups and charitable organisations across the UK. The aim of the march was to impose pressure on the eight world leaders to help ease Third World debt, eradicate poverty in Africa and arrest climate change. Following appeals by the organisers, the majority of marchers wore white clothing with the aim of encircling the city with a 'white band' to simulate the symbolic wristbands worn in solidarity with the MPH movement.

Gorringe and Rosie (2006) emphasise that, despite gloomy and alarmist press predictions of mayhem and vandalism, the march proceeded amidst a 'carnival atmosphere' and only one arrest was made during the entire day. The solitary incident of disorder occurred around 2.15 p.m. when 200 officers in riot gear corralled a group of 60–70 protesters in black clothing (variously described as foreign anarchists, members of the Black Bloc or Y Basta) into Buccleuch Street. Police 'spotters' had shadowed the group which eventually attacked a nearby bar. Waste bins were overturned and bottles hurled at the police, whereupon 200 riot police with short shields immediately arrived on the scene. According to one team of reporters, 'The incident gave an insight into the police preparations. Reinforcements were quick to descend on the scene, and officers who changed into riot gear to confront the rioters immediately changed back into uniform once the fighting was over to calm the situation' (Gray *et al.* 2005). Once the reinforcements had backed off, uniformed colleagues moved in to remove protesters' face masks, carry out body searches and take down everyone's personal details. People were allowed to leave only when these formalities had been concluded (BBC News 2005; Duncan 2005).

The peaceful nature of this event contrasted with the disorderly outcome of the so-called 'Carnival for Full Enjoyment' procession through the city centre on Tuesday, 4 July. This protest reflected collective indignation regarding the contributory role of financial institutions in the generation of world poverty and indebtedness. The Lothian and Borders Police, who had not been informed before-hand of the marchers' intentions, reacted to what they perceived as possible threats to major city centre financial institutions by using corralling-in and snatch-squad procedures to contain demonstrators (Seenan and Vidal 2005). At one point, demonstrators were forced into Princess Street Gardens where they overturned park benches and used them offensively against police officers. Participants and bystanders caught up in the conflict complained about the in-discriminate and overzealous nature of police tactics (*ibid.*).

The day of the heads of state meeting saw further violence, not only at the summit venue in Gleneagles, but also in Edinburgh city centre and in other Scottish towns and cities, such as Stirling and Bannockburn. Disorder occurred in the early morning at the latter two locations when protesters spilling out of nearby 'eco camps' vandalised cars and business premises. Soon afterwards, Tayside Police cited these events as a basis for calling off the planned march at Auchterarder. This was the first of a series of confusing messages which left would-be protesters uncertain as to whether the protest was being allowed to proceed as scheduled. March organisers and campaigning journalists later accused the police of using 'under-hand tactics' to discourage protesters from attending. Among these accusations were that police had boarded coaches in Edinburgh and Glasgow to announce falsely that the protest had been cancelled; and that occupants of vehicles en route to Auchterader had been informed by police that they would encounter impassable road blocks or that they would not be allowed into Auchterarder due to the violence that was already under way (Gordon and Duncan 2005).

The breaching of the fence at Auchterarder brought a further diversity of police tactics into play. Television news broadcasts showed how, in the initial phases, police officers fiercely lashed protesters about their legs to force them to retreat. Subsequently, however, the police assumed a far more tolerant attitude. Pictures broadcast by *Sky News Live* showed a pair of officers patiently lifting and carrying one male protester who was staging a sit-down protest in defiance of their order to move back. The station's 'on-the-spot reporter' clearly regarded the police handling of this incident as part of a general strategy:

> I have to say that the police are being very restrained on this. They're gently, gently, edging forward. We have seen a few instances where the horses have charged across the field, but generally the police are advancing and then stopping and letting the protesters move back, and then advancing. But the police are always making that movement forward and the protesters are always in that reverse direction. (Reporter, *Sky News Live*)

Sky News's subsequent live pictures demonstrated that, having cleared the field, police officers then started to reason with the crowd (and, for that matter, media personnel), persuading them to follow the narrow road running between the grassland and local houses, back into the centre of Auchterarder.

The focus and structure of the book

As the above discussion indicates, the nature of contemporary public order policing is too variable and complicated to lend itself to trite or superficial analysis. It is precisely for this reason that this book is dedicated to the careful and dispassionate explanation of the processes by which the police understand and react to instances of public disorder, of variations in police tactics and strategies, and of the possible ways that such interventions (and *non*-interventions) can serve to enhance or, alternatively, attenuate the potential for collective violence.

One leading academic commentator on public order policing recently disclosed how,

> In my experience, what police officers want from academic analysis is not a manual of how to fight battles on the streets – they know that well enough. Instead, they want and need a wider understanding of why disorder erupts at all and with what consequences. Fortunately, this is something about which academic research has much to contribute. (P. A. J. Waddington 2003: 394)

Evidence comprehensively suggests that police officers of all ranks continue to subscribe to 'theories' of disorder which pathologise the motives and actions of the crowd as fundamentally irrational or prone to 'manipulation' by ill-intentioned individuals or subgroups (Reicher *et al.* 2004; D. Waddington and King 2005). King and Brearley (1996: 99) speak for the overwhelming academic consensus by insisting that, in order to maintain credibility, public order theory must recognise the underlying rationality of the majority of crowd members. 'Further, the dynamic potential of crowds must be acknowledged and the possible impact of police and other action on this dynamic process appreciated in order to arrive at a workable solution to the problem of controlling public disorder.'

These academic principles are rigidly subscribed to in the first two chapters of this book, which constitute its theoretical foundation. Chapter 1 focuses on the wide range of political, institutional, cultural and practical variables which help to determine police strategic and tactical approaches to public order. It also explores the possible ways that particular forms of police behaviour may arouse or, perhaps, nullify the potential for disorder. These themes are further considered in Chapter 2, which highlights relevant theories of public disorder as a basis for comprehending the implications of particular contexts and dynamics of police–citizen interaction for the instigation and development of conflict.

Subsequent chapters follow the precedent set by my earlier publications of using case studies of particular events as mechanisms for the gradual construction of argument (e.g. D. Waddington 1987, 1992; D. Waddington *et al.* 1987, 1989). Thus, Chapters 3–7 each incorporate case studies of salient contemporary examples of public disorder (occurring from 1991 to the present day). The intended function of these cases is to illustrate and augment the theoretical bases established in Chapters 1 and 2. To provide continuity and focus of discussion, the examples are primarily British or American.

As P. A. J. Waddington (*op. cit.*) points out, in Britain a shift has occurred in the last 15 years away from picket-line confrontations

associated with de-industrialisation to political conflict involving environmentalist issues or opposition to 'globalisation'. Similarly, while
the 'community disorders' of the early and mid-1980s were typically
waged by the police and African-Caribbean youths, in the early 1990s
it was the turn of the police and white, working-class youths, and in
2001, the police and Asian youths after an initial involvement by the
Far Right (*ibid.*). A common feature of both eras is the ongoing
problem of football hooliganism – perhaps less so domestically, but
certainly involving British fans travelling abroad (Dunning 2002;
Williams 2002).

In the United States of America, sporadic rioting occurred between
1991 and 2001 in major cities like Washington, DC, Los Angeles, New
York (twice) and Cincinnati. These conflicts reflected deteriorating
relations between the police and a diversity of American ethnic
minorities (Gilje 1995). Not surprisingly, given its status as the
world's acknowledged political (and economic) 'superpower', the
United States has also been at the epicentre of anti-globalisation
protests, including those held in opposition to the war against Iraq.
As Noakes and Gillham (2006: 97) point out, it was the confrontations
between police and demonstrators at the 1999 World Trade Organisation (WTO) Ministerial Conference in Seattle which set a particular
kind of benchmark for subsequent protests in other major world
cities:

> The WTO protesters' opening-day victory, the scale and
> intensity of the clashes between demonstrators and the Seattle
> police and the subsequent political activism inspired by the
> WTO protests have made *Seattle* a rich signifier for both activists
> and police. For political activists, it became an aspiration – a
> new standard for effective protests against which demonstrators
> measured their subsequent efforts . . . Emboldened by *Seattle*, a
> subset of demonstrators in each city insisted on their right to
> disrupt these events, leading to repeated clashes between police
> and protesters.

With the exception of Chapter 6, the remaining chapters of the
book use existing publications (primarily academic, though some are
official or journalistic) to analyse the policing of these contemporary
forms of public disorder. This reflects an academic commitment to
focusing on practical instances of public order policing – as opposed
to discussing relevant issues merely in the abstract. Thus, Chapters 3
and 4 focus on the policing of the American and British urban

disorders of 1991–2001, respectively. Chapter 5 considers existing analyses of the police tactics and strategies used to control anti-global protests around the world in the wake of the 'Battle of Seattle'. The sixth chapter of the book represents something of a departure insofar as it sets out a case study, based on recently acquired data, of the policing of the June 2005 G8 Justice and Home Affairs Ministers' meeting in Sheffield. The purpose of this in-depth example is to re-emphasise the importance and interrelationship of variables discussed in earlier chapters. Chapter 7 completes our emphasis on relevant case studies by focusing on the policing of English football fans travelling to European destinations in support of the national team.

The concluding chapter of the book draws together those variables that are fundamental to our understanding the nature of the policing of public order events. Though by no means intended as a manual or prescription for effective public order policing, the conclusion also dwells briefly on the policy implications of the preceding chapters. As Reicher *et al.* (*op. cit.*: 559) point out, effective (that is, trouble-free) public order policing is beneficial both to the police and the wider society:

> A whole career can be ruined in the blink of an eye. Not surprisingly, then, many police officers approach crowds with some trepidation. However, whilst it is perfectly true that a riot can set back the relationship between the police and a whole community, it is also true that effective public order strategies can transform relationships for the better. Indeed, it may be that such strategies may be one of the best ways in which one can begin to turn around a spiral of negative inter-relationships with marginalised groups in society. In short, good public order policing can have an impact way beyond the crowd.

Sensible policy recommendations are only as good as the theory on which they are based. With this in mind, we turn, in the first instance, to an outline of academic explanations of variations in police public order tactics and strategies, and of their potential to quell or contribute to conflagrations of disorder.

Chapter 1

Public order policing: theoretical approaches

Introduction

Despite obvious signs of a growing commitment by public order police in Western societies to softening both their methods and the image they try to project of themselves to the public, conspicuous examples sporadically emerge of their unfailing determination to contain and, if necessary, confront disaffected and dissenting sections of society (della Porta *et al.* 2006; Earl 2006). This chapter sets out a number of theoretical bases for interpreting consistencies and discrepancies in styles of public order policing, for explaining police choices of strategy and tactics, and for understanding the nature and consequences of police conduct in potentially conflictual situations.

The chapter begins by outlining and explaining the late-twentieth-century shift in dominant Western public order policing styles towards negotiation and restraint. A second, supplementary section then describes the repertoire of preventative measures used by police to offset possible confrontation and reinforce their perceived legitimacy. The third section of the chapter identifies some of the main political, institutional, cultural and pragmatic determinants of coercive police strategies and tactics that deviate from the contemporary norm. The fourth section looks at possible reasons for, and consequences of, aggressive police conduct while 'out in the field'. This is followed by a brief discussion of the argument that paramilitaristic police methods are the best means of ensuring that police officers exercise requisite standards of discipline and restraint. The final section of the chapter outlines a model of public order policing that usefully draws together elements of the preceding discussion, as well as highlighting other relevant factors considered necessary to explaining tactical and strategic variations and their implications for possible conflict.

From escalated force to negotiated management

There is widespread agreement among American and European scholars that the last three decades have seen a major transformation in the dominant style of public order policing (e.g. della Porta and Filliuelle 2004; McPhail *et al.* 1998; Noakes and Gillham 2006; P. A. J. Waddington 2000a, 2003). The seminal study on this subject is that of McPhail *et al.* (*op. cit.*) who identify and explain the way in which American public order policing has departed from the uncompromising 'escalated force' model of the 1960s, towards a softer and more tolerant 'negotiated management' approach of the 1970s and after. This shift has involved a greater respect for the 'rights' of protesters, a more tolerant approach to community disruption, closer communication and co-operation with the public, a reduced tendency to make arrests (particularly as a tactic of first resort), and application of only the minimum force required in order to control a situation.

McPhail *et al.* attribute this transformation to the criticism and de-legitimisation of the escalated force approach by several government-sponsored commissions set up to look into the urban unrest of the 1960s and the university campus and anti-war dissent of the late 1960s and early 1970s. Concerned by their own apparent capacity to inflame crowds, provoke disorder and attract criticism, the police were particularly receptive at this stage to the possibility of using alternatives to the principle of overwhelming force. Senior officers now considered it sensible to slacken their authority so as to increase the predictability of protest events and minimise the risk of violence. Thus, as Noakes *et al.* (2005: 239) point out,

> Police would under-enforce the law and negotiate with protest groups prior to a demonstration in an effort to establish mutually agreeable terms and conditions under which the demonstrations would be held. To reach such an agreement, police would help protest groups cut through legal red tape, protect permit-holding protest groups from counter-demonstrators and ignore minor violations of the law during demonstrations in exchange for compromises from protesters on the route of a protest march or the location of a rally.

European academics have commented on parallel trends in their countries towards softer policing styles. In the Old World, 'During the decades from the 1950s to the 1990s, protest control evolved towards more flexible forms based on a more liberal understanding of demonstration rights' (della Porta and Fillieulle 2004: 220). Change was slow-moving in the United Kingdom where, only after bitter industrial conflict, notably with the miners (in 1984–5), and the anti-poll tax débâcle (of 1990), did the policing of dissent settle into a more conciliatory groove (D. Waddington 1998). King and Brearley (1996) attribute the 'drift' to a more paramilitaristic style of policing in Britain in the period from 1970 to 1990 to the accumulated 'lessons' learned as a consequence of key 'watershed' events. Thus, for example, the police decision to strengthen their 'mutual aid' capacity and create their central co-ordinating agency, the National Reporting Centre in Scotland Yard, was a consequence of their officers being outnumbered by thousands of 'flying pickets' during the 1972 miners' strike. Similarly, the Bristol riot of 1980 and the 'wave' of urban disorders in 1981 led, not only to improvements in protective equipment, but also the publication of a secret ACPO (Association of Chief Police Officers) manual on riot-control techniques.

King and Brearley's explanation of the subsequent reversal of this dominant orientation of the British police back towards a more negotiated form of management has much in common with conclusions drawn by their American counterparts. Among the lessons drawn on the basis of (say) the set-piece confrontations of the miners' strike and the poll tax riot was that escalated disorder resulting from uncompromising police tactics not only endangered human lives, but was also uneconomical in terms of police resources and damaging to police legitimacy. For such reasons, the 1990s saw a 'move within public order policing towards pre-emptive and proactive investigation and prediction, whilst at the same time developing a more flexible (in terms of different levels of response), highly trained and mobile public order force' (ibid.: 100). As one of King and Brearley's respondents put it, 'The image is now of a more caring cop on the street in view of the public, with reserves all tooled up and ready to go in the backstreets' (quoted in ibid.: 78).

European and American scholars now agree that this drive to restore, maintain or, preferably, enhance the legitimacy, of police and state alike, lies at the root of more benign control tactics and strategies (della Porta and Fillieule, op. cit.; D. Waddington op. cit.). The following section gives close consideration to the variegated (and sometimes controversial) types of preventative measures used by the police both to achieve this primary objective and to offset the likelihood of confrontation.

Preventative police policies

An overview of preventative measures

The British academic, Peter Waddington, makes the point that, despite the fact that the Public Order Act 1986 greatly expanded the police powers to ban marches and impose conditions on marches and assemblies, constabularies throughout the United Kingdom have seldom resorted to this legislation. Waddington attributes this widespread reluctance to the determination of senior officers to avoid encountering two highly undesirable forms of 'trouble' (1998: 119).

On the job trouble refers to such potential problems as injury, violence, injury and damage to property, all of which may arise as a consequence of doing police work. *In the job trouble* alludes to the possible criticism ('flak' or 'fallout') consequent on controversial police action. This may take the form of internal criticism by superior officers or external criticism (e.g. from the media, courts, politicians or a public inquiry). Generally speaking, 'Confrontation is, therefore, a "recipe for trouble": an arrest for a minor offence could spark off a riot in which damage and injury result and an inquiry that threatens careers. Hence, confrontation is avoided' (*ibid.*: 120).

Police reluctance to invoke public order legislation (see also Burke and James 1998) reflects a number of pragmatic calculations, such as the unavailability of sufficient officers and the possibility that resulting court cases might generate precedents to prevent its future application (P. A. J. Waddington 2003: 409). Another major reason is that police know that to invoke various statutes would be to run the risk of trouble:

> Whereas the law is conceived by legislators as a means of resolving problems, its enforcement can actually create greater problems for the police. The police regard it as far easier to have a crowd assemble at a known venue and time, even if it is predicted to be hostile and unruly, than to have the same people, or even a significant minority of them, dispersed throughout central London creating havoc. Banning a march is a recipe for creating confrontation and being seen to do so. If the crowd become disorderly, the police want sufficient 'insurance'

to deal with it adequately, but they seek to avoid allegations of provocation. *The crowd must be seen to relinquish public sympathy by their actions before the police can afford to take forceful action.* (P. A. J. Waddington 1994a: 381, emphasis added)

This overwhelming police desire to avoid 'trouble' also helps to explain why they are staunchly committed to pre-event negotiation with representatives of protest groups (P. A. J. Waddington 1994b, 1998). As a rule, the police tend to assert control, not by invoking legal powers and resorting to coercion, but 'by mobilizing their social and organizational resources' (1998: 120). Waddington explains how senior police deploy all manner of 'interactional practices and ploys', and use their 'home ground advantage' and 'monopoly of expertise' regarding, for example, the most 'suitable' route for a march, to secure the compliance of the event organisers. This procedure is by no means automatically or universally applied: the police will consider long and hard whether organisers are suitably sincere and capable of delivering their parts of any bargain. Where police perceptions of organisers are negative, the former will resort to hard-faced 'insurance' tactics – i.e. having adequate numbers of well-equipped officers in reserve.

Assuming that negotiations proceed in good faith, the police will persevere with the application of other preventative measures:

Attempts subtly to extend maximum control over protest do not cease once prior arrangements have been made. On the day of any demonstration, senior officers seek to perpetuate a non-confrontational style by overtly displaying bonhomie toward the organizer and the protesters generally, keeping the police out of view of the protesters, and controlling the progress of the march by the careful orchestration of traffic flow around it. Senior officers commanding the operation often greet the organizer of the march in full view of other protesters: hand outstretched, they address the organizer by his or her first name from some distance away, advance smiling broadly, and warmly shake the organizer's hand. They eagerly accept any invitation to brief marshals, not only to explain the respective responsibilities of marshals and police, but also to emphasize the collaborative relationship they want to exist between them. Any action that threatens to disrupt the appearance of amicable relations is stoutly rebuffed. *(ibid.*: 122)

13

Correspondingly, senior officers strive to offset the likelihood of confrontational behaviour stemming from their own ranks. One common strategy they use is to ensure the appointment of suitably reliable intermediate commanding officers. Much attention is then devoted to guaranteeing that all sectoral commanders share a common perspective regarding the management of the event in question. A similar amount of effort is devoted to ensuring that constables and sergeants are thoroughly briefed in terms of what is expected of them. Senior officers will candidly concede that part of the function of such ritual is to enable them to 'cover their backs' in the event of any confrontation and ensuing inquiry (*ibid.*: 123).

Waddington concedes that, in the final analysis, preventative strategies are less concerned with achieving a genuine process of 'give and take' than with ensuring that the police achieve their objectives via the least confrontational means at their disposal. Accordingly,

> On the face of it, public order policing in contemporary Britain remains a triumph of 'policing by consent'. However, political protest is still largely conducted on terms determined by the police. In other words, their interests are served and in doing so the interests of protesters are, at least, compromised. Protest is emasculated and induced to conform to the avoidance of trouble. In police argot, protest organisers are 'had over'. (P. A. J. Waddington 1994b: 197–8)

Interviews carried out by King and Brearley (1996) with specialist police public order officers confirm that this emphasis on preventative police measures had become widespread by the mid-1990s. Their respondents acknowledge the importance of direct communication with protest organisers, intelligence and evidence gathering, and relevant training methods as ways of avoiding confrontation during demonstrations. For example, pre-event training ensures that officers are aware of a 'sliding scale' of possible responses to incipient or ongoing disorder as an alternative to 'panicky overkill tactics' (*ibid.*, 83). Effective pre-event intelligence gathering can also help senior officers to gauge an appropriate (and cost-effective) level of response. Finally, evidence gathering (e.g. the use of video surveillance teams) means that officers do not feel obliged to respond to every incident occurring around them. They have the option to follow up an incident afterwards, rather than attempting an arrest that could prove escalatory (*ibid.*: 81–83).

At the community level, police have been increasingly concerned with the routine monitoring of 'tension indicators' as a way of anticipating and offsetting disorder before its actual occurrence (*ibid*.: 87–92). The concept was imported from America in the 1980s, where organisations like the National Institute of Justice maintained that certain 'early warning signs' often gave notice of impending disorder. Among such indicators were: increased intergroup conflict; the physical and verbal abuse of police officers; attacks on police or fire vehicles; increased media coverage of police-related incidents; and a decline in public co-operation towards the police (Field and Southgate 1982: 25). In the British context, this has involved the routine monitoring and processing of any social, economic, political and environmental signs of impending disorder. These are passed on to 'intelligence officers' by such diverse sources as colleagues on the beat, neighbourhood watch schemes, the media and pressure groups.

The Association of Chief Police Officers is officially committed to maintaining the use of tension indicators (ACPO 2000: 20). Her Majesty's Inspectorate of Constabulary (HMIC) have expressed enthusiasm for such schemes without necessarily being impressed by the current state of the art:

> Effective tension indicator systems are essential in predicting the possibility of disorder. They allow forces time to work with their partners to minimise and manage the risk of disorder. The Inspection saw a number of examples of tension indicators in forces, but each had its limitations and as such no one model can be confidently recommended to forces. Her Majesty's Inspector urges the ACPO, through the Public Order Sub Committee, to continue to work in this area to develop a tension indicator system that is up to date, and informs decision making. (HMIC 1999: 62)

Controversial preventative measures

The impression just given of senior police working in benign fashion to prevent possible confrontations with sections of the public is counterbalanced by studies highlighting the use of ethically more dubious strategies. James (2006) gives prominence to this theme by outlining the diverse strategies used by senior police as alternatives to invoking public order legislation (the Public Order Act 1986 and the Police and Criminal Justice Act 1994) to deter New Age travellers from occupying land within their areas. Some senior officers choose to let the travellers stay where they have settled. Less tolerant forces endeavour to avoid the financial and public relations costs incurred in mounting a direct 'show of force' by engaging instead in various forms of 'guerrilla tactics'. These include policies of 'disruption' (e.g. obtaining the mobile telephone numbers of travellers and constantly calling them up to impede communication between them), 'destabilisation' (such as springing drug raids to engender a constant fearfulness of engaging in counter-cultural activities), 'spatial exclusion' (simply moving travellers on to the next county), or 'bunding', where the police and/or landowners deny access to land by (say) digging a ditch in front of it.

Similar observations have been made in relation to environmental protests. Since the 1990s, the police have been confronted by an increasingly sophisticated and 'professionalised' opposition. The so-called *Militant Environmental Activist* (MEA) (Button *et al.* 2002) makes extensive use of websites, guidance manuals and media manipulation, using them alongside such 'ecotage' activities as sabotaging plant and equipment, spraying graffiti, tree-spiking and intimidating personnel, in pursuit of their objectives. Traditional public order strategies have therefore been rendered obsolete. Unable to predict how many protesters are likely to turn up at any given site, or the tactics that they will employ on their arrival, the police are actively pursuing 'intelligence-led' strategies involving surveillance of key activists, monitoring communications, cultivating informants and deploying undercover officers. Any legal injunctions brought against the protesters are usually enforced during the night in order to catch them unaware and avoid set-piece confrontations. Here, as with the New Age travellers, an element of disruption has been involved: innovative use has been made of laws to deter 'stalking' by men and women, and secondary picketing by trade unionists to dilute the presence and resolve of protesters (*ibid.*).

It is therefore apparent that the police will engage in all manner of preventative measures, of varying degrees of overtness and legality, to offset direct confrontation with the public. A variety of authors have emphasised that the police commitment to negotiated management, far from being monolithic and unchanging, will vary in relation to different situations and the actors involved in them. The next section explores some of the main contextual influences and pragmatic considerations impinging on police attitudes, tactics and strategies.

Contextual influences and pragmatic considerations

Police impressions of the public

One crucial criterion in police decision-making is the extent to which protesters have become institutionalised as part of the political mainstream (P. A. J. Waddington 1994b, 2003). Noakes *et al.* (2005: 247–8) make a useful distinction in this regard between *contained* and *transgressive* protests. The former typically involve organisers and participants already familiar to the police. Such people can be depended upon to negotiate all aspects of the proposed demonstration in advance, employ predictable tactics, and generally 'police' themselves in ways that discourage contraventions of prior agreements. Police perceptions of demonstrators will be all the more favourable where the latter are older in years, middle-class and subscribe to political positions that are not 'diffuse and abstract' in nature.

> In contrast, transgressive protest groups are those who: are unfamiliar to the police or have established a reputation for disruptive behaviour; are unable or unwilling to reach agreement with police prior to a demonstration; employ innovative tactics that they do not reveal in advance to police; or are deemed likely to challenge police control of public space and engage in direct action tactics. Police also read certain characteristics as possible indications of transgressiveness. 'Bad' protesters include: professional protesters; those seen as pursuing abstract, diffuse or radical goals; and young protesters, who are believed to be ill-informed and easily manipulated by others. (*ibid.*: 248; see also Earl and Soule 2006)

According to Noakes *et al.*, the negotiated management style is likely to be adopted in protests characterised by 'contained contention', where the police and protest groups share an established relationship based on familiar rules of engagement. In similar vein, P. A. J. Waddington (1994b: 175) explains how, in recent years, such organisations as the Trades Union Congress (TUC), National Union of Students (NUS) and the Campaign for Nuclear Disarmament (CND)-led Campaign to Stop the War in the Gulf all received co-operation and respect from the Metropolitan Police due to their readiness to 'play the game'. In contrast, many new social movements had not yet had an opportunity to form reciprocal relations with the police –

hence, as we shall see in Chapter 5, there exists a mutual suspicion between them, marked by a strong potential for disorder.

Political determinants of police strategy and tactics

Political influence is a second important determinant of police public order strategy and tactics. Peter Waddington acknowledges that there are some circumstances in which the police feel under a professional obligation to 'die in a ditch' – i.e. resort to firm and confrontational measures, regardless of their implications for either form of trouble. Such circumstances typically involve elements of implicit or explicit political pressure which act on the police. On an implicit level, this may be related to the symbolic significance attached to particular occasions, locations and personalities, of which royal ceremonials, government buildings, and visiting foreign monarchs or political dignitaries are classic examples: 'Here, in-the-job trouble would be enormous if disorder was to erupt. Under this pressure, police feel compelled not only to enforce the law rigorously, but also to take action which is legally dubious' (P. A. J. Waddington 1993a: 350). Alternatively, it may take the form of a more tangible political pressure:

> Behind the police are powerful forces – government, state institutions, powerful economic and social institutions – all of which have a vested interest in 'digging' proverbial 'ditches' in which they would have the police 'die'. The order that the police are duty bound to uphold inevitably favours those powerful interests and so the room to manoeuvre is limited. (P. A. J. Waddington 2003: 415)

Jefferson and Grimshaw (1984) offer a complementary account of the influences shaping public order strategy. They suggest that chief police officers formulate their policies with regard to the views of three significant 'audiences': *legal audiences* (the courts, police authorities and the Home Secretary); *democratic audiences* (politicians and the community at large); and *occupational audiences* (their immediate colleagues of all ranks and the wider police community). The mass media are seen as playing a crucial role in arbitrating between the views of the differing democratic audiences:

> The mass media are particularly influential in this process of the representation of interests. They are the most powerful

mediators of public opinion, in their self-claimed role of 'public watchdogs'; they also partly construct it, given their unparalleled ability to determine whether interests are reconstructed in negative ('sectional' or 'partisan') or positive ('universal' or 'public') terms. Public opinion, then, as represented in the media, is a highly influential determinant of a chief constable's response to democratic audiences. (*ibid*.: 86–87)

Each of these approaches stresses to some extent the importance of the political context in informing police decision-making *leading up to* a public order event. Indeed, taken together, they provide a comprehensive overview of the political factors impinging on police policy (see Figure 1.1). A recent example of the way that societal influence infiltrates this process concerns the events of September 2000 in the UK, when Britain experienced a sudden fuel crisis following a nationwide blockade of petrol refineries by thousands of farmers and road hauliers seething at the growing levels of fuel duties. Dohery *et al*. (2003) speculate that fundamental to the protesters' success in committing the New Labour Government to dealing with their demands were the attitudes of the oil companies, the police and the mass media. The sympathetic orientations of these parties also helped to ensure that the policing of the movement was far less repressive than it was (say) during the miners' strike of 1984–5.

The police contribution to this debate was exemplified by the comments of the president-elect of the Police Superintendents' Association, who clearly saw the police use of legislation as inappropriate:

Policing by consent is what it is all about in Britain. It would be appalling to go back to the way things were during the miners' strike. We don't want to get involved with that again. The government introduced laws to deliberately take on the miners in an industrial dispute and even then took nine months [sic] to defeat them. This is not an industrial dispute in the same way. It is a dispute involving an industry but there are different parties involved so those powers cannot be used. The government and the police have to respect the fact that these protests seem to have widespread public support. (quoted by Bagguley 2000: 19)

Ultimately, however, the government took a hard line against the protesters and police methods grew correspondingly uncompromising towards them (Doherty *et al*. 2003: 15–16).

On-the-spot decisions

The police's sense of accountability to different audiences also provides a useful basis for explaining the *on-the spot decisions* made by commanding officers caught up in the heat of public order events. Cronin and Reicher (2006) studied this process by engaging Metropolitan Police Service officers of the rank of chief inspector or commander in a 'table top' exercise requiring them to make decisions on strategy, tactics and how to deploy resources with regard to a march and rally of 5,000 anti-Fascists in opposition to a British National Party (BNP) candidate in forthcoming local elections.

Cronin and Reicher identify two forms of accountability impinging on the decision-making process. *External accountability* reflects a general concern with how audiences outside the police force – the wider 'community' – are likely to look upon police actions. This might include political representatives, direct political pressure or, more often, 'formal investigatory procedures', including public inquiries. *Internal accountability* refers to the views of fellow officers. Maintaining a good reputation among one's peer group of senior officers was seen as 'critical both to social acceptance and to career advancement' (ibid.: 185). Also important, though, were assumptions regarding the feelings of rank-and-file colleagues. Especially in situations of danger, involving possible risk of injury,

> The concern of senior officers was that, however good the strategies that they set, their ability to deliver these strategies depends upon the cooperation of junior officers. If junior officers disapprove of command decisions (which is particularly likely where permissive policing increases the likelihood of injuries to front line officers), then these officers can and do subvert the command strategy. (*ibid.*: 186)

Cronin and Reicher report that the amount of weight given to particular forms of accountability is likely to vary according to the phase reached in the occurrence of disorder. Thus, at the *non-conflict phase* of events, senior officers displayed a heightened preoccupation with the way that tactical interventions might be perceived by external audiences, especially as, 'To intervene where there is no violence can lead to accusations both of denying rights and of provoking violence' (*ibid.*). There was less of a concern at this stage of the proceedings with the possible views of junior officers. At the *incipient phase*, where conflict appears to be brewing, the different forms of accountability were more in balance, frequently placing officers in tactical dilemmas:

> While it might be slightly harder for external audiences to hold commanders to account for provoking violence that has already started, they can still be held responsible for escalating a minor problem by intervening too early. On the other hand . . . their own junior officers may undermine command strategies if they do not intervene. (*ibid.*)

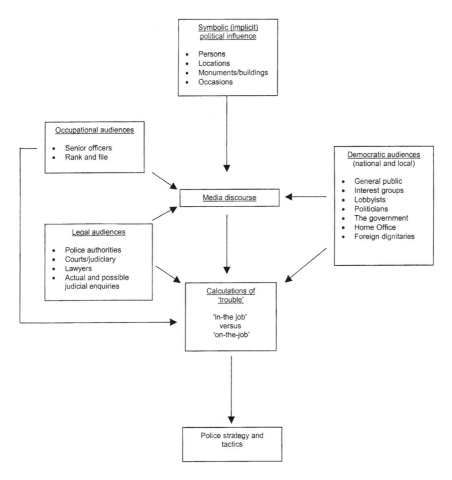

Figure 1.1 Political determinants of police strategy and tactics

One commonly stated solution to this dilemma was to have officers 'kitted up' in riot gear but carefully deployed out of sight to avoid unnecessarily provoking the crowd. By the time that the *conflict phase* had been reached, such a dilemma no longer applied. Senior officers generally assumed that neither external nor internal audiences were likely to criticise the police for inflaming violence at this phase. Rather, they were likely to criticise any failure to intervene given the dangers to police and public alike.

Once police commanders have taken the important decision to engage their junior colleagues in tactical intervention, the nature of any subsequent interaction with the public will have crucial implications for the instigation and development of possible confrontation. The following section sets out some possible explanations of police conduct in the field and of its implications for public disorder.

Explaining police conduct and its outcomes 'in the field'

Cultural predisposition

One common way of conceptualising police actions is by invoking the notion of the police occupational subculture or 'cop canteen culture', defined by Holdaway (1983: 2) as 'a residual core of beliefs and values, of associated strategies and tactics relevant to policing, [which] remains a principal guide to the day-to-day work of the rank-and-file officer'. Advocates of this approach maintain that such core characteristics of the police occupational subculture as its internal solidarity, machismo and action-orientation, its pragmatic approach to getting the job done, and its negative stereotyping of dissenting groups (be they black youths, miners or political demonstrators) are likely to play a part in creating or exacerbating confrontation (Reiner 1985). Police negativity is likely to be most keenly directed at those groups that respectable sections of society have designated as *police property*. This refers to those categories which are perennially stigmatised as 'problematic or distasteful' (including ethnic minorities, culturally dissenting youths and politically radical organisations). As Reiner points out, the wider public is generally disposed to give the police *carte blanche* to deal with their 'property' as they see fit.

Culturally-mediated typifications of crowd order situations and 'recipes' of how best to handle them are apparent in interviews with lower-ranking English Police Support Unit officers (Stott and Reicher 1998a) and endorsed by a questionnaire survey of similar personnel employed in English and Scottish forces (Drury *et al.* 2003). In each study, officers adopted the standpoint that the majority of people present in football crowds and at demonstrations typically comprised ordinary, 'respectable' people. This generally benign impression was heavily qualified by the belief that such individuals were likely to become irrational and violent once immersed in the crowd. At such times, the 'mindlessness' of the majority made them susceptible to sinister suggestion and manipulation by the deviant few, seen to be adept in the art of agitation. This perception of the crowd as inherently violent and easily led underpins the distrust and fear of junior officers and helps to explain the related beliefs that crowds must be strictly controlled, rather than being left to their own devices, and that all interventions should be uncompromising and decisive to prevent the 'contagion' from spreading.

Stott and Reicher (*op. cit.*) qualify their argument by insisting that it is unhelpful to assume that police views of crowd disorder and its management are entirely undifferentiated. They emphasise that senior commanders are more likely to balance the dangers confronting public order police against the risk (say) of denying fundamental civil liberties. Often, rank-and-file colleagues are exasperated by their superiors' reluctance to sanction interventions against crowds apparently acting in total breach of the law. One possible explanation is that junior officers, being literally on the front line, are the ones most liable to get hurt in the event of crowd disorder.

Experiential, practical and organisational considerations

Stott and Reicher's study illustrates some of the practical problems faced by rank-and-file officers when dealing with crowd disorders. For one thing, the difficulty involved in discerning precisely who among a crowd of several hundred actually threw a brick or bottle often creates a tendency to treat all members of the crowd with similar levels of hostility. Problems are exacerbated by another routine feature of riot policing – the necessity to wear adequate protection:

> Riot gear consists of fireproof overalls, a visored helmet and shield. Both the visor and the shield are made from Perspex which is characteristically scratched and scuffed from previous

use. Looking through the visor alone, but especially when the shield is held up as well, one's vision is blurred and it is hard to make out the features of individual crowd members. One is faced with a sea of indistinguishable faces and identifying who did what becomes even more difficult. In order to overcome such problems, the police do employ special surveillance techniques. Nonetheless, especially for those officers directly facing crowd members, the crowd is perceived and experienced as an undifferentiated entity. *(ibid.*: 521)

These problems become compounded wherever there is a tactical requirement to remove a particular threat in its entirety (e.g. by dispersing a crowd, shifting it *en masse*, or dividing it up into smaller units). Such tactics are difficult to pull off without treating the crowd as an undifferentiated entity. When this happens, police tend to rationalise their conduct on the grounds that, 'On being told to disperse, any well-meaning crowd member would have left. Hence, by the time the police intervene, anyone who is still there must have illegitimate motives and therefore is a legitimate target of police action' *(ibid.)*. Finally, junior officers protest that they simply do not have the necessary time or information at their disposal with which to make decisions regarding the 'guilt' or 'innocence' of specific individuals. 'If officers were to pause and deliberate on what each individual deserved while sweeping a street, the tactic would rapidly grind to an ineffective halt' *(ibid.*: 522).

Other experiential factors are highlighted by Marx (1970) in his comprehensive critique of the policing of the American urban riots of the 1960s. Marx argues that particular forms of police behaviour may have the unintended effect of contributing to disorder, rather than stifling its development. Thus, even at the pre-riot stage, the police are sometimes guilty of overdramatising the situation and needlessly drawing large crowds by arriving in great numbers, their car lights flashing and sirens loudly wailing. Invariably, their initial instinct is to forcibly disperse the gathering crowd, even where it might be more advisable to allow the public's understandable curiosity to be satisfied. Marx believes that too much prior planning and preparation may well prove detrimental, by inducing a premature 'siege mentality' among officers and creating a self-fulfilling prophecy.

According to Marx, once disorder is under way, signs of police reticence or weakness may be seized upon by opponents:

An additional problem may emerge if police lack the power to clear the street or, as in Detroit, to control it once it has been cleared. In Newark after an angry crowd pelted the police station with rocks, bottles, and a few fire bombs, police made several sorties into the crowd using their clubs, and each time withdrew back into the station. Such a seesaw motion, in demonstrating police ineffectiveness and the crowd's parity with control officials, may have emboldened rioters. (*ibid.*: 38)

Against this, *too much* force may have the unintended effect of 'creating martyrs and symbolic incidents' which draw other participants in due to a 'bystander effect'. An absolute failure to negotiate can have similarly catastrophic consequences – especially where there are specific and well-articulated grievances (concerning, for example, a particular instance of police brutality), where there is a degree of organisation among the rioters, and where potential mediators and/or 'counter-rioters' have identified themselves.

Marx sees a lack of co-ordination among units as especially inimical to effective riot control. One major problem confronting the police was that the decentralised and autonomous nature of regular patrol policing was not transferable to a situation requiring tight organisation and co-ordination. Further, specialist units drafted in to quell disorder often lacked familiarity with the local area and were not attuned to the particular sensibilities of its people. Compounding all this was the fact that complicated and largely untested procedures for mobilising and co-ordinating the various control agencies often malfunctioned:

Whereas the inability to admit failure, bureaucratic entanglements, petty rivalries, and political considerations all delayed the calling out of higher levels of force, the lack of prior planning and an unclear chain of command meant further delays once other control agents finally did arrive on the scene. Local, state, and national guard units did not merge easily. Guard units, accustomed to acting in patrols, were fragmented and guardsmen were isolated from commanding officers; police, who were usually organized as one- or two-man autonomous patrol units, were to become disciplined members of military units, relying on commands from superiors and not on their own discretion. While officers from different units were together, they were often responding to separate orders. (*ibid.*: 46)

Marx observed how, in some instances, senior officers froze due to the political enormity of the decisions they were required to make. During the Watts (Los Angeles) riot of 1965, for example, commanders were in a virtual state of denial, resulting in the misfeeding of information downwards: 'Early on the third day of the riot, field forces knew the situation was out of control but the downtown command post was still optimistic. This is the classic problem of information flow in a bureaucracy' (ibid.: 47). Technical problems also had a telling effect. Often, particular radio frequencies were overtaxed and the different agencies of social control (e.g. local police, state troopers and National Guard) were literally not on the same wavelength and therefore unable to communicate with one another. The extent of the resulting confusion is illustrated by the fact that police and guardsmen sometimes opened fire on one another, each labouring under the misapprehension that they were being targeted by snipers.

It was also apparent to Marx how the abnormal and disorientating nature of the situation in which officers found themselves was a key factor in riot development. The mere fact of being required to work taxing 12-hour shifts, with the distractions and discomfort of hunger and uncertainty to contend with, was demanding in itself. Police officers were often fazed, as well, by the size and severity of the disorder and found themselves rushing from place to place, frequently in response to deliberate false alarms: 'As large numbers of people taunted, defied, insulted, and attacked them and they saw their fellows injured and in some cases killed, patience thinned and anger rose. Rumors about atrocities committed against them then spread' (ibid.: 49). The situation was then ready for escalation as priorities like not losing face, avoiding humiliation, taking control of 'turf' and exacting revenge all emerged. Such contexts invariably produced weakened or ruptured chains of command and com-munication, and senior officers found their capacity to effectively control their men considerably undermined (ibid.).

Finally, Marx comments on the lack of internal and external accountability acting on officers involved in the riots. The costly and time-consuming nature of civil damage suits against the police made this an unlikely avenue of redress for individuals on the receiving end of police atrocities. Insofar as formal mechanisms of accounta-bility were concerned, Marx notes that even the now-defunct Civilian Review Boards tended to have no formal powers of enforce-ment and could not instigate inquiries into police conduct. Similarly, police internal review procedures were not sufficiently independent to inspire public confidence or police apprehension. Thus, as Marx (*ibid.*: 54) points out, 'Knowledge that they are unlikely to be subjected to post-riot sanctioning may have lessened restraints on their use of violence.'

The paramilitary policing debate

How to ensure that public order police carry out their responsibilities with the utmost discipline, proficiency and restraint is therefore an issue of great significance. This matter is central to the so-called paramilitary policing debate. The staunchest advocate of the paramilitary approach is Peter Waddington (P. A. J. Waddington 1987, 1991, 1993a, 1994a and b). Waddington usefully characterises this style in terms of its emphasis on: the use of protective shields and clothing by specialist units, trained in the use of squad formations and controlled force; intelligence gathering, surveillance and planning; and, crucially, the imposition of direct command and control by immediate senior officers. Within the modern public order policing hierarchy, it is the most senior officer, the 'Gold' commander, who is responsible for determining overall strategy. Forward ground command is undertaken by 'Silver' who is charged with the actual implementation of such strategy. He or she is assisted in this task by 'Bronze' commanders, each of whom has responsibility for particular units operating within designated pieces of territory (P. A. J. Waddington 1994b: 26). It is thus evident that, 'Instead of leaving individual officers to take uncoordinated action at their own discretion, a paramilitaristic approach deploys squads of officers under the direction and control of their own superiors' (P. A. J. Waddington 1993b: 353).

This emphasis on clear lines of command and effective co-ordination is regarded by Waddington as the key to eradicating inherent tendencies for officers to 'lose it' in the heat of the battle:

Policing civil disorder engenders fear, anger and frustration amongst officers who are often too close to the action to understand what is occurring. The feeling that one has lost control and is at the mercy of unpredictable events only heightens anxiety. The opportunity to take forceful action allows not only for the expression of these emotions, but is exhilarating in its own right. For all these reasons, it is essential that officers engaged in public-order situations are carefully supervised and controlled, for internal controls on behaviour are unlikely to prove reliable. (P. A. J. Waddington 1991: 137)

Waddington maintains that the traditional, non-paramilitary style of policing involves the risk of disorganised forays by individual police officers acting on their own discretion. Such actions often fail to discriminate between the 'innocent' and 'guilty', thus serving to undermine police authority and provoke violent crowd reactions. He considers it more advisable to deploy well-trained, effectively led, paramilitaristic units, operating on the basis of sound intelligence and pre-formulated strategy and tactics (P. A. J. Waddington 1993b: 366). 'Real time' intelligence is regarded as imperative, due to the fact that 'evidence gatherers and intelligence cells, working in co-ordination with arrest squads, target particular offenders in an unruly crowd and direct officers selectively to arrest those individuals for which evidence exists' (*ibid.*: 356–7). Sensations of injustice are therefore minimised. Other probable benefits are: the unlikelihood that *ad hoc* actions undertaken by officers, individually or in groups, will cause panic and anger among civilians; and the fact that senior officers in charge of paramilitary units will be held directly accountable for the actions of their subordinates (P. A. J. Waddington 2000a: 166).

The case for *avoiding* the use of paramilitary methods is robustly argued by another British criminologist, Tony Jefferson, who asserts that paramilitarism has an 'inherent capacity to exacerbate violence'. Jefferson (1987: 51–3; 1990: 84–6) posits an 'ideal-typical sequential account' of four distinct phases in the customary paramilitary scenario. He refers to these as: *preparation, controlling space, controlling the crowd,* and *clearance.*

In the *preparation* (or 'standby') phase, apprehensive units of (mostly male) police officers, all harbouring strong expectations of trouble, anxiously exchange 'disparaging stories' about the enemy and trade 'precursory justifications' for their forthcoming inter-vention. In such a tense climate, the sight of armoured police vehicles and 'tooled up' riot personnel enhances the possibility of a self-fulfilling prophecy (Jefferson 1987: 51). Preliminary attempts at *controlling space* – i.e. demarcating those areas where it is permissible for the crowd to congregate – can be equally provocative, especially when carried out with truncheons drawn and shields at the ready (Jefferson 1990: 85). Jefferson contends that verbal or physical retalia-tion by protesters will serve only to confirm the police anticipation of trouble and reinforce their readiness for battle (*ibid.*).

Once the event is under way and police are engaged in *controlling the crowd*, there is every possibility that other elements of the para-military approach will exacerbate existing anger and indignation. The spectacle of horses, dogs and officers in riot gear is likely to turn police into the 'legitimate' targets of stone-throwers. Snatch-squads will inevitably intervene, though not in the disciplined and restrained manner envisaged by Waddington. This is because such units not only have the law on their side, but also possess 'a conception of supportive teamwork and an occupational culture which requires that the most aggressive and bull-headed individuals be supported in the field and defended in the aftermath, and an ideology of the demonstrator as violent sub-human undeserving of either respect or sympathy' (Jefferson 1987: 52).

The attempted restoration of order will require nothing less than a 'massive and highly oppressive police presence' (Jefferson 1990: 85). Having achieved this, the police will then make up their minds as to when the point of the protest has passed and it is therefore time to instigate the *clearance* phase. Given their existing feelings of indignation at the way they have been treated, some demonstrators may prove resistant to police orders. Superior force will undoubtedly ensure short-term success for the police but that does not necessarily produce a conclusion of the matter. Protesters will return, more determined and better prepared, on a subsequent occasion (Jefferson 1987: 53).

The degree to which paramilitarised policing methods might serve to nullify or promote existing tendencies to violence may ultimately depend on various contingencies already highlighted in this chapter. It seems reasonable to suppose that, in situations where the legitimacy of police actions is recognised by a sizeable majority of the crowd, decisive use of reasonable force is unlikely to be resisted by anyone other than a misbehaving minority. Such use of force will, in turn, be more reasonably applied in circumstances where the prevailing climate of political opinion is sympathetic to the crowd and where briefing by senior officers emphasises the need for tolerance and restraint. Alternatively, political climates advocating the uncompromising policing of dissenting groups (such as that prevailing in the 1984–5 miners' strike) will undoubtedly encourage the type of unrestrained aggression predicted in Jefferson's worst-case scenario.

An explanatory model of differing styles of policing

Several aspects of the above analyses have been incorporated into *A Model for the Explanation of Protest Policing Styles*, developed by the Italian academic, Donatella della Porta in conjunction with her colleagues (della Porta 1995, 1998; della Porta and Fillieulle 2004; della Porta and Reiter 1998). The model (see Figure 1.2) encompasses several variables, including: the dominant legal framework; institutional characteristics of the police; the prevailing police and societal cultures; governmental and other political influences; public opinion and the media; and police–protester interaction. It serves the useful functions of reiterating and showing the interrelationship between variables already referred to in this chapter, and of introducing important complementary factors, hitherto unmentioned.

Among the institutional factors thought relevant to explaining particular styles of protest policing is the *legal framework* in which control strategies are implemented. Of particular importance are the *constitutional rights of demonstrators* (e.g. the extent to which legislation permits them to freely assemble and express their political points of view). For example, della Porta and Reiter (1998: 10–11) point out that in Italy a battery of fascist laws remained on the statutes until the mid-1950s, restraining the right of protest and permitting coercive intervention by the police.

A second major variable is that of police organisational structure. Three aspects of this (centralisation, accountability to the public, and militarisation) are central to the model. *Centralisation* refers to the degree to which control over the police is centrally directed by the national government or is subject to the discretion and influence of local police commanders and/or civilian authorities. *Accountability to the public* concerns the degree to which police officers can technically be made answerable for their actions (e.g. because of the requirement to wear identification numbers, because their actions are subjected to a process of independent review, or due to the availability of a robust civilian complaints procedure). Finally, *militarisation* of the police refers to the extent to which the police operate according to military-style discipline or in liaison with the army. As della Porta and Reiter explain,

> In general, a militarily organized police force is considered to be more prone to brutality since it implies a hierarchical organization with 'blind' obedience to order. Looking at the evolution of

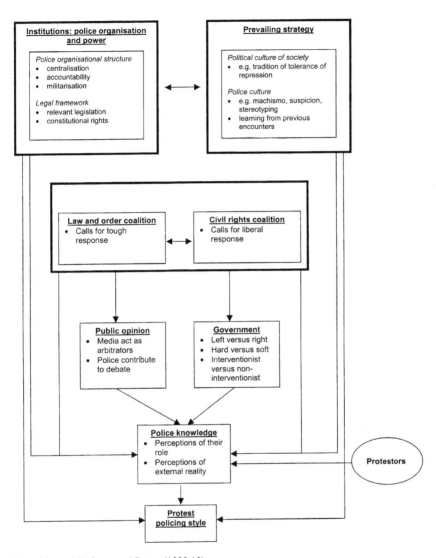

Adapted from della Porta and Reiter (1998:10)

Figure 1.2 Adapted version of della Porta and Reiter's Explanatory Model of Different Styles of Policing

the British police, however, several scholars noted that militarization, with its implication of stricter control on rank-and-file officers, could actually help prevent brutality. (*ibid.*: 11)

In-built tendencies within the *police occupational culture* to machismo and suspicion may generate a predisposition to repressive behaviour. della Porta and Reiter recognise that the culture is functional to police work. In particular, the need to make snap decisions almost inevitably encourages the formulation of shorthand stereotypes and typifications of protest groups and situations likely to prove dangerous or troublesome. Accordingly, they provide guidelines for possible interventions (*ibid.*: 14).

A second aspect of culture – this time, the wider *political culture of the host society* – is fundamental to understanding longstanding styles of protest policing. As della Porta (1995) points out, protest policing is very much influenced by national history and tradition. For example, the World War II fascist regimes in Italy and Germany each left an 'institutional and emotional legacy' encouraging the police to come down hard on public displays of protest. della Porta explains that such legacies are never fixed or immutable and that 'traumatic events can stimulate learning processes'. Moreover, challengers to the political orthodoxy may find themselves and their methods of pro-testing initially subjected to repressive policing, before they are gradually accepted into the mainstream (*ibid.*: 74).

A more contemporary political determinant of the nature of protest policing is the prevailing *configuration of power* – chiefly, the influence wielded by the government of the day. Though ostensibly neutral, protest policing is heavily subject to government influence. della Porta and Reiter (1998: 15) explain that the management of demonstrations tends to be less repressive when left-wing govern-ments hold office. However, this rule is by no means hard and fast: 'the Left' may sometimes strive to appease proponents of a 'law and order' approach or establish its credentials as the 'party that is fit to govern'.

Police policies, as well as the direction given to them by govern-ment, are further influenced by the opinions of other parties, such as the protesters, their opponents, and all manner of other political and interest groups. These opinions are typically filtered through the mass media. It is by such means that 'civil rights coalitions' advocat-ing tolerant policing or, alternatively, 'law and order coalitions' seeking tougher police interventions, attempt to hold sway. The media acts as an arbitrator in this debate, 'partly as a "spokesperson" of one or the other coalition and partly with their own "autonomous" logic' (*ibid.*: 18).

della Porta's (1998) interviews with Italian police officers show how the latter base their choices of tactics and strategy on the anticipated public reaction to their policies. Nevertheless, police actions sometimes deliberately fly in the face of dominant public opinion: 'This is especially true when the police enjoy unlimited government support and receive clear directives, that is, if they know that the difficulties of the job, considerable if they have to suppress a large minority, are outweighed by the possible trouble that could result if they fail to follow the government's orders' (*ibid.*: 19). Indeed, della Porta makes the related point that, whatever the actual tenor of popular opinion may be, the Italian officers see themselves as 'King's police' – ultimately loyal to, and answerable to, the government of the day.

At the micro level of analysis, della Porta and Reiter refer to the context and nature of the interaction between police and protesters as other important variables influencing the policing of protest events. They argue, for example, that the prohibition of a demonstration is often a key factor in encouraging subsequent 'violent dynamics' (*ibid.*: 20). More generally, they observe that police officers 'seem to be equipped with an elephant's memory' in terms of allowing any history of previous interaction with protest groups to shape current strategy and tactics (ibid.). Memories of having come off 'second best' may rankle among the police and invite pressure from their detractors:

> Individual incidents may have long-term repercussions on police attitudes toward protest. If the image of a 'weak' police – especially when 'promoted' by political entrepreneurs – can produce fear in the public and calls for more 'effective' repression, the impression of having been 'defeated' will also have important consequences within the police. These consequences go beyond immediate reactions such as promises to take revenge, and extend to tactical and structural changes. (*ibid.*: 21)

In attesting to the significance of interactional dynamics, the model reasons that conflict escalation is invariably due to indiscriminate or heavy-handed police dispersal tactics. Such actions sometimes result from problems in co-ordinating different units of officers, from uncertain chains of command or lack of clarity of tactical objectives. There is a further risk involved in introducing officers from outside forces who do not share local sensibilities or knowledge of the area. In cases where peaceful demonstrations have been 'infiltrated' by smaller, radical groups, police tactics aimed at neutralising the activities of the violent core may contravene the rights of the majority and draw them into the conflict. Looking ahead to the next time the police and protesters meet, there is a danger that atrocities committed by one side or the other this time may produce a 'reciprocal adaptation' of their tactics (della Porta 1995).

The above variables form the cornerstones of what della Porta and Reiter (1998: 22) refer to as *police knowledge* – 'that is, the police's perception of their role and of the external reality'. This knowledge forms the basis on which strategy and tactics for dealing with particular protest events and participants are determined and implemented.

Conclusions

This chapter has demonstrated how methods of policing public order in Western democratic societies have undergone a significant transformation in recent years. In America, the United Kingdom and other western European states, uncompromising police tactics and strategies for managing public order have given way to a 'negotiated management' style, emphasising prevention and accommodation, while retaining a readiness to deal resolutely with potential or actual disorder (the 'iron fist in the velvet glove'). Academic theorists on both sides of the Atlantic interpret this transformation as a manifestation of the police desire to reduce the scale (and cost) of resources required for dealing with large-scale disorder, to eradicate the risk of danger to themselves and others, to restore public confidence and enhance their own legitimacy.

Ordinarily, the police will try to anticipate or offset the possibility of community disorder or violent protest by various preventative measures, such as: the use of tension indicators and other forms of intelligence; communication, liaison and negotiation with community representatives and demonstration organisers; ensuring the careful selection of commanding officers; providing adequate training and briefing for junior officers; and employing real-time evidence gathering. Sometimes, the police will resort to methods of questionable legality to harass or destabilise groups in preference to engaging them in direct confrontation.

Studies reviewed in this chapter emphasise that police tactics and strategies are politically contingent. The police are apt to use more repressive and potentially escalatory tactics in situations involving transgressive (or 'bad') protesters. A complementary explanation suggests that police decision-making is based on the likelihood of on-the-job or in-the-job trouble accruing as a result of their actions. While generally averse to confrontation, the police are prepared to 'die in a ditch' in situations where they are exposed to implicit or direct forms of political pressure requiring them to deal uncompromisingly with the public. A slightly more expansive variation on this approach specifies that senior police are sensitive to the perceived wishes of different 'audiences', including sections of the public, political and legal authorities, and their own colleagues (all mediated via the mass media), when formulating their policies. Interviews with frontline commanders illustrate that on-the-spot decisions undertaken prior to or in the heat of conflict are likewise based on guesswork regarding the feelings of junior officers and the possible reactions of superior officers, as well as the likelihood of official or internal 'inquests' into the event.

Contingent factors of this nature will have a bearing on the type of tactical intervention chosen by the police. Once junior officers have been called upon to act, their conduct is liable to be affected by a variety of cultural, experiential and emotional factors predisposing them to conflict. Studies suggest that particular aspects of the police occupational culture (notably, its emphasis on machismo, solidarity, action and challenge, and inherent tendency to see crowds as volatile and in need of strict regulation) help to create a predisposition to violence. Such considerations are fundamental to the so-called paramilitary policing debate. Advocates of this approach maintain that it represents the surest way of ensuring police discipline, the safety of the public and the legitimacy of the police. Opponents castigate it as intensely provocative and repressive, a sure-fire way of heightening the potential for conflict.

della Porta's model of protest policing consolidates and extends our knowledge of the policing of public disorder – in particular, by placing more emphasis on the importance of police accountability, of the dominant political culture of the relevant society, the prevailing configuration of power between left and right, and the way that political discourse, as mediated by the mass media, shapes police policies towards dissenting groups. The model's utility lies in its ability to highlight the interrelationship between explanatory variables. Such are the major insights residing in the policing literature. In the following chapter, we turn our attention to theories of public disorder *per se* in search of complementary ways of understanding policing methods and their consequences.

Chapter 2

Theories of public disorder

Introduction

This chapter explores the extent to which *theories and models of public disorder* (as opposed to more focused explanations of police conduct) can enable us, not only to understand the types of contexts and dynamics that give rise to confrontation, but also to appreciate how particular forms of policing may have the capacity to enhance or reduce its possible occurrence.

In commenting on the possible causes of the British inner-city riots of 1985, Benyon (1987: 23) remarks how:

> It is noticeable how frequently pathological language is used in discussions of law and order. There are 'outbreaks' of disorder, and 'epidemics' of crime, and a 'crisis' can occur if the 'contagion' spreads too far . . . Disorder is seen as a disease of the body politic but, like so many ailments, it may be rather easier to recognise than to cure. To continue the medical metaphor, diagnosis determines treatment, but if the condition is not fully understood there is a danger that the prescribed remedies merely treat the symptoms of the disorder, rather than curing its causes.

We saw in the previous chapter how there appears to be a general tendency among police officers to conceive of public disorder as a by-product of the highly contagious state of 'mindlessness' supposedly resulting from immersion in a crowd. Police rank-and-file respondents interviewed by Stott and Reicher (1998) maintained that disorder was due either to this process or to the Machiavellian antics of rabble-rousing individuals. Such 'lay theories' of crowd disorder have their academic counterparts in the convergent traditions of 'classical psychological reductionism' (Reicher *et al.* 2004; D. Waddington and King 2005) and 'mob sociology' (Schweingruber 2000). Each of these perspectives attributes crowd violence either to the onset of a potentially dangerous 'mob mentality', to the sinister machinations of 'agitators', or to the deviant or criminal characteristics of the 'riff-raff' who typically come looking for trouble.

The common source of most of these perspectives is Le Bon's (1895) major work, *The Crowd: a Study of the Popular Mind*. This posits that, whenever people form together in crowds, their conscious personalities automatically disappear to be replaced by a sinister, uncivilised and potentially barbaric 'group mind'. The reasons for this are threefold: first, the anonymity deriving from crowd membership separates individuals from any personal responsibility for their actions; secondly, being in crowds makes people less resistant to 'hypnotic' powers of suggestion that may compel them to behave in reckless and unsavoury ways; and finally, crowd behaviour and the powerful emotions it evokes tend to spread contagiously, causing virtually everyone present to recklessly join in.

Reicher (1987) speaks for countless academics in criticising the inherent bias of any approach that both discredits crowd disorder as irrational and disinvests it of any underlying meaning or justification. He further objects to the way in which theories cast in the Le Bon tradition absolve the police and other agents of control of any responsibility for the violence and, therefore, serve to justify repressive crowd control measures. Reicher and other authors, like Billig (1976), are rightly cynical of the underlying theoretical presumption that rioting occurs because a multitude of people are coincidentally experiencing a heightened state of arousal. Such a standpoint does little to explain the degree to which collective action is generally underpinned by identifiable social aims and involves scores of people acting in concert. Reicher and his colleagues are equally scornful of the 'agitator view' of crowd behaviour (Reicher *et al.* 2004), which sees crowd members as apt to be 'led astray' by unscrupulous individuals keen to take advantage of their temporary 'suggestibility'. Reicher's (1984) own study of the St Paul's (Bristol) riot of 1980 powerfully demonstrates that crowd participants are invariably unresponsive to the directives of individuals not regarded as sharing their aims and ideals.

Finally, it should also be noted that doubts were cast on the validity of the so-called riff-raff approach by the Kerner Commission on the 1960s American urban riots. The commission discovered that, far from being 'criminal types, over active social deviants, or riff-raff – recent migrant members from an uneducated underclass – alienated from responsible Negroes [sic] and without broad social or political concern' (Kerner 1968: 73), the 'typical rioter' was economically on a par with the average non-rioter, was comparatively better educated, politically more active, and invariably a lifelong resident of the city.

The commission emphasised the more general point that rioting is actually a more complicated social phenomenon than lay theories give it credit for. In its view, urban disorder was invariably the result of an interaction between several underlying causal conditions, most notably: a longstanding 'reservoir of grievances' concerning police harassment, poor housing, and unemployment or under-employment (i.e. people occupying jobs incommensurate with their skills or qualifications); frustration deriving from a perceived inability to change matters via the political system; an increasingly tense social atmosphere, involving a sequence of negative incidents between local people and the police; and finally, a triggering or 'precipitating' incident representing the 'final straw' in the context of police–community relations. It is therefore apparent that, in order to have credibility, theories of disorder must be capable of incorporating the full range of variables necessary to the explanation of any given confrontation. Moreover, they must strive to make appropriate conceptual linkages between the relevant contexts of disorder and the role of human agency (including that of the police).

Notwithstanding its similar tendency to see public disorder as inherently pathological, Smelser's (1962) *Theory of Collective Behaviour* theory constitutes a comprehensive and imaginative attempt to elucidate the contexts and dynamics of disorder and the possible contribution of police strategy and tactics. This groundbreaking sociological approach is reviewed in the first section of this chapter. Subsequent sections explore the nature and utility of other multi-variate approaches appearing in the wake of Smelser's model. These include a pair of American explanations (Hundley 1968/1975; Spiegel 1969) and corresponding European examples (Otten *et al.* 2001; D. Waddington *et al.* 1989). While undoubtedly influenced by Smelser's approach, these models strive to accentuate the fundamentally *rational* nature of crowd disorder and place stronger emphasis on the police's role in the causation of violence. Finally, consideration is also given to the so-called *Elaborated Social Identity Model* (ESIM) (e.g. Stott and Reicher 1998), which establishes a social psychological basis for understanding the entrenched feelings of mutual hostility and escalating violence consequent on police public order interventions.

Smelser's theory of collective behaviour

Smelser's Theory of Collective Behaviour constitutes an attempt to transcend the naivety of traditional psychological and sociological perspectives by highlighting the significance of the context of crowd violence, as well as the triggering (or precipitating) incident or event responsible for sparking it off. It is therefore ironic that the theory still manages to draw extensively on the tenets of mob sociology and classical psychological reductionism.

The theory is entirely consistent, for example, with the riff-raff approach to rioting. Its underlying premise is that 'hostile outbursts' are essentially pathological and apt to involve 'deviant groups' – i.e. the poorly socialised and sections of society undergoing some disturbing form of transition in their lives (e.g. adolescents, the unemployed or recent migrants). The theory identifies six determinants of disorder: *structural conduciveness, structural strain, the growth and spread of a generalised hostile belief, precipitating factors, the mobilisation of participants for action,* and *social control.*

The first of these, *structural conduciveness,* refers to features of a relevant situation which might facilitate or, otherwise, constrain an outbreak of disorder. Disorder is more likely to occur where: there is an agency present on which to attach blame for a troubling state of affairs; there is an absence of official channels for addressing the relevant grievance; and social conditions allow for the aggrieved people to communicate and act in concert. The presence of these structures enhances the possibility that collective feelings of *structural strain* (i.e. frustration resulting from a flouting or transgression of the group's rights, or when its economic or social needs have not been met) will culminate in disorder.

Smelser's third determinant, the *growth and spread of a generalised hostile belief,* concerns the process by which the source of the social strain is identified, blame is assigned, and a suitable course of action decided upon. Displaying his obvious deference to the group mind approach, Smelser characterises such hostile notions as 'magical beliefs (which) distort reality and "short-circuit" the normal paths to the amelioration of grievances' (Skolnick 1969: 253). He further insists that, in formulating these beliefs, crowds have a tendency to wrongly scapegoat particular outgroups (primarily, the police).

With the potential for disorder thus established, it now requires the combined effect of two other processes – a *precipitating factor* and the *mobilisation of participants for action* – for a hostile outburst to occur. Precipitating factors are defined by Smelser as incidents, rumours or 'sudden threats or deprivations' which serve to sharpen and exaggerate the generalised belief. These are not sufficient in themselves to cause disorder. In order for this to happen, participants must be suitably mobilised for action by processes of leadership and communication advocating aggression. Here, crowd members are susceptible to the deliberate or unwitting influence of prominent individuals or representatives of formal institutions (shades of the 'agitator theory' of disorder).

The degree to which the resulting disorder continues to spread is ultimately dependent on the style of *social control* exercised by the authorities. Smelser (1962: 267) advocates the police undertake the following course of action:

(a) Prevent communication in general, so that beliefs cannot be disseminated. (b) Prevent interaction between leaders and followers, so that mobilisation is difficult. (c) Refrain from taking a conditional attitude towards violence by bluffing or vacillating in the use of the ultimate weapons of force. (d) Refrain from entering the issues and controversies that move the crowd; remain impartial, unyielding and fixed on the principle of maintaining law and order.

Elsewhere, we have raised a number of criticisms of Smelser's theory (D. Waddington 1992: 13; D. Waddington *et al.* 1989: 174–177). These include the objections that: (i) it is ill-considered and dangerous to conceive of society as an integrated whole, of rioters as 'deviants' and of disorder as irrational; (ii) the theory is insensitive to cultural differences between civilians and the police, as well as to historical relations between them; (iii) the theory tends to portray the police as an unwitting and/or scapegoated party to the violence; and (iv) there is a danger that uncompromising police interventions in the manner prescribed by Smelser will only serve to escalate disorder.

Smelser's theory was formulated prior to the 'long hot summers' of the 1960s (approximately 1964–1968) when rioting perennially broke out in the African-American communities of major American cities. Other academics subsequently enjoyed the obvious advantage of being able to draw on their own observations and Kerner's analysis of the literally hundreds of riots breaking out in this period as the basis of theory building. We now turn to two well-known examples of this type of theoretical development.

Hundley's model of the dynamics of 'ghetto riots'

Hundley (1968/1975) based his explanation of riot dynamics on interviews with residents of four American cities (Chicago, Cleveland, Detroit and Newark) who had either witnessed rioting first-hand, or who were familiar with the area prior to the outbreak. This data allowed him analytically to distinguish between three aspects of rioting: (i) general preceding conditions; (ii) immediate or proximate conditions; and (iii) internal dynamics.

Like Smelser, Hundley (1975: 229–232) specifies a number of background conditions seen as necessary for rioting to occur. These are that:

- potential participants must perceive that a crisis exists (they must subjectively experience some form of inequality, discrimination or deprivation);
- they must believe that legitimate channels for expressing grievances are closed off to them;
- they must share the view that rioting is likely to produce beneficial change(s);
- they must be in close enough proximity to each other for communication to occur;
- there must have been a substantial breakdown in police–community relations (with the police being perceived as brutal, impolite or disrespectful).

Hundley (*ibid.*: 232) also nominates four immediate or 'proximate' conditions considered fundamental to the outbreak of rioting, namely:

- the generation of rumour (the 'communication of hostility and dissatisfaction') proposing rioting as a possible solution to such salient ghetto problems as slum landlords or police brutality;
- the occurrence of an event that typifies enduring grievances: 'The significance of this event is that it immediately focuses the attention on an overt act of suppression that is met with

open hostility not because of the act itself, but because it is representative of a long history of such acts' (*ibid.*: 232–233)

- the gathering together of large numbers of people around the event; and
- communication of particular grievances among the crowd (by informal leaders or the 'most verbal' speakers present), leading to an agreed course of action.

The actions of police officers are thought to have a crucial influence on the way that conflict subsequently develops:

In the beginning stages of riot formation, the presence or absence of police officers can have various effects. In most instances, the very presence of the police creates an event, provides a point of focus, and draws people together among whom rumour can be easily transmitted. In other cases, sending too few officers to a scene results in actions being uncontrolled because not enough policemen are available to break the developing crowd structure. We suggest that if the police activity is seen by the rioters as legitimate, then the presence of small quantities of police will not precipitate a riot. However, even if the original police activity is viewed as legitimate, but the policemen are observed as being rude, impolite, unfair, or brutal, then these activities can precipitate a riot. It appears that the police officers, in their attempt to enforce a higher authority, are perceived by ghetto residents more as a causal factor than a deterrent of riot behaviour. (*ibid.*: 237)

Hundley further maintains that, in situations where the police allow deviant behaviour to go unpunished due to their own ineffectuality (e.g. by half-heartedly chasing offenders or levelling verbal insults), these 'non-control' activities will serve only to exacerbate existing hostility. A total police withdrawal will invariably escalate the situation. Indeed, such tactics are only likely to succeed where police contact credible community leaders and furnish them with meaningful concessions to put to their constituents.

There are compelling similarities between Hundley's analysis and Marx's observations on the American riots, introduced in the previous chapter. However, Hundley endorses Smelser's recommendation that the police must focus on dividing the crowd up into smaller units and preventing communication among the aggrieved. Certainly, this is preferable to mounting a military-style frontal attack. Once rioting is in full sway, the best policy is for the police to call in external support: 'Apart from the sheer force of numbers, calling in the national guard indicates the success of the rioters, since they have beaten the "boys in blue"' (*ibid*.: 238).

Spiegel's stage theory of the riot process

Spiegel (1969) used survey techniques and interviews to obtain the views of white and black residents of three unspecified cities in which rioting occurred. Central to Spiegel's approach is the idea that riots (or hostile outbursts) occur in the presence of a 'pre-existing hostile belief system'. Such beliefs relate to instances of 'value conflict', where one section of society is treated in a manner which is 'beyond the pale of accepted norms' (*ibid*.: 120). Spiegel cites the examples of police incivility and brutality towards black 'ghetto' residents that are rarely displayed towards whites. The problem for those on the receiving end is that such grievances are not often brought to the attention of relevant authorities. This is partly because the mass media seldom run stories exemplifying or highlighting such problems. Additionally, city administrators prefer to deal only with moderate (i.e. out-of-touch and ineffectual) community representatives, tending to dismiss more dissenting or militant spokespersons as 'Black Power agitators'.

Where preconditions of this nature exist – and, especially, when resentment has been stoked up by recent rumour – the riot process is liable to be activated. Spiegel identifies four stages of rioting (the *precipitating incident*, the *street confrontation*, the *Roman holiday* and the *siege*) but emphasises that the majority of conflicts do not go beyond the end of stage two.

The first of the specified phases is that of the *precipitating incident*:

The hostile belief system is connected, on the one hand, with the value conflict and, on the other, with the incident which precipitates a riot. It embodies the value conflict, giving it form, substance and energy. It sets the stage for the precipitating incident which then becomes a concrete illustration of the beliefs. A police officer shooting and killing a young black suspected car thief (as in San Francisco in September 1966) or beating and bloodying a black taxi driver (as in Newark in July 1967) confirms and dramatizes the expectations incorporated into the hostile beliefs and triggers the uprising. (*ibid*.)

The second phase, the *street confrontation*, then follows as other residents 'swarm' to the incident and a 'keynoting' process rapidly takes place. Riot 'promoters' begin to articulate resentments and recommend courses of action. Against this, opponents of conflict plead for tempers to cool and for greater consideration to be shown. At this point, the crowd becomes affected by contagion. The way in which city administrators respond is a key determinant of future behaviour. Where representatives show a genuine readiness to listen to complaints and propose credible solutions, there is a chance that hostilities will subside. However, 'If they fail to show up and are represented only by the police, who are already heavily involved in the hostile belief system, the level of agitation tends to rise' (*ibid.*: 123). Indeed, there is a danger that police conduct in dispersing civilians may add weight to calls for an intensification of conflict, thus propelling the riot into its next phase (*ibid.*).

In situations where the hostile keynoting extends to fever pitch, it is probable that the riot process will take a 'quantum jump' into phase three, *the Roman holiday*. Typically at this stage, the younger males in the crowd regroup away from the scene of the initial incident and begin hurling projectiles at symbolic targets (e.g. white-owned stores, cars driven by white civilians or police officers) with 'an angry intoxication indistinguishable from glee'. Law enforcement officers are taunted and every successful strike by a thrown missile is wildly celebrated. The crowd is too excited to contemplate acts of looting, though these soon become evident at phase four (*ibid.*: 123–124).

Spiegel contends that where Roman holiday behaviour is met by under- or over-control by the police, the riot will enter its fourth phase, a state of *siege* (*ibid.*: 124). Customarily, this will involve summoning in state troopers and the National Guard, each of whom is likely to be subjected to sniper fire. A curfew will be imposed but this will not stop ghetto residents from hurling fire bombs. Eventually, though, 'The siege runs its course, like a Greek tragedy, until both sides tire of this fruitless and devastating way of solving a conflict' (*ibid.*: 124).

Of paramount significance are Spiegel's general conclusions regarding the police's role in suppressing or inflaming disorder. The possibility of escalation is greatest when the police response takes the form of either under- or over-control. In the former case, police under-activity sends out an invitation to would-be rioters to behave with impunity. In the latter, the law enforcement agencies intervene too soon and with 'counterproductive brutality':

> Police and state troopers are rushed to the scene and begin to manhandle everyone in sight. Since the action is out of proportion to the event, it generates an intense reaction . . . Short of the use of overwhelming force, overcontrol usually leads to increased violence. Black people in the ghetto see the police as violent and strike back with increasing intensity. (*ibid.*: 122)

According to Spiegel, the police must endeavour to strike an effective balance: they should strive to be firm but discriminating in their actions from the outset, making arrests selectively and without unnecessary use of force (*ibid.*). These views are, of course, highly convergent with those of Marx and Hundley.

British explanations of riot causality

The 'tinder and spark' metaphor for understanding the US urban disorders was subsequently borrowed by British theorists of the UK inner-city riots of 1981 and 1985 (see Benyon and Solomos 1987 for an overview of these events). Benyon (1987: 33) distinguishes, for example, between the *trigger* event which usually 'sparked off' each riot and the background social conditions which provided the *tinder* for a major conflagration. In his words, 'The *immediate precipitants* or *trigger events* in each case involved police officers and black people' (ibid.), whereas the tinder comprised five interrelated factors, namely: racial disadvantage and discrimination; high unemployment; widespread deprivation; political exclusion and powerlessness; and mistrust of, and hostility to, the police, due to the aggressive application of 'stop-and-search' procedures, harassment and abuse (*ibid.*: 33–34).

Benyon's 'five common characteristics' provide a useful foundation for understanding the origins of disorder. However, related British studies also highlight the importance of other variables, such as cultural differences between the police and African-Caribbean youths, an ideological climate encouraging hostility between police and youths, and the particular dynamics and locations of the daily interactions acting as precursors to the riots.

A link between urban deprivation, black youth counter-culture, political marginalisation, racial discrimination and the type of militaristic policing ultimately held responsible for the rioting is posited by Lea and Young in their model of *The Collapse of*

Consensus Policing (Lea and Young 1982; Lea and Young 1993; Kinsey *et al.* 1986). Lea and Young take the view that the relative deprivation experienced by second-generation African–Caribbeans in this country gave rise to a 'street counter culture', where the 'positive search for identity and survival in the harsh conditions of the inner city' produced proclivities towards street robbery and interpersonal violence (Lea and Young 1982: 8–9). They argue that this state of affairs was unlikely to have materialised had the youths not also lacked 'any viable tradition of ethnic politics' through which to defend or further their interests (*ibid.*: 15).

According to Lea and Young, it was the soaring crime statistics involving African-Caribbean youth, in conjunction with prejudicial police attitudes, which encouraged 'an exaggeration of the contribution of black persons to the actual crime rate' (*ibid.*: 9) and led to the police adopting tough, 'high-profile strategies', predicated on closer community surveillance and random stops and searches. The inherent danger of such strategies is that:

> Once police actions blur the distinction between suspect and innocent, then the community comes to see any attempt at an arrest by officers as a symbolic attack on the community per se and, as a consequence, the phenomenon of collective resistance to the arrest of an individual begins to emerge. And by this stage, riot is on the agenda. Events assume the status of a vicious circle of cumulative causation. The deterioration in police–community relations leads to a drying up of information which in turn forms the background to the development of aggressive 'military' policing. This reinforces the tendency of the community to dry up as an information source and the general alienation further undermines the basis of consensus policing, leaving military style action as the only viable strategy available to the police. (*ibid.*: 12)

A similar explanatory approach is set out by Brogden *et al.* (1988), who also recognise a logical connection between economic crisis and an increasing 'survival crime' among African-Caribbean youth. However, crucial to their explanation is the idea that a media-led 'moral panic' served to transform the victims of recession (black youth) into 'folk devils' warranting harsher and more repressive policing. Very quickly, the police and youths become mutually resentful and distrustful. A 'deadly dynamic' is set in motion whereby 'Police enter encounters expecting trouble and act aggressively to pre-empt it. Black youth similarly expect trouble and create the necessary ("disrespectful") mind set to cope' (*ibid.*: 141).

Keith (1993: 17) takes issue with 'left realist' academics like Lea and Young for failing to show sufficient sensitivity to relevant geographical and historical factors: 'Left Realist explanation can only incorporate processes which take place at no place, always in the present.' Keith's own ethnographic analysis of conflict between the police and members of predominantly black communities in Brixton, Hackney and Notting Hill (all London) in 1981 focuses on the importance of 'Front Lines' in the genesis of disorder. According to Keith, these front lines, such as Railton Road (Brixton), Sandringham Road (Hackney) and All Saints Road (Notting Hill), are regular meeting places where the role and self-image of black people are 'acted, re-enacted, defined and re-defined, every day'; they are 'locales at which resentment of power relations was transformed into resistance of power relations' (*ibid.*: 159).

Crucial to Keith's analysis is the distinction between *metonymic* (historical) and *syntagmatic* (relating primarily to the present) ways of viewing the world. For residents of black communities, attitudes are informed by a lived experience and folklore stretching back possibly through decades; whereas as far as the police are concerned, the histories of particular locations are of little interest, and the communities themselves are stereotyped as 'troublesome' or 'dangerous'. Keith rejects those descriptions of the riots which regard the immediate trigger events as 'irrelevant or inconsequential'. The importance of the triggering incident is that it is an act which is read similarly by a large number of people as symbolic of a wider historical state of affairs: 'Trigger events are not epiphenomenal or incidental to the development of violence. They provide a key element in the signification of action, the meaning of the *riot* set against its spatial and social context' (*ibid.*: 169).

Taken collectively, these approaches identify the nature and interrelatedness of numerous variables crucial to understanding the British riots. A more comprehensive attempt to nail down the type of variables necessary to explain, not only inner-city riots, but episodes of public disorder more generally, was undertaken during the 1980s by myself and co-workers based in the northern English city of Sheffield.

The flashpoints model of public disorder

The multivariate approaches of American theorists like Smelser and Hundley provided inspiration for our work on the *Flashpoints Model of Public Disorder*, developed during the 1980s and 1990s (see, for example, D. Waddington 1987, 1992, 1996; D. Waddington *et al.* 1987; 1989). The main objective of the model was to incorporate relevant variables into a general framework for explaining the circumstances in which disorder is likely to break out or, alternatively, fail to ignite. Accordingly, the model embraces six interdependent levels of analysis: *structural, political/ideological, cultural, contextual, situational* and *interactional*, running from aspects of face-to-face interaction at the micro core, through a series of more macro contextual factors.

The *structural* level concerns those types of macro-sociological factors, such as material inequalities, political impotence and inferior life-chances, which lie at the root of collective grievances and resentments in society. We may also include here circumstances giving rise to an 'ideological alienation from the state' – a position from which certain groups (e.g. peace campaigners or environmental activists) object to social issues on the basis of moral principle. Latent social conflict is more likely to become manifest where the state appears indifferent to such grievances, forcing the relevant section of society to conclude that they have no real stake in the existing social order.

The depth of such disaffection depends on activities occurring at the *political/ideological* level of analysis. This level refers to the way in which key political and ideological institutions (notably, prominent politicians, senior police, members of the judiciary, the media and other opinion-shapers) respond to the politically or culturally dissenting group (or groups) in question. The degree of legitimacy accorded to the group's demands and strategies is crucial here. Processes of vilification and denunciation will not only fuel their resentment but are liable to encourage police repression.

The *cultural* level emphasises the importance of the ways of life and thought which groups develop on the basis of shared conditions and experiences. It assumes that cultures (or subcultures) inform their members' definitions of themselves and 'outsiders', influence their attitudes to using violence, and imbue them with knowledge of the 'rules' of in- and out-group conduct relevant to particular situations. Thus, 'If the groups involved have differing or in-compatible definitions of the situation, appropriate behaviour, or legitimate rights, then the potential for conflict is increased' (D. Waddington *et al*. 1989: 162).

This is clearly of relevance to encounters between police officers and dissenting sections of society (e.g. black youths, pickets and demonstrators), who perceive each other in terms of fundamentally negative stereotypes. This danger of possible conflict is enhanced in those instances where police officers from outside forces, perhaps lacking sensitivity to local cultures, are drafted in on a temporary basis. Though competing definitions are undoubtedly problematic, conflict may still be avoided where both parties subscribe to a 'pattern of accommodation' which shows due respect for the rights and objectives of all concerned and sets up tacit norms prescribing appropriate conduct.

The *contextual* level focuses on those dynamic communication processes leading up to an event which may enhance its potential for disorder. These include: the transmission of rumour, a history of negative relations and/or recent incidents between police and civilians, contentious statements by the parties involved, and media sensitisation. Factors of this nature may lead to advance preparations on both sides for a 'worst possible scenario'. The possibility of a self-fulfilling prophecy may diminish due to the moderating effect of pre-event liaison, especially when it helps to establish 'rules of accommodation' to the satisfaction of both sides.

The *situational* level refers to spatial or social determinants of order or disorder. It starts by acknowledging the possible symbolic significance of the location of police–civilian encounters. Such places may represent cultural 'turf' to be defended by disaffected youths, or 'no-go areas' to be recaptured by the police. Their physical configurations may lend themselves to greater or lesser degrees of police surveillance or the entrapment of fleeing demonstrators. They may contain particular 'targets of derision', such as controversial dignitaries or buildings, which the police are determined to protect.

The organisation and tactical dispositions of police and civilians may also be key factors. Disorder is less likely to occur wherever the latter are self-managed by stewards and their organisers disavow violence for the duration of the event. Likewise, order is more likely to be maintained where the policing is low-profile (or 'soft hat'), with riot-clad reinforcement, dogs and horses kept discreetly out of view, and junior ranks are supervised according to clear lines of communication and command. Two final and related variables are the actual and perceived situational objectives existing on both sides. For example, while senior officers may consider it necessary to keep protesters well away from a political venue, both for the safety of political rivals and in order to maintain the flow of rush-hour traffic, the demonstrators may regard this as a cynical suppression of their 'democratic right' of expression.

The *interactional* level deals, as its name suggests, with face-to-face activities between members of the police and public:

> These will vary in degrees of respect, co-operation, restraint or provocation. In highly charged situations, a particular incident (the throwing of a brick, an arrest or police charge) may spark off disorder. Such 'flashpoints' are interpreted symbolically as indicating the underlying attitude of the other side. Important are intensifiers – i.e. characteristics of the individuals involved (whether high-ranking or from a 'vulnerable' category, such as a woman, old person or child), or the way in which they are perpetrated (e.g. an especially rough or degrading arrest). The conflict promoted by such actions may still not prove irreversible. Escalation may yet be prevented by reactions ['pacifiers'] indicating that other members of the group, especially leaders, regard the original action as out of line. (D. Waddington and Critcher 2000: 106)

As I have previously pointed out (D. Waddington 1992: 20), such accompanying feelings and emotions as 'power, liberation, elation and revenge' are best interpreted with reference to variables existing at the preceding levels of analysis, such as the particular grievances affecting the dissenting group, its marginalisation from conventional politics and the history of its recent encounters with the police.

My colleagues and I have systematically applied the model in endeavouring to explain numerous public order events, some in or around Sheffield, others based abroad; some violent, others not (Critcher 1996; King and Waddington 2005; D. Waddington 1987, 1992; D. Waddington *et al.* 1989). Elsewhere, Baker (1991) has used the model to explain police–picket relations in an Australian industrial dispute, Sheptycki (2005) has applied it in a cross-cultural comparison of violent political protests in Canada and Bolivia, and Lo Shiu-hing (2006) in a case study of the policing of the anti-WTO protests in Hong Kong in 2005. We therefore feel justified in claiming to have devised an explanatory framework 'which [is] flexible enough to encompass a variety of types of disorder while at the same time allowing for the uniqueness of each situation' (D. Waddington *et al.* 1987: 159).

Criticisms of the model by Keith (1993), Otten *et al.* (2001) and P. A. J. Waddington (1991, 1994b, 2000a, 2003), have been dealt with in previous publications (King and Waddington 2005; D. Waddington 1996, 1998). Such objections focus on the fact that the model tends to assume that all riots are triggered by a single flashpoint when, in fact, they are often the result of more than one main incident. P. A. J. Waddington has also justifiably argued that some riots commence in the absence of an identifiable flashpoint, while others flare up long after the 'precipitating incident' has first occurred, thus rendering the notion of a 'flashpoint' of little conceptual value. As I have previously stated in response:

> It ultimately makes no difference whether 'the final straw' in the evolution of a riot takes the form of a highly emotive arrest which induces a spontaneously violent reaction . . . or involves a less immediate, though equally arousing, symbolic event (e.g. the shooting of a black woman by police officers in Brixton in 1985, or the acquittal of police officers in Los Angeles in 1992) which provokes a collective expression of indignation by people not initially in close proximity to each other. Either way, the significance of such precipitous developments lies in their capacity to crystallise enduring sensations of injustice. (D. Waddington 1998: 387)

Nevertheless, it is still accepted that there is a need for the model to allow for such variations in the nature of precipitating incidents or events, and for possible time-lags or 'lulls' (Horowitz 2002) between the trigger and the onset of wider confrontation. Likewise, it is also important to assume that there may be several flashpoints in the course of one particular event, some of which do not ignite, others of which may initially ignite only to then die down, and one or more of which explode so intensely as to consume the whole event.

A Dutch model of the dynamics of disorder

A specific criticism levelled against the flashpoints model by Otten *et al.* (2001: 16fn) is that it lacks a 'thorough treatment of the important phase of mobilisation and (self) organisation of crowds (and police)'. These authors purport to have adapted the model in order to rectify this shortcoming. In fact, as we shall see, their own framework of analysis has much in common with the other approaches previously referred to in this chapter. Their *Model of the Dynamics of Disorder* is applied to two case studies: celebrations by Feyenoord fans of their team's success in winning the Dutch football championship (Rotterdam, 25 April 1999), and an ethnic community disorder (Amsterdam-West, 23 April 1998). For the purpose of illustration, we focus on the latter.

This case study centres on a police arrest of three Moroccan youths in an impoverished neighbourhood which led to 'massive disorders'. Rumours that the officers had used unnecessary violence in making these arrests swept through the neighbourhood and led to local residents occupying a centrally located road roundabout in protest. Following a brief standoff, police used force to disperse the protesters and confrontation then ensued. Otten *et al.* make the point that 'One of the intriguing questions, which caught the policymakers' and societal attention, is how such outbursts of community discontent can result from a seemingly innocent incident involving a few youths' (*ibid.*: 24). The authors address this question with reference to six levels of analysis: *incubation, tension, precipitating event, onset, adjustment* and *learning*.

The first of these (*incubation*) deals with factors contributing to strained long-term police–community relations. Otten and his colleagues make the point that here was a local community comprising Moroccan, Turkish and Surinamese migrants alongside a relatively elderly indigenous Dutch population. Relations between the police and ethnic minority youths had progressively deteriorated due to concerns over rising crime statistics and complaints by the elderly that they felt threatened and intimidated. Early in 1997, a special police supervisor had been appointed to restore law and order. Local police patrols were duly stepped up and civilian 'police observers' deployed as part of a street surveillance exercise. The ineffectiveness of such measures placed yet more pressure on the local mayor and police to get a grip on the situation.

The second level is concerned with the way in which recent incidents can produce a gradual build-up of *tension* in relations between the police and one or more sections of the civilian population. Here, such a situation arose when the police implemented a policy of systematically stopping Dutch-Moroccan youths on mopeds (motorised pedal cycles). The number of traffic violations rose accordingly and scores of vehicles were impounded. The youths retaliated by subjecting officers to verbal abuse and harassment – so much so that police observers were forbidden from entering a central shopping mall to protect them from possible harm. The overall rise in tension was exemplified by an incident at the beginning of April in which a drunken youth fell on his face during an argument with a female observer and his injuries were widely interpreted by his peers as evidence of police brutality.

The key *precipitating event* (defined as an incident that fuels resentment on both sides and, perhaps, introduces a territorial dimension to the conflict) occurred on Thursday, 23 April in a local playground where several youths were gathered around a fire they had just ignited in a wire wastebasket. In contrast to many of their contemporaries, these young men enjoyed a local reputation for good behaviour. The problem occurred when the youths were approached by three police observers who were in the course of doing their rounds. One of the officers had just referred to a civilian counterpart as 'an idiot' when the locally detested police supervisor arrived by motorcycle and commanded the youths to leave the area. When one young man defiantly stood his ground, he was immediately arrested.

Bystanders were quickly sucked into the struggle: an angry crowd of 40-strong surrounded the supervisor and his colleagues. This was due to indignation caused by the fact that that the arrestee's father had been kicked in the stomach while trying to intervene. Each of the three observers was physically assaulted, at which point the supervisor threatened to draw his firearm. Within two minutes, police reinforcements arrived and order was temporarily restored. Several of the youths were handcuffed and whisked away to the county police office.

Otten *et al.* define the *onset* phase as that part of the proceedings where communication occurs: information is disseminated and rumour starts to circulate resulting in the mobilisation of the crowd. In this case, the process involved the crowd reaching an agreement to converge on the nearby police office. Included in their ranks were a number of elderly protesters who regarded the police action as unjustified. The crowd number was also swollen (to an overall total of 'a few hundred') by the sight and sound of an encircling helicopter which drew in many curious bystanders.

On arriving at the station, the crowd discovered that the premises were unoccupied. They also failed in their attempt to contact the police by phone. Thus thwarted, they decided to occupy a central roundabout in a bid to induce the police into entering negotiations. A traffic bottleneck then developed and members of national and local media converged on the scene. In the meantime, exaggerated rumours of police atrocities began circulating. One senior police officer was eventually drawn into discussions with some of the older Moroccan men. However, he steadfastly refused their demands to set the prisoners free, explaining that he had no way of guaranteeing that the youths would respond to their parents' authority.

The penultimate, *adjustment* phase of the proceedings involves attempts by the authorities to reassert control. This particular stage was reached when youths started throwing rocks and, after several warnings, the police charged in to successfully disperse them. Finally, the *learning* phase refers to the post-riot process of reflection, evaluation and policy formulation. In the present example, this involved an official inquiry by the Crisis Research Centre, Leiden University, which led to the implementation of a raft of youth programmes and a review of police strategy and tactics.

Otten *et al.*'s approach places a similar emphasis to the American models reviewed in this chapter on the post-flashpoint mobilisation of the crowd. This process is further dealt with by the final model to be considered in this chapter, which focuses on the ways in which the nature of police–citizen interaction and their reciprocal interpretations of each other's behaviour has implications for the escalation of disorder.

The elaborated social identity model

The Elaborated Social Identity Model (ESIM) assumes that the identities and norms of behaviours that crowd members bring to a situation are liable to be transformed during interaction with an out-group (e.g. Reicher 1996; Reicher and Stott 1998). It stands to reason that, 'Since the out-group in question is typically the police, any adequate explanation of crowd conflict must include not only the actions of crowd participants themselves, but also those of the police' (Drury *et al.* 2003: 1481).

The ESIM maintains that, in crowd order situations, the police are apt to interpret the identities and actions of participants in ways that differ substantially from the crowd's own reading of itself and its behaviour. For example, while a benignly intended sit-down protest may be regarded by those involved as a perfectly legitimate course of action, the police are liable to interpret it negatively – as a potential threat to public order – and act accordingly. Then,

> Once conflict has begun, the ESIM suggests that it can escalate through the change in the social location of crowd members that

comes about through the out-group action. In the first place, where out-group action toward in-group members is perceived by the in-group as indiscriminate, then in-group members will come to define themselves as a common social category sharing a common relationship of threat in relation to the out-group. This may mean that previously disparate subgroups and individuals come to see themselves increasingly as a single (superordinate) group or that an already existing single group may come to see itself as increasingly homogeneous. (*ibid.*: 1481–1482)

Reicher (1996) illustrates the importance of social interaction in the transformation of identity, and its resulting implications for social relations, by focusing on the so-called Battle of Westminster, of 24 November 1988, when demonstrators opposed to the introduction of a new system of student loans engaged in violent clashes with police in central London. This march had originally been organised by the National Union of Students (NUS) to follow a route from the University of London, across the Thames via Waterloo Bridge to a rally in Mary Harmondsworth Park. However, a breakaway section of marchers, including small numbers of the Socialist Workers Student Society (SWSS), moved off towards Westminster Bridge (and thence to the Palace of Westminster), taking the remainder of the procession in its wake.

A so-called sessional order prohibits demonstrations from occurring within one mile of the Palace of Westminster while Parliament is sitting. It is usually a matter of police discretion as to whether people are allowed to approach Parliament in small groups. On this occasion, the Chief Superintendent in charge felt that, although the majority of the marchers were law-abiding, the SWSS was intent on causing trouble.

The contrasting perceptions of each group at this point are fundamental to explaining the resulting disorder. The marchers clearly believed that they had a 'right' to cross the bridge and, therefore, regarded police attempts to obstruct them as illegitimate. Equally, the police objected that the students had *no right* to be on the bridge and considered their presence as illegitimate. A 'pattern of action and reaction' was then generated:

It was because the police saw the student crowd as dangerous that they blocked off Westminster Bridge and stopped anyone crossing it. Hence the police not only held particular views of the crowd, they also had the power to act accordingly. What is more, in using this coercive power, they acted indiscriminately upon the demonstration as a whole. Demonstrators were contained on the bridge irrespective of their original affiliations or intentions. When police horses pushed the crowd back, students were equally liable to get shoved aside or knocked over whether they had sought confrontation or not. The police tactics therefore ensured that all demonstrators shared the same experience . . . the indiscriminate nature of the police tactics can be used to explain how a fragmented mass of demonstrators came to form a psychologically homogeneous crowd. The fact that the basis of their common experience was a denial of perceived rights explains why the members of this crowd were willing to enter into conflict with the police. What is more, in being brought together as a common category and in being able to presuppose the support of others in the category, crowd members gained the confidence to challenge the police and try to break their lines. (*ibid.*: 130)

To begin with, participants had regarded themselves as an aggregate of small groups which were easily differentiated from a militant minority who were antagonistic towards the police. However, following police intervention, most of the crowd saw themselves as a single social category, distinguishable now from a small minority *not opposed* to the police. Variations in people's willingness to engage in violence are explained by Reicher via two important qualifications to his argument. First, he assumes that participants committed to principles of non-violence may have been unprepared to respond in like manner to extreme provocation. Secondly, interviews suggest that it was those participants who recognised the futility of shoving against better organised police lines who were disinclined to engage in confrontation. 'Equally, the shoving increased as the police were moved back and police lines seemed vulnerable. In other words, conflict only occurs when it is seen as efficacious' (*ibid.*: 129).

Conclusions

By and large, the above review of American and British theory lends weight to Taylor's (1981: 171) observation that single-factor, or 'univariate', explanations of public disorder are not adequate to do justice to such a complicated social phenomenon. The contents of the chapter generally endorse his standpoint that 'a distinction may be made between two types of causes of riots, namely, the long-term preconditions and the more specific accelerators or precipitants' (ibid.). Smelser's seminal Theory of Collective Behaviour emphasised that the importance of such incidents lay in their power to crystallise hostile social beliefs relating to conditions of 'social strain'. Subsequent American and British theorists have placed greater emphasis on the fact that flashpoint encounters invariably exemplify problematic relations between the police and a relevant section of society. These incidents tend to be all the more incendiary to the extent that they involve police interventions that are especially 'brutal', 'impolite' or otherwise 'go against the pale' of acceptable behaviour.

What this chapter also indicates is that the nature and impact of the triggering incident immediately giving rise to disorder cannot be entirely understood without due reference to a potentially wide range of accompanying background variables. American scholars, like Smelser, Hundley and Spiegel, have each emphasised the significance of such relevant underlying conditions as subjective deprivation, the absence of social or political channels for redressing grievances, and recent histories of poor police–community relations. These factors are said to work alongside more proximate variables, such as rumour and situations which enable requisite processes of communication and mobilisation to occur.

Complementary theorising by British academics also highlights the significance of deprivation, discrimination, disadvantage and political marginalisation. These theories and models also recognise the importance of emerging counter-cultural opposition and ideological pressures on the police to tactically respond in ways detrimental to the maintenance of order. The Flashpoints Model of Public Disorder in particular has endeavoured to synthesise these and other variables, such as relevant communication processes (e.g. rumour, media sensitisation and the recent history of police–public relations), and situational factors, like the symbolic and historical significance of the particular location.

American models of the 1960s are in slight disagreement regarding the effect of specific police tactics following the immediate precipitation of a riot. Smelser, Hundley and Spiegel all conclude that outbreaks of disorder appear to be most effectively quelled by firm but discriminating police intervention, aimed at dividing up the public into smaller, more manageable groups, preventing leadership and restricting the spread of communication. For Smelser, this involves taking a no-holds-barred attitude without any signs of bluff or vacillation. The remaining two theorists maintain that unrestrained, head-on charges invariably provoke hostile counter-reactions, while half-hearted and understaffed interventions can easily signal a lack of police conviction. Smelser further asserts that control is more effective where police officers refrain from entering negotiations with the crowd, while Spiegel contends that placatory discussions are best carried out by civilian intermediaries, particularly where police–community relations are at issue.

European theorists, like myself and Otten *et al.*, take the contrasting view that the greater the police emphasis on police negotiation and communication with the crowd, the lesser are the chances of violence escalating. The flashpoints model assumes that well-timed pacificatory gestures by the police can often serve to repair breakdowns in police–public relations, primarily by signalling the former's willingness to accommodate the goals and values of the crowd. Otten *et al.* assert that the police's failure to communicate and explain their actions to crowd members, especially in ways that are sensitive to cultural sensibilities, is often a major contributing factor to the escalation of a riot. The Elaborated Social Identity Model, formulated by Reicher and his colleagues, is useful in showing how, following police interventions seen as unjust and/or indiscriminate, a wholesale shift occurs in the social identity of the crowd, which not only enhances solidarity against the police, but also imbues those present with the belief that they have the collective capacity to stand up to the authorities.

The conclusions drawn both in this chapter and its predecessor provide tentative foundations for understanding police behaviour and its consequences in the context of major public disorders of the past two decades. With these preliminary theoretical ideas in mind, we now turn, in search of an even better understanding, to our case studies of major public disorder in the 1990s and beyond, starting with the American urban disorders of 1991–2001.

Chapter 3

The American urban riots, 1991–2001

Introduction

One of the main case studies in this chapter is that of the infamous Los Angeles riot of April 1992. This disorder closely followed the acquittal by an all-white jury of a group of white Los Angeles Police Department (LAPD) traffic cops who had been covertly videotaped while in the process of beating up the African-American citizen, Rodney King. During three days of rioting, 52 people died and television audiences looked on in horror as live footage showed white motorists being dragged from their vehicles by blacks, and beaten and stabbed with the police apparently nowhere to be found. The extent and severity of this violence was undoubtedly exceptional. Yet, as Gale (1996: 2) points out,

> Many Americans are sadly aware that the violence in Los Angeles in 1992 was no isolated incident. It was only the most spectacular event in a long time of urban riots that have erupted periodically during this century . . . One is hard put to name another country in which urban interracial mob violence has been such a recurring theme.

The United States has experienced two contrasting forms of urban violence in the last 11 decades. Janowitz (1969) helpfully categorises these disorders into two contrasting types. His *communal* riots are so called because they typically involved conflict between rival ethnic groups (notably blacks and whites) over contested areas of territory. Though significant examples of these occurred at the turn of the twentieth century and as isolated examples in the 1930s and 1940s, they were most commonplace between 1915 and 1919. By contrast, *commodity* riots generally involved attacks by black ghetto dwellers on white-owned properties and symbols of public authority, notably the police. This type of rioting was characteristic of the 'long, hot summers' of 1964 to 1968, involving 500 such riots across the USA which accounted for over 250 lives (Gilje 1996; Gurr 1989).

Since 1990, there have been four major examples of commodity rioting. The Mount Pleasant (Washington, DC) and Washington Heights (New York City) riots of May 1991 and July 1992, respectively, were unusual insofar as they involved altercations between police officers and members of local *Hispanic* communities. The St Petersburgh, Florida, riot of 1996 and the Cincinnati, Ohio, disorder of April 2001 conformed to a more familiar pattern, having been triggered when white cops shot dead African-American suspects of crimes.

The two exceptions to this form of rioting are the Crown Heights (New York City) disturbance of August 1991 and the Los Angeles riot itself. The former fits the prototypical definition of a commodity riot, insofar as it centred on a dispute between blacks and Hasidic Jews. Police inaction in the early phases of the riot subsequently provoked fierce complaints by the Hasidic population and drew contrite reactions from city authorities. The Los Angeles riot constituted something of a hybrid example, being strongly reminiscent of the 1980 Miami riot, which was similarly provoked by the acquittal of police officers who had brutalised a black motorist (Porter and Dunn 1994). Like the Miami riot, the LA riot also involved sustained attacks on neighbouring ethnic groups (in Miami, it was Cuban expatriates and whites; in LA, whites and Koreans) in addition to widespread looting and devastation of property. A justifiable comparison may also be drawn between the Crown Heights and LA riots, in that they each provoked intense criticisms of police inaction and disorganisation, later acknowledged in official reports (Girgenti 1993; Webster 1992).

The remainder of the chapter is devoted to exploring the lessons of these slightly contrasting types of disorder for public order policing. To avoid wasteful duplication of discussion, only two of the four commodity riots are discussed in close detail, these being the Washington and Cincinnati riots, about which information is more plentiful. Academic, journalistic and official accounts and analyses are used in all four of the following case studies to explore the possible significance of police structures and organisation, police–community relations, police tactics and strategies, and wider socio-political issues, including the role of the media. The chapter resists the obvious impulse to address the riots in chronological order. The relevant literature on the commodity riots focuses primarily on the processes *building up* to them, while studies of the Crown Heights and Los Angeles disorders also concentrate on police activities *during the riots*. We therefore begin by focusing on the former category, starting with the Mount Pleasant confrontation.

Commodity riots

The Mount Pleasant Riot, Washington, DC, May 1991

The incident that sparked two days of rioting on Sunday, 5 May 1991 in the Mount Pleasant area of Washington, DC involved the shooting by a black 'rookie' female police officer of a young Salvadoran male who was allegedly resisting arrest on charges of public drinking. The policewoman maintained that the man had pulled a knife, moments before she shot him in the chest. Civilian witnesses insisted that the prisoner was already handcuffed at the time of the shooting. Either way, a crowd formed around the incident and proceeded to attack the police (*The Economist* 1991; Gilje 1996; United States Commission on Civil Rights 1993).

Following this incident, the police were instructed by the city mayor, Sharon Pratt Dixon, not to risk escalating the situation by making arrests. The mayor adopted a conciliatory approach by meeting with representatives of the Mount Pleasant Hispanic community a day later and acknowledging that grievances against the city government were well-founded. However, soon after this meeting, demonstrators attacked police vehicles and personnel and were fired on with riot gas as several hours of violence unfolded. It was not until midnight that the mayor finally declared a curfew. On the following evening, people living in the locality were required to be indoors by 7 p.m. or risk being arrested. This measure proved effective, bringing to an end a riot in which 230 people were arrested and 60 vehicles damaged or destroyed (Drummond Ayres Jnr 1991; *The Economist* 1991).

In the wake of the riot, judgements of the mayor's actions were divided between those who commended her restraint in not escalating the disorder and those who condemned her for 'encouraging' the rioters by adopting too passive a posture (*The Economist* 1991: 41). Such commentators were virtually unanimous, though, in identifying long-term antagonism between the police and local community as a primary cause of the riot.

The Mount Pleasant area was heavily populated by refugees from El Salvador who had fled the civil war in their country in the early 1980s. Many of them had worked in the tertiary trade or construction industry until a law was passed in 1988 which penalised employers for taking on 'illegal immigrants' but which provided an amnesty for any employees hired before 1982. As the majority of Salvadorans had settled in the USA *after* 1982, most were suddenly forced out of their jobs. The resulting high level of unemployment was cited as a probable reason for the growing tendency of large numbers of Salvadoran males to hang around on street corners and in parks, drinking beer and provoking complaints by the police, traders and other local residents of drunkenness and other forms of anti-social behaviour:

> At the same time, Mount Pleasant was being yuppified and the new arrivals put pressure on the police to 'clean up' the area. Already driven from newly fashionable Adams-Morgan (just down the road) by yuppification, the Hispanics began to feel that they were being pushed from Mount Pleasant too. (*The Economist* 1991: 44)

Salvadoran and other Hispanic residents of Mount Pleasant complained of police harassment and discrimination. They maintained that Hispanics were forever being stopped to have their immigration papers checked, or were routinely being booked for minor traffic violations. One Mexican-American quoted by Castaneda and Henderson (1991) complained that, 'If you look Spanish or speak Spanish, they're suspicious of you.' This was echoed by a Honduran construction worker who told Jordan (1991): 'The police believe we're all dumb, illegal and drunk . . . They don't treat us as well as they treat blacks. We call them, they come two hours later. If we are standing around on the streets, they tell us to move on. They don't do that to blacks.'

Cultural and linguistic differences may also have been instrumental in bringing the conflict to the boil. Hispanics complained that, in places like El Salvador, it was customary for groups of males to do their drinking in public without fear of legal intervention. In contrast, the police regarded the drinking as a source of street fights, litter and domestic abuse (*ibid.*). The fact that the main groups of antagonists literally spoke two different languages was also a crucial factor. There were no Spanish-speaking officers involved in the original arrest and no others arrived on the scene until an hour or more had passed (Castaneda and Henderson 1991).

These were among the main contributing factors highlighted in an official report of inquiry published two years later:

> Witnesses at the Commission hearing alleged instances of police misconduct, including harassment, racial and demeaning language, excessive use of force, and the abuse of discretionary arrest power against the Latino community. Testimony also focused on the low number of Latinos and bilingual personnel in the MPD to communicate with a growing Spanish population, and the inadequacy of current police training and monitoring of police misconduct. (United States Commission on Civil Rights 1993: 20)

Another police–civilian encounter, this time involving the arrest and fatal shooting of a Dominican-born American by an undercover NYPD narcotics agent, was the catalyst for six days of rioting in the Washington Heights area of New York City, on 3 June 1992 (Hevesi 1992; Katz 1993; McGowan 1993). Subsequent riots in Florida and Ohio were even more reminiscent of the commodity riots of the 1960s, insofar as they involved African-Americans and the police. Rioting in St Petersburgh, Florida, on 24 October 1996 followed the shooting in broad daylight of an 18-year-old African-American, TyRon Mark Lewis, by one of two white police officers who had stopped him at an intersection, allegedly for speeding in a suspected stolen car (Post and Younce 1996). This was the sixth in a series of shootings of this nature, the latest having predated the riot by only a week (*ibid.*). The St Petersburgh disorder was superseded in scale by the Cincinnati riot of five years later which, as we shall now see, was similar in other important respects.

The Cincinnati (Ohio) riot, April 2001

The Cincinnati, Ohio, riot of April 2001 was America's largest urban disorder since the Los Angeles conflict of 1992. The four days of rioting in the city's Over-the-Rhine area followed an incident occurring around 2.20 a.m. on Saturday, 7 April, when a 19-year-old African-American male (Timothy Thomas) was shot at close range in the chest, having been pursued down an alleyway by a white Cincinnati police officer (Patrolman Stephen Roach). The teenager had been wanted on 14 misdemeanour counts, including 12 traffic violations. The shooting followed a 10-minute chase involving nine other officers. Initially, Roach had defended his action by claiming that Thomas had gone for a gun in his waistband. Subsequently, he admitted that he had shot Thomas by accident, having been startled by his sudden appearance from round a corner. Thomas was rushed by ambulance to hospital where he died of his wounds (Walsh 2001).

Growing community tension peaked on the following Monday, 9 April, when angry protesters, including Thomas's mother, assembled outside City Hall to demand a public explanation of her son's killing. Council members were prevented from leaving the building for three hours as the protesters waited in vain for an answer. Later that evening, hundreds of residents assembled outside Over-the-Rhine's District 1 police station, where they were confronted by a waiting line of police officers, some on horseback, others in cruisers. Protesters threw stones and bottles at the police and smashed in the station's front door. The station flag was pulled from its mast and rehung upside down. After approximately one hour, police in riot gear opened fire with tear gas, bean bags and rubber bullets, and 10 arrests were made (McDonald 2001; Walsh 2001).

The following afternoon (10 April) saw a resumption of violence when a hitherto static demonstration by 20–50 young black men suddenly set off north with police officers in tow. At a road intersection, the protesters started throwing bottles and garbage at the police, causing the latter to back off. Such behaviour was repeated at a nearby set of traffic lights. Sensing the police's reluctance to intervene, parts of the crowd headed downtown where they overturned garbage cans, vendors' carts and newspaper boxes. They then set about smashing the windows of banks, restaurants and bars and looting stores (Conte 2001). A number of white motorists were hauled from their cars and beaten. Police with linked arms or on horseback used tear gas, bean bags and rubber bullets to disperse the rioters. Sixty-six people were arrested (Walsh 2001).

Sporadic incidents also broke out on the following night, during which time a police crackdown resulted in 82 arrests. On the following morning, the local mayor announced a city-wide curfew allowing only those people travelling to and from work to use the streets between the hours of 8 p.m. and 6 a.m. (*ibid.*). The city was placed under a state of emergency and 125 state troopers brought in as back-up (White 2001a). No fewer than 800 people were arrested for violating curfew conditions (*ibid.*).

Further controversy was caused on 14 April, the day of Timothy

Thomas's funeral, when the police geared up for a possible confrontation by flying a helicopter overhead and positioning riot officers two blocks away. After the service, a procession of 30 mourners marched to Liberty and Elm Streets. Six members of the Cincinnati SWAT team and an Ohio Highway Patrol officer soon arrived, leaped out of their cruisers and fired bean bag ammunition into a crowd of 20 peaceful marchers. Two adults and two children were injured in the process (Clark and O'Kain 2001; Hart 2001). The police later asserted that officers were responding to instructions to clear the streets of a large crowd which was blocking an intersection. Civilian eyewitnesses claim that the police pulled up and, without any warning, singled out black participants as targets (Edwards 2001; Hart 2001).

In order to fully understand the causes of this riot, we must first consider the socio-economic conditions affecting Cincinnati's African-American population and explore their implications for police–community relations. Of the city's 331,000 residents, just over 40 per cent are African-American (Walsh 2001). Disproportionately high numbers of blacks are concentrated within the city's highly impoverished Over-the-Rhine area (Lazare 2001). White (2001b) makes the point that, at the time of the riot, average income for the city as a whole was $26,774, while that of Over-the-Rhine was $8,600. High unemployment, resulting from the 'dramatic loss' of manufacturing jobs, was occurring just when the budget for youth programmes had been slashed (White 2001c).

Symptomatic of this growing poverty was the fact that drug-related arrests in Over-the-Rhine had averaged 2,300 per year since 1995. The police response to gathering public concern about the proliferation of drug activity is interpreted by White (2001b: 10–11) as indicative of a wider class conflict:

> The actions of the police cannot be understood outside of understanding the function they serve in a city that is so sharply polarized between economic classes. Like every other American city, Cincinnati in the 1990s has undergone a deepening class division between the haves and have-nots. It is under these conditions that the police have emerged as the chief enforcers of a social policy to marginalize the poor and protect the private property and well-being of the affluent. (*ibid.*: 10–11)

This theme is reinforced by Cottle (2001) who comments on the pre-riot proliferation in Over-the-Rhine of new firms, particularly internet companies, keen to take advantage of low rentals; of young professionals and property developers buying up the cheap but full of character Victorian housing within easy commuting distance of the city's central business district; and of the accompanying growth of bars, restaurants and nightclubs. This increased gentrification of the area had been accompanied by a parallel transformation of police activity:

> In Over-the-Rhine, the increase in police presence (and police vigilance) in recent years has been dramatic. Not only does the city put extra officers on patrol during the entertainment district's peak hours, but many off-duty officers moonlight as private security guards for area businesses. Few of the patrol-men come from the neighborhood, and critics charge that they are more concerned with protecting its (white) club-hoppers and house-renovators than its longtime (black) residents. In fact, according to may of those old-timers, protecting the newcomers has led to increased police harassment of black youth. In a sense then, Cincinnati's riots were emblematic of a new kind of racial conflict, born of creeping prosperity. (*ibid.*: 2)

White (2001b) reports that, in addition to being hired in their off-duty capacity to guard patrons and their cars, the police carried out block-by-block sweeps for drugs and alcohol of apartments owned by business corporations. These services were paid for at police overtime rates. Following such incidents as the robbery and killing of a young white musician employed at a local nightspot, the City administrators passed a 'draconian local ordnance' giving the police 'almost unfettered discretion to banish people' who had been arrested for drug-related offences (Lazare 2001). Arrests for such offences could lead to a person's exclusion from the area for a period of 90 days, and an actual conviction for one full year. Between September 1996 and January 2000, over 1,500 people were excluded in this fashion (White 2001b).

Poor police–community relations resulting from these policies were further aggravated by institutional pressures:

> As in other cities, such as New York, Cincinnati police officers are expected to make arrest goals or quotas. Police officers are also rewarded for high volumes of arrests, while facing discipline for failing to achieve an 'expected' number of arrests. The end result is that the police arrest more low-income and

minority persons, who are less likely to fight the charges in court. (White 2001b: 14)

The problem – as identified by a former police officer, turned Head of the city-sponsored Human Relations Commission – was that police officers tended to cruise the area with more concern for catching troublemakers than with building positive relationships with its people. Such officers used a questionable *modus operandi*: 'They drive up in their cars real fast, slam on the breaks, and see who runs . . . The one who runs must be wanted' (quoted by Cottle 2001: 3). In the six years leading up to the disorder, the Cincinnati police had killed 15 suspects, all of them black, including four since the previous November. Three weeks before the riots took place, local civil liberties organisations joined with the American Civil Liberties Union (ACLU) in filing a lawsuit through the civil courts, alleging 30 years of racial profiling by the Cincinnati police (White 2001c). As the legal director of the Ohio ACLU has stated, measures like the drug exclusion war form part of 'a tapestry of abuses that has led to a culture of hostility between the African-American community and the police. It's one more way in which over-policing has brought the community to the brink' (Cottle 2001: 4).

Communal rioting: the Crown Heights riot (New York City), August 1991

The last significant American example of a communal riot took place in a major borough of New York City in August 1991.

An overview of the riot

The Crown Heights area of central Brooklyn is largely populated by citizens of African-American and African-Caribbean heritage. Also resident in the area is a smaller, though densely populated, community of members of the Lubavitch Hasidim sect of Orthodox Jews. The four days of rioting in Crown Heights from 19–22 August 1991 reflected a mutual animosity between black and Jewish residents, as well as problematic relations between each of the rival ethnic groups and the police. The following account of the riot is largely based on an official report by the State Director of Criminal Justice (Girgenti 1993), complemented by more recent academic analyses of events (Conaway 1999; Shapiro 2002; Shapiro 2006: esp. 36–69).

The trigger of the riot occurred at approximately 8.20 p.m. on the evening of Monday, 19 August 1991, when the Grand Rebbe of the worldwide community of Chabad Lubavitch, Rabbi Menachem Schneerson, was returning to his headquarters, having just paid his weekly visit to the graves of his wife and father-in-law. As they drove through a traffic intersection, one of three vehicles in the Rabbi's motorcade (a station wagon) collided with another car before veering on to the sidewalk and striking down two seven-year-old black children, Gavin Cato and his cousin, Angela. Some bystanders later alleged that the traffic light was at red when the station wagon entered the intersection (Conaway 1999; Girgenti 1993).

The car's driver and its two passengers were instantly surrounded by a hostile crowd as two police officers (both male) also arrived on the scene. The officers were soon joined by two ambulances, one belonging to the city's Emergency Medical Service (EMS) and the second a Hatzolah-sponsored vehicle which was first to arrive on the scene by several minutes. Before long, members of the 150-strong crowd started to assault the three occupants of the station wagon, prompting the police to radio to colleagues for assistance. Two of the officers responding to this call bundled the three Jews into the Hatzolah ambulance and instructed the driver to remove them for their own safety. The ambulance hurriedly drove off to the city's Methodist Hospital where the station wagon's driver was given an alcohol breath test by the police, the result of which was negative.

Gavin Cato was taken by an EMS ambulance to King's County Hospital but was pronounced dead soon after his arrival. Angela Cato was taken to the same hospital by a third vehicle and subsequently survived her injuries. A rumour soon spread that, in the confusion surrounding the accident, Gavin Cato's father had been pushed out of the way by a police officer. A second rumour – that the Hatzolah ambulance crew had bypassed the critically injured Gavin to administer treatment to their fellow Jews – also rapidly circulated the crowd. Following this, Lubavitcher bystanders were angrily bombarded with rocks. The crowd was too large for the 15–20 or so police officers to manage. Indeed, their senior officer ordered them to withdraw for their own safety (Girgenti 1993: 61–62).

During the ensuing hours, Jewish civilians were systematically assaulted and their cars and houses vandalised. Yankel Rosenbaum, a 29-year-old visiting rabbinical student from Australia, was surrounded and set upon by 15 youths. He was stabbed four times and later died in hospital. However, when police commanders gathered at 4 a.m. in the local 71st Precinct Station House to review the situation, their general consensus of opinion was that this had been nothing more than a spontaneous eruption, quite common for the area, 'that proper tactics had been employed', and that the conflict would now gradually wind down (*ibid.*: 65).

This was an over-optimistic prognosis. On the following day, the City Mayor and his staff met up and decided on a strategy for disseminating information into the community to counteract the spread of rumour. Police twice intervened that afternoon to separate rival demonstrations by blacks and Jews. On the second occasion, black demonstrators began throwing bottles and stones at a 100-strong detail of police, eventually forcing them to flee for cover. The Commander of the Brooklyn South Patrol Borough later explained that this had been a deliberate act of restraint, designed to avoid exacerbating the situation. However, junior officers complained of having been 'sitting ducks': only those colleagues standing in the front row of the detail had been equipped with protective shields and even they had been forced to relinquish them whenever they were more urgently needed elsewhere (*ibid.*: 76).

Wednesday afternoon saw a resumption of violence, including an attack on the Police Commissioner's car, which forced him to take refuge alongside junior colleagues in a school building. Following this incident, the Commissioner conducted a personal tour of the neighbourhood, an experience which finally persuaded him of the necessity of a tactical reorientation. This decision may also have been encouraged by growing signs of frustration among rank-and-file officers aggrieved at the Department's failure to allow them to take a more proactive stance.

On Thursday morning, the Police Commissioner approved a revised strategy for dealing with the disturbances. The riot area was divided up into four zones, each under the command of a hand-picked officer. Far greater numbers of officers were deployed than on previous evenings, many of them in the form of mobile response teams. Assembly laws were invoked to move on or disperse gathering crowds and more arrests were enforced that day than in the three preceding days put together. According to Girgenti (*ibid.*: 105), 'The increased police presence and different tactics, coupled with a new get-tough approach, let area residents know that rioting and lawlessness would not be tolerated.' The following morning heralded an 'uneasy calm' and, by Saturday, the violence had completely subsided (*ibid.*: 106).

The sources of community tension

The Girgenti Commission underlines the significance of the resentment felt by black residents towards their Jewish neighbours and the police. Part of this resentment concerned perceptions that the Hasidic community was over-represented in the local polity and could therefore exercise unfair political clout. A second source of indignation related to competition over local housing, which was greatly in demand by Lubavitchers, who – due to the typically large size of their families and religious constraints on their use of motor cars – were always on the lookout for large properties within walking distance of their synagogues. According to Girgenti, many black home owners felt intimidated and antagonised by 'unsolicited, persistent and aggressive campaigns' by their Jewish neighbours to buy up housing stock and 'drive them out' of the community (*ibid*.: 45).

A third major bone of contention related to black perceptions of 'a conspicuous pattern of "preferential treatment" of the Lubavitchers by the Police Department and the City' (*ibid*.). Black residents habitually objected to the inconvenience caused by the police practices of closing off streets and re-routeing public transport on Jewish Sabbaths and Holy Days, and providing a police escort of Rebbe Schneerson on his visits to the graves of relatives. Closely related were accusations of police 'double standards' in their enforcement of the law. Crown Heights blacks would often refer to the strangulation by police officers in 1978 of a black civic leader who was trying to intervene during the arrest of his brother for a motoring offence. They argued that no Lubavitcher would ever have been subjected to such a horrifying ordeal, and that the incident was 'indicative of the limited value placed on black lives' (*ibid*.: 46).

The police were also paying close attention to activities in black neighbourhoods following Lubavitcher complaints about growing levels of crime and drug use in the area. Prior to this, the Lubavitchers had informally established a civilian anti-crime patrol. Critics alleged that this was 'little more than a vigilante group set up to harass black men', although it was also a matter of record that Lubavitchers had been campaigning assiduously for increased police protection (*ibid*.). Blacks also objected to another innovation by the local Hasidics – their decision to instigate a privately funded Hatzolah voluntary ambulance service. Resentment here focused on the belief that the service operated exclusively for the benefit of the Lubavitchers and was indifferent to the needs of other ethnic groups.

Given these background conditions, Girgenti is undoubtedly justified in concluding that:

The accident of the evening of August 19, 1991, was the catalyst for a disturbance largely because it epitomized many of the perceptions pre-existing in the black community about the Lubavitchers, the police and the Hatzoloh ambulance service. The police escort was perceived by many blacks as illustrative of the accommodation that the Police Department and the City routinely make to the Lubavitchers. That police did not arrest the Hasidic driver was regarded by many in the black community as yet another application of a 'double standard' in law enforcement. Finally – what many that night found most outrageous – the first-responding Hatzoloh ambulance was rumoured to have refused to treat the black victims in favour of the Hasidic driver and his passengers. (*ibid*.: 47)

Analysing the police response

The Girgenti Report is equally emphatic in characterising the policing of the Crown Heights disorder as 'inadequate' (*ibid*.: 206). It states that officers responding to the violence erupting at the scene of the accident were too slow to prevent the spread of the disorder. Indeed, over half of the 400 officers eventually deployed to the incident did not arrive until after 11.30 p.m. Part of the reason for this delay was a failure by senior officers to activate the NYPD Rapid Mobilisation procedure. This procedure provided for specific radio codes to be used to call in officers as a matter of priority. However, senior officers explained to Girgenti that most officers were either unfamiliar with, or did not understand, the relevant codes. It had been 20 years since the codes had last been used.

In the absence of a well-defined and clearly articulated mission statement outlining NYPD's philosophy for managing public disorder, the Field Commander operated according to his personal predilection for restraint and non-confrontation. Girgenti argues that the problem with this approach was that it did not allow for any proactive steps that might have been taken. 'As a result, field supervisors were either forced to improvise in order to deal with the specific problems confronting them, or simply remained passive. The Department's response was, consequently, uncoordinated and ineffective' (*ibid*.: 207). It was only after the introduction of Thursday's proactive arrest policy that police tactics became imbued with a confidence and clarity of purpose.

Compounding the problems of poor communication and co-ordination was the fact that recent personnel changes had placed temporary (and inexperienced) officers in crucial positions of authority. In particular, a newly appointed Chief of Department had not yet taken up his post following the retirement of his predecessor. This left the Chief of Detectives to assume interim responsibility as Acting Chief. The fact that the new Chief of Patrol – an officer responsible for the first-line supervision of operations in Crown Heights – had also just been appointed meant that key officers were serving in unfamiliar roles (the Chief of Patrol was also unfamiliar with the area). As a result, 'They were inclined to accept the information and plans they received rather than adopting more assertive roles' (*ibid.*: 18).

Lack of feedback, communication and co-ordination meant that, at crucial stages of the riot, the police underestimated the extent and seriousness of the disorder and the need for an urgent change of strategy. The report maintains that any one of the senior tier of commanding officers could have insisted on regular progress meetings but that the ultimate responsibility for calling them belonged to the Commissioner:

> After each of the first two nights of rioting, there was no meeting of the Headquarters Executive Staff with [the Field Commander] to critique how the police had handled the events. This kind of review in a structured setting is an essential practice so that the police executive can obtain the collective wisdom of principal advisers. Neither Commissioner Brown nor any member of the Executive Staff assembled the Department's management team to examine this urgent situation, review police performance, and determine appropriate police action. (*ibid.*: 254)

On a more positive note, the report praises the efforts of senior police to 'listen to concerns, calm the community, and control rumors' (*ibid.*: 236). These included a rumour that Gavin Cato's cousin had also died as a result of the car accident, but that confirmation of this fatality was being withheld for fear of arousing further hostilities. The fact that such speculation 'built upon long-perceived injustices' made it all the more difficult to dispel (*ibid.*).

A hybrid example: the Los Angeles riot, April 1992

The Crown Heights riot was eclipsed in size and severity less than one year later by the Los Angeles riot of April 1992.

The background to the riot

Aside from the 52 people killed during the LA disorder, 2,383 people were reported injured; property damage was estimated at up to $1 billion; and 9,456 people were arrested, of whom 37 per cent were Latino, 30 per cent were black and the remainder white or 'others/unknown' (DiPasquale and Glaeser 1998; Oliver *et al.* 1993). Oliver *et al.* (*op. cit.*: 120) characterise the riot as a 'response not to single but rather to repeated acts of what is widely perceived in the community to be blatant abuse of power by the police and the criminal-justice system more generally'. However, they also trace a causal link to 'broader external forces', notably the effect of economic restructuring, financial disinvestment and 'conservative federal policies', which accelerated neighbourhood decline, marginalised ethnic minority youth and brought them into sharp conflict with the police.

According to these and other authors, recessionary activity between 1978 and 1992 created thousands of job losses in the auto, steel, rubber and electrical plants of Los Angeles, producing a 50 per cent unemployment rate among young black males (*ibid.*; see also Callinicos 1992; Davis 1988, 1992a,b,c; Gale 1996). While urban re-development occurred in the relatively affluent areas of downtown and westside LA, the far needier South Central area was overlooked by the planning agencies. Cutbacks were also made in the funding of community-based organisations (CBOs), designed to help disadvantaged and disaffected youths back into the economic and social mainstreams. Furthermore, increasing numbers of middle-class blacks had migrated to the more affluent suburban areas of LA, leaving a void of political representation (Davis 1988). The overall effect of these developments was to create a substantial residuum of ethnic minority youth, lacking gainful employment, political representation or a stake in the social order – hence their propensity to join gangs engaged in drug trafficking and other criminal activities (Oliver *et al. op. cit.*: 127 and 131).

As Oliver *et al.* and several other authors (e.g. Callinicos 1992; Sears 1994) point out, blacks and Latinos were each resentful of a more prosperous ethnic minority, the Korean community within Los

Angeles. Since arriving in their thousands in the 1970s, Koreans had secured a firm toehold in American society by creating scores of small businesses. The practical support of close-knit families and the presence of 'Kye' credit systems (set up by established Asian entrepreneurs) gave Korean small traders a head start on their competitors in their attempts to establish commercial roots in poorer, working-class areas (Freer 1994).

Cultural differences between the Koreans and other ethnic minorities were chronically problematic. Black and Latino customers complained of the rude and disrespectful attitudes displayed by Korean shopkeepers. They also objected to the fact that, unlike the one-time Jewish traders in the ghetto, Koreans rarely employed local non-Koreans (Davis 1992: 8; Oliver et al. 1993: 132). Sears (1994: 244) points to the possibility that: 'Underlying much of this conflict also was blacks' anger about being denied access to the American dream; once again African Americans were being passed by, as ambitious migrants from many lands and cultures found fertile economic ground in America.'

Also highly significant was the proliferation of gang-related crack cocaine trafficking and the moral panic it induced. Strident demands for hard-nosed policing to sort out the gangland turf wars were underpinned by a prejudicial ideology asserting that '"family failure" in the ghetto, abetted by indulgent welfarism and the decline of paternal role models, has created a feral population of grave social menace' (Davis 1988: 45). According to Davis, a 'numbers game' was entered into by police, politicians and the media, which gradually exaggerated the extent of gang membership from 10,000 to 100,000.

Public alarm reached fever pitch when gang members accidentally gunned down a Japanese-American woman caught in the cross-fire outside a theatre in the up-market Westwood Village. Local merchants and politicians clamoured for the police to invoke curfews. Only the Southern California chapter of the ACLU presented the political case for the black youths but their voice was lost amidst the outcry:

> Within weeks the LAPD, led by its CRASH division and under the banner of Operation Hammer, mounted full-scale retaliatory raids on the black community. In April 1988, 1,000 extra cops were sent into South Central, and in a single night they rounded up 1,453 black and Latino teenagers. Since then a state of siege has persisted in South Central, where each night – and often during the day – any teenager on the street is fair game for an

LAPD roust, 'jack-up' or bust. An astonishing total of more than 50,000 youths have been detained in Operation Hammer's ongoing manoeuvres. (Cooper 1992: 15)

This sustained paramilitaristic intervention resulted in the alienation and resentment of an entire generation of ethnic minority youth. The uncompromising brand of law enforcement encouraged by the LAPD Chief of Police, Daryl Gates, was relatively unaffected by countervailing opposition to his methods. This was because a unique city charter dating back to the 1920s limited the capacity of the Mayor of Los Angeles to fire his incumbent chief of police and thus placed Gates in a singular position of autonomy (D. Waddington 1992: 196).

Perceptions that the LAPD operated as a 'law unto themselves' were perpetuated on 3 March 1991 when a speeding car driven by 25-year-old African-American, Rodney King, was forced to stop after a protracted chase by two California Highway Patrol officers. By the time the vehicle came to rest, the arresting officers (actually, a husband and wife) had been joined by three LAPD cruisers while a police helicopter circled overhead.

King's two passengers immediately obeyed police instructions by getting out of the vehicle and lying on the ground. However, the driver's strange, unco-operative behaviour (he is said to have gyrated his buttocks at the arresting female officer) suggested that he may have been drunk or even have ingested PCP (phencyclidine), a pain suppressant with the potential to imbue the user with superhuman strength. Tentative attempts by officers to handcuff King and then debilitate him by firing taser darts all failed in their objectives. King was then subjected to a succession of more than 50 baton blows and assorted kicks and stomps that resulted in severe head, leg and abdominal injuries. Unbeknown to the attending officers, the whole incident was captured on videotape by an amateur photographer, George Holliday. On the following day, Holliday took the tape to a local police station but the station desk sergeant expressed indifference. Holliday therefore took the tape to a local TV station (KTLA) which broadcast a 68-second segment that same evening (Fukurai et al. 1994).

In the following few weeks, a highly relevant sequence of events dramatically unfolded. First, on 14 March, an LAPD sergeant and three junior officers were charged with having used excessive force in arresting Rodney King, and the sergeant with having submitted false reports of the incident (Miller 2001). Soon afterwards, a 49-year-old Korean shopkeeper, Ja Du, shot dead a 15-year-old African-American girl, Latasha Harlins, whom she accused of trying to shoplift a carton of orange juice. Ms Du's version of events was contradicted by the store's security video which showed that the unarmed girl had been shot in the back of the head. Consequently, she was charged with murder. Finally, on 1 April, Mayor Tom Bradley attempted to offset the possible impact of the King incident on racial unity by appointing an independent commission on the Los Angeles Police Department, under the prominent legal attorney, Warren Christopher.

The outcome of each development was highly significant. On 9 July 1991, the Christopher Commission released its report. Among its recommendations were: that undisciplined LAPD officers should be expelled from the department, that greater civilian control should be exercised over the force, and that there should be a heavier emphasis on community policing methods. The report was also critical of Chief Gates for encouraging a departmental ethos celebrating the excessive use of force. The commission advocated that the City Charter be redrafted to limit police chiefs to no more than two five-year periods in office. Gates responded to this in writing to say that he planned to retire in April 1992, though he subsequently announced that he might stay in post until later in the summer (Cooper and Goldin 1992: 43–44; Locher 2002: 111).

In November 1991, the trial of Ms Du took place and she was given an unexpectedly lenient suspended prison sentence. The case for her defence was that the shop had been burgled no fewer than 39 times and that shoplifting had been a chronic problem. Moreover, Du's son, Joseph, had recently been assaulted by gang members, who threatened to kill him should he dare to testify against them (Cannon 1997: 117). Later that month, the defence team in the Rodney King case succeeded in securing a change of venue for the forthcoming trial. Following arguments that negative pre-trial publicity was likely to prevent officers from receiving a fair hearing, the trial was switched to the predominantly white, middle-class area of Simi Valley. With the exception of one Latino and one American-Filipino, the eventual jury was all white (Fukurai *et al.* 1994).

The trial of the four LAPD officers took place in the spring of 1991. Commentators generally accept that the prosecution team was guilty of complacency and that the case for the defence was stronger than everyone realised (*ibid.*). At the time of his arrest, King was on parole for robbing a general purpose store and the alcohol levels in his blood were in excess of the legal limit. Moreover, few people had realised that the video transmitted on local radio was an *edited* version of the Holliday recording, which omitted a blurry but crucial ten-second opening to the incident showing King charging at an arresting officer (Cannon 1997: 23).

Somewhere between 3 o'clock and 3.15 p.m. on 29 April 1992, the King verdicts were announced: the defendants were acquitted on all charges bar one, which related to the excessive use of force by one of the accused. The Los Angeles riot of 1992 was now only minutes away from igniting.

The riot process

Morrison and Lowry (1993: 36) make the point that 'Demographically, South Central Los Angeles was ripe for civil disturbance: it contained a critical mass of young males who had no regular occupation, little reason to feel bound by social rules, and the physical energy needed to stone, loot, burn, and run from the police.' These authors maintain that the first two recorded incidents of the riot occurred at Hyde Park (near Crenshaw Boulevard and Florence Avenue) and at the intersection of Normandie and Florence. The former was logged at 3.43 p.m., when the police were informed that bricks were being thrown at passing vehicles. A white pedestrian was beaten up before the crowd moved off to a shopping centre and started looting.

The second incident broke out at 4.17 p.m. A number of commentators (e.g. Cannon 1997; Useem 1997) have identified it as the riot's 'flashpoint' or 'catalyst' for the wider conflagration that occurred. Useem is correct to assert that, had the incident been rapidly contained, the high level of anger prevailing in the ethnic minority may well have exploded into violence at some other location. He nonetheless acknowledges that events at Florence and Normandie constituted the 'heart of the riot', and that one reason for its incendiary effect was that here, 'participants refused to disperse, in effect taking control of the area as their own. When police arrived, the group drove the police out. In contrast, rioters/protestors at other locations generally fled after having committed a crime or after police entered the area' (*ibid.*: 363–364).

It is therefore important for us to understand the way in which events developed at this location. The following commentary is based on what is arguably the most exhaustive and compelling overview and analysis of the riot – by Cannon (1997). Cannon's account is based on interviews with protagonists, the findings of the

Webster Commission (Webster 1992) and an internally published LAPD debriefing document called 'Analysis of the Los Angeles Police Department's Planning, Preparedness and Response to the 1992 Riot (The First Six Hours)'.

Cannon makes the point that, within five minutes of the verdicts, crowds of angry protesters were making their feelings known at various locations throughout Los Angeles, including the 77th Street Division police station at South Central's 77th and Broadway and the Lake View Terrace site of the Rodney King beating. In the vicinity of Florence and Normandie, growing tension was manifested in a proliferation of minor incidents. First, at approximately 4.17 p.m., five young blacks robbed beer from a Korean 'Liquor and Deli' store at Florence and Dalton Avenues, having hit the store owner's son on the head with a bottle. One of the perpetrators is said to have yelled 'This is for Rodney King!' just before the owner activated a silent alarm button, drawing officers based at the 77th Street Division police station to the crime (*ibid.*: 281).

The two African-American officers who responded to this robbery had just finished interviewing the victims and were on the point of leaving the store when they were called to a disturbance a mere 100 yards away at Florence and Halldale. A small number of other officers, including four sergeants, were first to arrive at this incident, where they discovered that a black youth was using a baseball bat to crush in the windscreen of a car occupied by two whites. One of the sergeants blamed the sudden arrival of a TV news crew for trans-forming the mood of the crowd. A second maintained: 'We were the friendly neighbourhood cops one minute, the next minute we were lunch meat. It didn't take a genius to figure out we needed to do something . . . We got out of there' (quoted in *ibid.*: 283).

Two other pairs of officers were still in the process of responding to the original call for assistance when they drove their two cars through the Florence-Normandie intersection. These officers suddenly came under a shower of rocks and bottles and instantly sent out a distress call. Within five minutes, they were joined by 30 colleagues occupying 18 patrol cars. Two of the newly arriving officers immediately set off in pursuit of one of the missile throwers, a 16-year-old black youth whom they recognised as a local gang member. They captured and handcuffed the youth, face-down, before placing him in a police vehicle.

At this point, officers tentatively formed a 'skirmish line' around their cars but were soon in danger of being overwhelmed by an increasingly angry crowd. The Field Commander for Florence and

Normandie, Lieutenant Michael Moulin, arrived from the 77th Street station to discover a situation of intense panic and alarm:

> 'I found utter chaos, an intersection that was uncontrollable,' he said afterward. 'The officers were being subjected to bricks, to huge pieces of concrete, to boards, to flying objects.' Moulin knew how ill-equipped the officers were. 'Most of the policemen had no helmets. They had no bulletproof vests, no tear gas, no face shields . . . I think we're going to have to use deadly force, we could have a massacre here. So I ordered a pullout.' (quoted in *ibid*.: 287)

Thereafter, the crowd turned its attention to robbing and beating civilians. Cars containing black drivers were allowed through the intersection while those containing whites, Asians and Latinos were not spared. By 5.59 p.m. there were reports of 500 male blacks throwing bottles at passing cars.

Back at the divisional headquarters, Moulin and his station captain debated what to do next. The latter insisted afterwards that he had commanded his colleague to return to the intersection with the aim of restoring order. Moulin contradicted this, stating that his orders had been merely to go back in and 'assess the situation' before establishing an emergency command post at Fifty-fourth Street and Arlington Avenue (*ibid*.: 292). Whatever the truth of the matter,

> During the forty-five minutes after this retreat the LAPD lost its chance to stop the riots in its tracks. As disorders spread beyond the Florence-Normandie flash point, isolated teams of officers skirmished with rioters and two of them conducted an especially brave rescue, but the 77th Street Division overall operated without effective direction and had scant communication with units outside the area. (*ibid*.: 293)

By now, the Florence-Normandie intersection was completely under gang control. Television news helicopters hovered overhead, sending live coverage across the nation. These broadcasts were sometimes accompanied by frenzied commentary appealing for the police to 'do something' to help the hapless victims of the ongoing rebellion. This was never more apparent than when, at approximately a quarter to seven, an 18-wheeled vehicle, driven by 36-year-old Oliver Denny, tentatively entered the intersection to be instantly bombarded by rocks. Within minutes, Denny had been dragged from his vehicle and kicked and beaten by several assailants (one of whom used a claw hammer, another a slab of concrete) before being left bleeding and unconscious in the road (*ibid.*: 305).

This incident temporally overlapped with a second confrontation in which a crowd of 150 protesters rushed the city's main police headquarters, the Parker Center. A skirmish line was set up to hold them at bay, which resulted in a 50-minute standoff. However, at 7.30 p.m., a section of the protesters upended and set fire to a guard shack located in the station car park. A quarter of an hour later, the remainder of the crowd descended on a nearby hotel and put through its windows. Police succeeded in pushing the demonstrators away from the station and hotel. The crowd then broke up and started to attack and vandalise cars and buildings, including those of the *Los Angeles Times* and Criminal Courts. By organising themselves into mobile units, the police regained control of the area (*ibid.*: 314–15). The police response had been relatively effective; but, as Cannon explains, 'since the Parker confrontation came on the heels of the Denny assault and was also widely televised, it reinforced a public impression that Los Angeles was an undefended city under siege' (*ibid.*: 315).

Understanding the LAPD's response

Ironically, while millions of Americans looked on, horrified by the live televised unfolding of events at Florence and Normandie, officers were gradually pouring into a field command post established close by. Indeed,

> By midnight as many as 1,790 officers were sent to assist at the 77th area. These were held in a bus yard without deployment. The consequences of this decision were far reaching; for not only were these officers unavailable to the 77th area, they had been drained from their sectors and these were undermanned while their manpower languished awaiting redeployment. (Miller 2001: 196)

Useem (1997: 365) contends that the LAPD's tactical manual incorporated a plan for dealing with the type of incident occurring at the crucial intersection. This provided for officers from the city's élite Metropolitan Division to arrive in tactical support elements (TSEs) and break up riotous behaviour into smaller, more manageable sectors of activity. Thereafter, ordinary uniformed patrol officers were supposed to form cordons around each sector, thus preventing the incidents from spreading and aggregating.

Several authors point out that the LAPD completely failed to implement this plan and that its most senior officers scarcely engaged in any advance training or preparation for the riot (Cannon 1997; Miller 2001; Useem 1997). A major reason for this was that a breakdown in communication occurred between Chief Gates and many of his senior officers, and between Gates and Mayor Bradley, following investigations by the Christopher Commission. According to the Webster Commission on the riot, 'For almost one year before the 1992 civil disturbance, the top LAPD commanders appear to have functioned with a seriously impaired working relationship characterized by poor or non-existent communication and little co-ordination of their respective commands. This prolonged period of infighting and isolation severely impacted the LAPD's command and control' (quoted in Cannon 1997: 275). Weekly meetings of executive staff were cancelled in the four weeks leading up to the disorder (Useem 1997). Also contributing to this force-wide condition of inertia was the general supposition that, as the officers were almost certain to be found guilty, it would have been wasteful of resources to have engaged in unnecessary forward planning and preparation (Cannon 1997).

One notable exception was the attitude of the assistant chief in charge of operations, Robert Vernon, who was extremely aware of the strategic importance of the élite Metropolitan Division in the management of any riot. He therefore instructed the 'Metro' to update its riot plans and brush up its training and tactics in readiness for a 'major unusual occurrence'. Vernon issued similar directives to the captains of all LAPD divisions, though the majority are said to have ignored him (ibid.: 269–270). Lieutenant Michael Moulin, the Field Commander at Florence and Normandie was one of many 77th Street Division officers who later complained that they had received no briefing or training for the possibility of disorder (ibid.: 270; Useem 1997: 369).

Within the Metro Division itself, commanders treated the possibility of disorder far more seriously than their counterparts elsewhere. Metro personnel were put through intensive training at secret locations two weeks prior to the King verdict. In order to avoid creating a self-fulfilling prophesy, Metro commanders committed their officers to making a decisive but well-disciplined intervention at the first sign of any disorder. One particular lieutenant urged the LAPD high command to deploy Metro units in personnel carriers between 10 a.m.

and 6 p.m. on the day of the trial outcome. He recommended that such officers be given protective clothing and equipped with AR-15 assault rifles (Cannon 1997: 273). Nevertheless, the decision was taken to deploy the Metro *at night* – in 'soft patrol mode'.

As a result, 76 of the Metro's 233 officers were not even on duty when the flashpoint at Florence-Normandie occurred. Most of the remainder were deployed further afield, such as the San Fernando Valley or at the LAPD's Parker Center headquarters. Cannon makes the point that, had they been more sensibly deployed, Metro officers could have responded speedily to the incident in which the youth was wielding a baseball bat, making it unnecessary to contemplate any form of retreat. Alternatively, 'they might have moved back to Florence and Normandie after the original retreat and dispersed the gang members when the mob was relatively small' (*ibid.*: 294).

The overall lack of planning and preparation proved equally disastrous in terms of its effect on police communication and co-ordination. At the field command post established by Lieutenant Moulin, the few existing telephone lines were quickly overloaded, while all but one of the cellular phones available required recharging. Equally, there were no fax machines, computers or photocopiers. This meant that each time a command officer needed to talk to a colleague, they were forced to contact them in person. When Moulin requested 100 hand-held radios for use in outside vehicles, he was told that only a mere seven were on hand (Cannon 1997: 310).

A key contributing factor was the lack of effective leadership. While the riot was in progress, 12 of the department's 18 area captains were attending a training course some 60 miles away. A 'tactical alert' requiring all officers to report for duty was not declared until almost 7 p.m., meaning that hundreds of officers had gone home by the time the rioting broke out. Included among them were officers from the South Bureau who had been trained to staff a command post. Most significantly of all, Chief Gates had left town at 6.30 p.m. to attend a fund-raising event. Thus, according to Useem,

The swirl of political events in and around the LAPD diminished the agency's capacity to respond effectively to civil disorders. Specifically, the events that comprised the 'King incident' resulted in enormous pressures on the department, pushing it in just about every direction except toward riot preparation. These pressures could have been resisted, but the agency was internally divided and distracted from its core task of the maintenance of the public order. Thus, although an assistant chief recognized the need to prepare the department for a riot he thought inevitable, he could not effect this agency wide. When the riot broke out, the institutional core was hesitant. The department drifted through the first half dozen hours of the disturbance, stumbling at Florence and Normandie. (1997: 373)

An eventual decision to call in the National Guard was taken by Mayor Bradley in consultation with other LAPD senior officers at a time when Chief Gates was still airborne in an LAPD helicopter. It was only when a dusk-to-dawn curfew was enforced by members of the California National Guard, federal troops, LAPD officers, and other state agencies that the riot was finally quelled (Schnaubelt 1997: 10).

Conclusions

Four of the six major American riots occurring between 1991 and 2001 conformed to Janowitz's category of commodity riots. Riots of this nature broke out in Washington, DC, New York City, St Petersburgh (Florida) and Cincinatti (Ohio). A fifth disturbance, in the Crown Heights area of Brooklyn, was in many ways the prototypical community riot. What made it somewhat unusual, though, was the fact that,

> In a typical riot, there is a tremendous level of destruction of physical objects such as stores, buildings and especially windows. In Crown Heights, such vandalism was relatively limited. Participants sought human targets for their attacks. The violence was not blind or random: it was calculated and focused. (Locher 2002: 92)

The Crown Heights riot was largely driven by inter-ethnic enmity between local blacks and Hasidic Jews. Antagonism between rival ethnic groups (African-Americans and Koreans) was also an underlying issue in the Los Angeles riot. While this dimension of the disorder is consistent with Janowitz's definition of a community riot, the arguably more prominent matter of police–community relations imbued Los Angeles with an unusual, hybrid quality. Despite these differences of character, each of the riots mentioned in this chapter highlights the contribution of police structures and practices in the genesis of large-scale urban disorder.

In each of the cases considered, community relations were brought to the boil by specific police tactics designed to manage sections of the urban poor. More accurately, it was in their handling of the social symptoms or side-products of deprivation and political marginalisation (heavy drinking in Mount Pleasant and drug use in the other locations) that the police helped to generate the 'cultures of hostility' that eventually culminated in violence. Political and departmental pressures encouraged particular styles of policing that were inimical to achieving respect, trust and the confidence of the local communities. 'Respectable' audiences, ranging from middle-class whites and local restaurant owners to representatives of beleaguered Jewish enclaves, urged the police to deal uncompromisingly with the 'lawless' in their midst. In the case of the Cincinnati riot at least, arrest quotas and 'clean-up' targets provided added incentives for clamping down on the underclass.

Such pressures gave a hefty impetus to police strategies involving racial profiling and prior assumptions of guilt. This tendency was compounded by the absence of police accountability, whether this took the form of restricted civilian input (in Los Angeles), a lack of procedures for monitoring police misconduct (in Washington), or concern about the fact that privately employed, off-duty police officers in Cincinnati were answerable to no one but their employers. In the Mount Pleasant riot, linguistic and cultural differences were additional sources of aggravation. There is compelling evidence to suggest that, over time, sections of all these communities became acutely aware of a 'tapestry of abuses'. Animosity towards the police gradually accumulated; and where evidence arose that the law was not being evenly enforced (as with black perceptions of the leniency accorded to Jews and Koreans in Brooklyn and Los Angeles, respectively), inter-ethnic hostility became endemic.

Police–civilian interaction gave rise to 'flashpoints' where everyday encounters symbolically crystallised enduring grievances against the police (and, in the case of Crown Heights and Los Angeles, rival ethnic groups). Our case study of Los Angeles indicates that academics were misguided in supposing that there was an absence of a specific triggering incident. Nevertheless, Gale (1996: 154–55) is justified in emphasising that collective memory had a significant part to play:

Rioters had many months to absorb the beating incident. Yet even after a cooling-off period, the most deadly and most destructive urban riot in modern times resulted. The 1980 Miami and Los Angeles disasters demonstrate that urban interracial mob violence erupts not solely in response to immediate antagonizing events; it can happen even in the aftermath of the opportunity for reflection, investigation, and thoughtful inter-action between races and classes. Even with a year to cool inflamed passions, the propensity to strike out was too powerful to be denied.

It may be precisely because the triggering incident constitutes the 'final straw' that conflicts resulting from perceived police atrocities may be difficult to reverse. The evidence of the Mount Pleasant and Crown Heights riots suggests that interventions by the police or city authorities, designed to dispel rumour and/or ameliorate known grievances are unlikely to succeed in cases where trust has irrevocably broken down. Likewise, the case studies of Mount Pleasant, Crown Heights and Los Angeles endorse assertions by the likes of Marx, Smelser, Hundley and Spiegel that, where initial police responses to the riot are perceived as weak, slow or otherwise ineffectual, this will embolden rioters and encourage an unrestrained expression of their grievances.

The apparent causes of the recent American riots are generally consistent with the theoretical insights reviewed in Chapter 1 and, especially, Chapter 2. However, official reports on the Crown Heights and Los Angeles riots further enhance our knowledge by emphasising the importance of effectively disseminated police mission statements and departmental plans for dealing with disturbances. The absence of, or failure to use, such guidelines in these cases had devastating repercussions. In both instances, organisational flux in the build-up to the riots proved detrimental to planning, training and preparation, and, ultimately, the clarity and conviction of operational command during the actual disorders. The trickle-down effect of organisational disarray was felt at ground level where bemused and demoralised officers ultimately complained of indecision and poor resources. Ironically, guidelines embedded in NYPD and LAPD documentation comprised possible strategies for containing outbreaks of disorder on a sectoral basis. In Crown Heights, such an approach was eventually used to telling effect on the fourth night of the riot. The absence of such an approach in Los Angeles meant that it was left to the combined efforts of the National Guard and permanent armed forces to belatedly quell a disorder in which more than 50 lives were lost.

Chapter 4

The British urban riots, 1991–2001

Introduction

The 11-year period from 1991 to 2001 saw a similar pattern of rioting on the opposite side of the Atlantic to North America. A decade after the inner-city riots in places like Brixton (London), Handsworth (Birmingham), Toxteth (Liverpool), Moss Side (Manchester) and Chapeltown (Leeds) (see for example Benyon and Solomos 1987), Britain experienced renewed rioting, though this time on mainly white, working-class housing estates scattered across England and south Wales. In the space of a single fortnight spanning late August and early September 1991, there were riots in Cardiff, Oxford, Birmingham and South Shields. Nine more riots then occurred in the three-month period from May to July 1992 in such widely dispersed towns and cities as Coventry in the Midlands, Salford, Burnley and Blackburn in Lancashire, and Stockton-on-Tees in the north-east of the country (King and Brearley 1996; Power and Tunstall 1997).

Unlike their predecessors of the early 1980s where saturation policing and police harassment were primary issues of contention, the latest disorders were triggered by sudden police interventions (following long periods of apparent indifference and inaction) in response to growing public concern over the theft of motor vehicles and/or their use in criminal or improvised 'leisure activities' (Lea 2004; D. Waddington 1992). An overview of these riots, and explanation of the particular forms of policing that gave rise to them, is provided in the first section of this chapter, which uses studies by Campbell (1993) and Power and Tunstall (1997) as its basis of analysis.

The remainder of the chapter is then devoted to analysing the policing of the most recent British 'riot wave'. In the late spring and summer of 2001, there were riots in northern Pennine towns and cities once renowned as centres of the textiles trade. Following minor disturbances in Bradford (West Yorkshire) on 14–15 April, there were more serious disorders in Oldham (Greater Manchester) on 26–29 May, Burnley (Lancashire) on 23–25 June, and Bradford again on July 7–9. Another small disorder also broke out in Leeds (West Yorkshire) on 5 June.

As Kalra (2003: 145) points out in relation to the three most serious of the riots,

> Those arrested were predominantly aged 17–26, predominantly local and mainly of Pakistani and Bangladeshi heritage. The areas where the riots took place were also on the margins of, or otherwise near, areas occupied by Asian Muslims. Indeed, even though the causes of the riots are multiple, and the incursion of Far Right groups has been cited in all of the subsequent policy reports, ultimately the conflict in all three areas was played out between predominantly Asian Muslim young men and local police. Clearly, the relationship between the police and sections of the young male Asian Muslim population is something that needs to be explored further.

In the wake of the riots, there was a plethora of official inquiries into their causation and possible remedies. Two of these were primarily local in their emphasis: Clarke (2002) examined the Burnley riot while Ritchie (2001) focused on Oldham. Two others (Cantle 2001; Denham 2002) had a more general orientation. Kalra and other writers (e.g. Bagguley and Hussain 2003; Lea 2004) have commented on the tendency of these reports to highlight such factors as Asian 'self-exclusion' from mainstream (white) society, an absence of credible political leadership and representation within such communities, intergenerational conflict and growing youth criminality as the underlying sources of the crisis. What is absent from, or subordinated by, these official analyses is corresponding discussion of the police role in the generation of disorder. Nevertheless, this is handsomely compensated for by complementary, and sometimes competing, academic discourse focusing on the contributory effect of police policy prior to and during the riots.

As a necessary prelude to our discussion, the second section of the chapter sets out the social context of the riots by focusing on the relevant underlying conditions giving rise to youth disaffection and hostility in their relations with the police. This part of the discussion includes a brief analysis of an early manifestation of the growing problem – the Bradford riot of 1995. It also begins to examine the way that the mass media, in conjunction with senior police, helped to create a stereotypically negative impression of Asian youth which attracted the unhealthy attention of the Far Right and so created a highly combustible atmosphere. The third section elaborates on this theme by showing how Oldham police's particular method of interpreting and disseminating crime figures on 'racist incidents' made a significant contribution to the eventual riot. A fourth section then focuses on the misguided police tactics and strategy employed during the Burnley riot which were predicated on an equally dangerous and misleading interpretation of the activities of Asian youth.

The chapter excludes any mention of the most recent noteworthy riot occurring in Great Britain – the Lozells Road disorder in Birmingham in November 2005. By all accounts, this was a classic instance of a 'community riot' between African-Caribbean and Asian youths, which followed rumours that a young black woman had been 'gang-raped' by customers in an Asian-owned hairdresser's and beauty salon (Vulliamy 2005). Newspaper reports scarcely mention any possible police involvement in the riot. In the absence (at the time of writing) of journalistic, academic or official accounts of police activity, there is no point in making further reference to this event.

The 1991–92 riots on white, working-class housing estates

The locations in which the youth riots of 1991 and 1992 took place are characterised by Power and Tunstall (1997) as 'stigmatised' council housing estates experiencing common problems in the form of political and physical neglect, low incomes, high welfare dependency, poor job prospects and low educational attainment, especially among boys. More than 50 per cent of families living on these estates were headed by a single parent and there had been a growing tendency for older residents to migrate out of the areas concerned.

Both Power and Tunstall and Campbell (1993) recommend that we focus on the variations in the ways that young men and women responded to the effects of economic crisis, as these are fundamental to helping us to explain the disorders. These authors emphasise that young women did not play any direct part in the rioting – other than to attempt to restrain their menfolk and deter them from attacking local buildings. Power and Tunstall attribute this non-involvement to the greater likelihood that the girls would do better at school and be more successful in landing jobs. The high rate of teenage pregnancies also provided young mothers with a sense of purpose and esteem not available to their male counterparts. The lives of young men seemed rudderless in comparison:

> They felt they had nothing and were going nowhere. They were very far from any formal job market. They were alienated from training, maybe through fear of further failure. They were often hostile to adults, maybe through fear of or an expectation of rejection. These attitudes led them to reject authority. (*ibid.*: 43)

Campbell extends this argument to suggest that much of the criminal activity predating the riots, notably the theft and public flaunting of motor cars, symbolised a masculine reassertion of power, status and domination of community space to compensate them for the loss of occupational identity and wage status once conferred on them in times of full employment. Appearances of masculine potency and self-sufficiency were further sustained by drug-dealing, shop-lifting and burgling within their own community, and meting out reprisals on anyone daring to inform the police.

Campbell and Power and Tunstall all agree that police inaction in dealing with the youths also played a central role in the genesis of disorder. Police officers in these areas were exasperated and dismayed by their limited powers to bring the youths to book. Local information had dried up and, far from being a deterrent, the prospect of court appearances was welcomed by the youths as offering opportunities to flaunt and enhance their notoriety. The police presence was therefore alien and sporadic – 'not close enough to the community or permanent enough within it' (Power and Tunstall 1997: 45). Consequently, crime and disorder tended to 'rumble on' indefinitely until finally reaching fever pitch, at which point police in riot gear waded in with overwhelming force:

> In areas where cars were stolen and driven dangerously around estates, buildings were set on fire, drugs were peddled and small groups of young men were out of control, tension between older residents and groups of law-breaking youths built up to a point where eventually residents demanded police action to suppress behaviour they themselves could not control. In the 13 areas, incidents mounted to a point of extreme conflict

within the community over behaviour standards and expectations, which then triggered police intervention. It was scarcely
surprising that the police, attempting to intervene in an already
long-running situation of disorder, failed to impose their
authority without a struggle. Police attempts to re-establish
control over an area were often seen by young people as a
challenge to fight back. (*ibid.*: 15–16)

This was an example, *par excellence*, of 'too little policing followed by
too much policing' (*ibid.*: 45). Escalation was now inevitable for, as
Campbell (*ibid.*: 193) points out, the police and the youths were two
rival cultures that 'needed each other' to endorse their avowedly
masculine self-imagery.

The textile town riots of 2001: general background

Social conditions

The origins of the social conditions giving rise to the confrontations
in Bradford, Oldham and Burnley are explained by Kundnani (2001).
He comments on the cruel irony of the fact that migrant labour
brought over from Pakistan and Bangladesh in the 1960s and
1970s to work the undesirable night shifts of the textile trades had
progressively become redundant due to capitalism's preference for
employing cheaper labour back in their countries of origin. As
Kundnani puts it, 'The work once done cheaply by Bangladeshi
workers in the north of England could now be done even more
cheaply by Bangladeshi workers in Bangladesh' (*ibid.*: 106). By such
means were low-paid local economies transformed at a stroke into
severely impoverished communities – among the 20 most deprived
areas in the United Kingdom.

On top of this, segregationist policies, first encouraged decades
earlier by the racist practices of estate agencies and local authority
housing departments, were given fresh impetus by 'white flight' out
of neighbourhoods associated with the dying textile trade and into
the outlying suburbs. Too intimidated by the prospect of making
similar moves on to the predominantly white suburban estates, Asian
residents simply stayed put, the upshot being that 'The geography of
the balkanised northern towns became a chessboard of mutually
exclusive areas' (*ibid.*: 107).

Amin (2002, 2003) explains how these conditions of poverty and segregation gave rise to accompanying inter-ethnic animosities. Mutual resentment festered as Asians complained of pro-white discrimination in employment and housing, while whites developed 'a language of victimhood' based on perceptions of preferential welfare and regeneration spending on Asian areas (Amin 2002: 965). Most seriously affected by de-industrialisation were the cohorts of relatively unskilled and unqualified young Asian males. This section of the British Asian population felt profoundly aggrieved towards the elders of the communities, whom they regarded as subservient to white society and out of touch with their own (Jan-Kahn 2003). Generally speaking, Asian youth of the 1990s was unwilling to accept the designation of second-class citizenship conferred on previous generations:

> When racists came to their towns looking for a fight, they would meet violence with violence. And with the continuing failure of the police to tackle racist gangs, violent confrontations between groups of whites and Asians became more common. Inevitably, when the police did arrive to break up a melee, it was the young Asians who bore the brunt of police heavy-handedness. As such, Asian areas became increasingly targeted by the police as they decided that gangs of Asian youths were getting out of hand. The real crime problems faced by Asian communities – not only racist incursions but the growing epidemic of heroin abuse – were ignored. Among young Asians, there grew a hatred of a police force that left them vulnerable to racism, on the one hand, and, on the other, criminalised them for defending themselves. (Kundnani 2001: 108)

A forerunner: the 1995 Bradford riot

Strongly indicative of the increasingly troubled relations between male Asian youths and the police was the rioting that broke out in the West Yorkshire city of Bradford in the summer of 1995. It is informative to consider the details of this riot, as disclosed by the independent Bradford Commission (1996).

The immediate trigger for this disorder was an incident commencing at approximately 9.25 p.m. on Friday, 9 June 1995, when two police officers driving round the Manningham area of Bradford passed a group of eight Asian youths playing football in the street. The officers maintained that they approached the youths because some of them had sworn in their direction. During the ensuing argument, four youths were arrested. A sister of two of these prisoners claimed that police had pushed her and struck her baby in the course of making their arrests. A growing crowd of onlookers was instructed to 'get back indoors' or risk being arrested. One witness, a white resident, complained that the police's 'unnecessarily aggressive attitude' had generated feelings of hostility and defiance. Within 10 minutes, police reinforcements – including a dog handler – arrived on the scene and whisked the arrestees off to the nearby Central Bridewell police station. Civilian respondents maintained that an elderly man standing in the doorway was briefly threatened by the police dog. They also claimed that the police vehicles quickly left in convoy, preferring to depart by driving over a pavement at the end of a cul-de-sac, their tyres squealing in their haste to get away.

The Bradford Commission's report is highly critical of the police's intervention, especially because

> There was no differentiation made between curious local residents who later became protestors, responsible people trying to calm things down, and trouble-makers. All members of the public there were treated with equal hostility and contempt by the police. No attempt was made to explain what the police were doing, even when the arrests had been accomplished and all the activity of the other officers had ceased. Even the manner of exit, across the traffic barrier pavement, was necessarily provocative. The police swept in, and then swept out, having acted throughout as though the local residents were of no account, and incapable of understanding an explanation. (*ibid*.: 38: 4.8.17)

Community resentment was reinforced by a rapidly spreading rumour that the police 'attack' on the Asian woman's baby had resulted in its hospitalisation or even death. Two contingents of local residents – one, a group of Asian young men demanding the immediate release of their four peers; the other, older men concerned by police conduct earlier that evening – converged on Lawcroft House, a local police station closer in distance than Central Bridewell. Members of the older party were invited in for discussion. Shortly afterwards (between 10.30 p.m. and 10.45 p.m.), seven more arrests were made outside the station of people accused of failing to respond to police instructions to disperse (*ibid*.: 42: 4.10.7). According to the Commission, these arrests were the 'clinching factor in uniting young and old in openly expressing anger against the police' (*ibid.*: 42: 4.11.1).

Rioting by local youths spread from Lawcross House to nearby Oak Lane, where fires were lit in the road and a car showroom attacked. Disorder continued until 4 a.m., with local officers having been joined by reinforcements from elsewhere in West Yorkshire. During the night, youth and community representatives and local politicians held discussions with the police. These continued on the following day when a local MP, a city councillor and two youth representatives explored with police the possibilities of dropping all charges against their prisoners of the previous day, suspending the two arresting officers and apologising to the sister of the arrested youth.

Following the breakdown of these talks, 300 youths already gathered outside Lawcross House started breaking down a nearby wall and hurling bricks at the police. Rioting spread once more to Oak Lane where youths drew a barricade across the road. As officers and police vehicles moved slowly in their direction, the youths threw stones and petrol bombs. Disorder eventually extended into Bradford city centre. At 12.45 a.m., the police succeeded in setting up roadblocks around the area, though violence continued to flare up sporadically until 2 a.m.

The Commission concluded that 'the disorders took place again on the Saturday night because the police were unable to convince the local representatives that their concerns were understood and would be taken seriously . . . and because the police failed to relate to the aggrieved residents themselves' (*ibid.*: 58: 4.18.3). The police tactics deployed were criticised as 'provocative', 'impersonal' and 'inflexible'. Outside forces were regarded as having been tense and unfamiliar with the locality and its people. In contemplating possible lessons for the future, the Commission conceded:

> It is easy to be wise after the event. We therefore do not criticise the decisions which led to the lack of adequate police deployment to protect the city centre, given the difficult situation the police faced. We do, however, think that the vulnerability of the city centre, and the unpredictability of violent gangs and looters, should be specifically considered by the police in the event of future threats of disorders, particularly when the build up of trouble indicates that some of the trouble-makers are not very local, but from a wide area of the city and beyond. (*ibid.*: 62: 4.18.24)

On Sunday, 11 June, the potential for further disorder was apparent. However, local control was now entrusted to more senior police leadership; dialogue between senior police and local representatives was more constructive, and officers patrolled the city in normal uniform. A hostile crowd of 600 gathered outside Lawcroft House. Officers without riot gear (but still wearing protective body armour and brandishing long side batons) were deployed in response. Ringleaders advocated further violence. However, a series of speakers, including local councillors and the Bishop of Bradford, successfully appealed for further discussion. Then, as midnight approached, eight members (four Asian and four white) of the recently formed Interfaith Women for Peace turned up at Lawcroft House, bearing candles and a makeshift banner proclaiming 'Peace', in Urdu, English and Arabic. According to the Commission, 'this very public intervention was particularly striking', marking a termination of the disorders (*ibid*.: 63: 4.21.1).

The Commission identifies a number of watershed experiences and events of the preceding 25 years which, in their view, helped to shape Asian orientations to the police and other sections of white society, and influenced outside attitudes and behaviour towards them. Mention is made of such developments as: the anti-racist riots in Southall, London, of 1976 and 1981; the Iranian revolution of 1979/80, the 'Honeyford affair' of the mid-1980s, where comments by a Bradford-based head teacher linked poor educational standards to the high ratio of schoolchildren from ethnic minorities; demonstrations and book burnings in response to the publication of Salman Rushdie's *Satanic Verses*; and the Gulf War of the early 1990s.

The report also refers to the effect of long-term antagonisms between Kashmiri youths and the police (based on 'inappropriate, unfair, or racist treatment by individual officers') in lending credence to rumours at the outset of the riot and fuelling indignation and anger throughout its duration (*ibid*.: 158: 6.17.6). It is sceptical, though, of reports of extensive drug-related gang activity among Asian youths and, in particular, the degree to which it supposedly reflected animosity towards the white community (*ibid*.: 104: 5.21.13).

The political and ideological context

This final theme is addressed by Webster (1997) who presents evidence to suggest that a growing commitment to self-defence among young Asians from the late 1980s to the mid-1990s was misconstrued by neighbouring white communities and authorities, notably the police, as 'black racism on whites'. According to crime statistics for Keighley in West Yorkshire between 1988 and 1995, the frequency of attacks by whites on Asians decreased while 'Asian on white violence rose correspondingly. Webster interprets these trends in terms of a growth of informal vigilantism by loosely organised Asian youths, aimed at deterring white racism and creating 'safe areas' for Asian people.

In the meantime, however, senior police and the mass media were depicting places like Keighley, Bradford and Oldham as no-go areas, heaving with territorial rivalries between drug traders and racial hostility towards whites. For example, a profile of Bradford's Muslim community appearing on BBC television's *Panorama* programme in 1993 portrayed them as 'an "underclass in Purdah", where drug abuse and crime was rife' (*ibid*.: 80). Following the Bradford disorder, the Chief Constable of West Yorkshire was the latest in a long line of senior police to allege that growing 'criminality' among Asian young men was due to the fact that they were rebelling against the authority of their parents and community elders (*ibid*.: 67). Thus, as Webster maintains,

> A growing perception began to be shaped in the minds of white youngsters, the police and local agencies, which associated Asian self-defence and territorialism with street disorder and criminality through white perceptions of an Asian 'offensive' and experiences of being attacked by Asians. White territorialism inadvertently generated those very conditions that whites complained about to the study; that attacks on Asians had declined and attacks on whites had increased, enabling white young people to portray racism as something that black people inflict on whites in the form of violent racism and abuse aimed at whites, and that Asians were a threat to public order (*their order*). A further consequence was a growing perception among the police and local agencies of Asian gangs' involvement in drug use and criminality. (*ibid*.: 76)

Regarding this final point, Alexander (2004) also notes that the focus of moral panics over aspects of Asian life has shifted from issues around arranged and/or forced marriages, domestic violence and absconding young women on to that of the criminal and violent 'Asian gang'. The implications of this changed ideological emphasis for the worsening of police–community relations that culminated in the disorders of 2001 are exemplified by the first of our examples, that of the Oldham riot.

The Oldham riot

The background to the riot

The flashpoint of the Oldham riot was an incident occurring on the evening of 26 May 2001 when two Asian brothers, aged 14 and 11, were walking past a chip shop situated on the borderline of the Roundthorn and predominantly Asian Glodwick districts of the town. The following description of this incident and the wider reaction it provoked is based on a diverse range of sources (e.g. Ahmed *et al.* 2001; CARF 2001; Kundnani 2003; *Oldham Advertiser* 2003; Oldham Partnership Board 2001).

According to these commentators, trouble broke out when one of the boys was struck on the leg by a brick deliberately aimed at him by a 16-year-old white youth. The victim was immediately accompanied by his 19-year-old brother to a nearby house which the perpetrator was seen to have entered. One of the permanent occupants of the house, a 36-year-old white woman, was sitting talking to a group of visiting friends when she heard the Asian brothers knocking on her door. Instantly, she took exception to their arrival and became racially abusive towards them. A small number of other Asian youths then appeared and also entered the argument, whereupon one of the woman's house guests decided to call the police. Feeling that other measures were also necessary, the occupant firstly phoned up her mother and then her 25-year-old brother, informing the latter, 'There's some trouble at the house. Some Pakis have kicked the door in' (quoted in *Oldham Advertiser* 2003).

The woman's brother had more reasons than normal for feeling incensed by news of the 'attack' on his sister. At the time of receiving the call, he was engaged in a drinking spree in Oldham town centre. His 12-strong group of co-revellers included members of the right-wing British National Party (BNP) and of the politically similar Combat 18 organisation who had travelled up from London to join ranks with the Fine Young Casuals, a hooligan 'crew' associated with Oldham Athletic FC. Having been alerted by telephone, the group sped off to outer Glodwick in three taxis. They arrived at around 8.10 p.m. and instantly set about smashing the windows of Asian residences and an Asian-owned hairdresser's. Among those besieged in their homes was a 34-year-old pregnant woman who was subsequently treated for shock.

Police quickly arrived on the scene and promptly arrested the majority of the 10 or so white offenders. Meanwhile, Asian youths poured into the area, responding to rumours that the police were either unwilling or unable to prevent ongoing white atrocities. Asian anger was exacerbated, first by the arrest of two of their number, and then by a police decision to throw a protective cordon around a van-load of white prisoners. Finding themselves outnumbered, the police rapidly withdrew from the scene at approximately 8.45 p.m.

By 10 p.m., a 500-strong crowd of Asian youths had formed in central Glodwick, where they threw stones at police and passing vehicles. Street barricades were erected and youths hurled petrol bombs and other objects at opposing police lines. Rioting continued until 5 a.m. the following morning. During this time, four public houses and the offices of the *Oldham Evening Chronicle* were attacked and 32 police vehicles damaged. At the subsequent trial in Manchester on 13 June 2001 of nine white men and one white women, each charged with affray for their part in the Oldham riot, the Judge remarked that there had been 'simmering unrest particularly among the Asian community' in the build-up to the riot, and that 'It only required a spark to ignite the fires that ensued' (Kundnani 2003).

The context of the riot

Ray and Smith (2004) ask why it was the case that rioting broke out in Oldham but not in the ostensibly similar neighbouring town of Rochdale, which is characterised by similar degrees of ethnic segregation and deprivation, relative to other parts of Greater Manchester. For them, the answer to this question lies in the unique way in which local police and media both commented on and interpreted a supposed proliferation in the Oldham area of racist attacks by Asians on members of nearby white communities.

Crime statistics analysed by Ray and Smith suggest that, since 1994, the number of incidents involving white victims of racial incidents had been higher in the Q Division (Oldham) than in any other division of Greater Manchester Police. For the year 1999–2000, statistics showed that 52 per cent of the 646 victims of racial incidents in the Oldham area were 'white'. Of all of the white victims recorded across Greater Manchester as a whole, 38 per cent were from

Oldham. Moreover, just under half of the Asian 'suspects' involved in such incidents were said to have been living in the town (*ibid.*: 687).

Not only Ray and Smith but other commentators also (e.g. Ahmed *et al.* 2001; Kalra 2003) have argued that it was not the publication of these figures *per se*, but rather the particular *interpretation* imposed on them by police spokespersons and the media, that heightened the potential for rioting. In commenting on previous figures (released in 1998), purporting to show a greater frequency of attacks on whites, the local Chief Superintendent for Q Division had maintained that:

There's evidence that [Asian male youths] are trying to create exclusive areas for themselves. Anyone seems to be a target if they are white. It is a growing polarisation between some sections of the Asian youth and white youth on the grounds of race, manifesting itself in violence, predominantly Asian. (quoted by Ahmed *et al.* 2001: 8)

It was a similar story in January 2001 when the police released figures showing that 62 per cent of racial incidents were 'Asian on white'. A special report for the Chief Constable of Greater Manchester emphasised that these were part of 'an ongoing trend involving primarily Pakistani and Bangladeshi teenagers' (*ibid.*). A press statement by the Chief Superintendent of Q Division underlined that 'gangs of Asian young people were causing resentment in the town' (quoted in Kalra 2003: 149).

This police-sponsored definition of the problem was reproduced in local newspapers:

During the 1990s, local media reporting in Oldham had emphasized the 'threat' of Asian violence with headlines such as 'RACIST ATTACKS BY ASIAN GANGS' (*Oldham Chronicle*, 17 March 1998) and 'HUGE RISE IN RACE ATTACKS ON WHITE MEN' (31 January 2001). The latter story repeated a frequent theme that racist crime in Oldham had reached 'record levels' with a massive increase (to 60 percent of all incidents) in violent attacks on whites. This, it suggests, reveals a 'worrying trend' in such violence over the past few months, in which gangs of between five and 20 Asian youths would target victims. (Ray and Smith *op. cit.*: 691)

Ray and Smith argue *à la* Webster (1997) that, in such a climate of accusative police definition-making and media reporting, Asians came to see no point in reporting incidents to a police force whose minds already seemed tightly made up against them. Feelings of distrust and alienation played a key part in encouraging Asian youth vigilantism as an alternative to irresolute police protection of Asian communities. The upshot was that: 'The repeated representation of these young men as a threat to social order and in particular to innocent whites promoted fear, suspicion and hatred among sections of the white population – a possibility not lost on far right political groups, whose interest in Oldham long preceded the violent conflicts of the spring of 2001' (Ray and Smith *op. cit.*: 693).

The build-up to the riot

The release of the crime statistics in January 2001 was later criticised by the official report on the Oldham riots as 'unnecessary, mis-leading, in view of the difficulty with all such statistics, and distinctly unhelpful in those circumstances at that time'. According to the panel, 'very serious consideration should have been given to the impact of releasing such figures before it was done and we do not believe that this was handled as carefully as it should have been' (Ritchie 2001: 43: 8.23). There is no doubt that the publication of the figures gave rise to a climate of tension, hostility and mutual recrimination in which the Far Right was extremely conspicuous.

On 3 March, the BNP staged its annual northern rally in Oldham. Afterwards, the majority of its 150-strong audience congregated out-side Oldham police station to protest against Asian attacks on whites. Later that month, the National Front announced its intention to march through Oldham on 31 March. Widespread opposition was voiced by politicians, religious, trade union and community leaders and the police and the Home Office eventually banned the march (CARF 2001). However, it was symptomatic of growing media interest that the 19 April edition of BBC Radio 4's *Today* programme included a report by its Home Affairs correspondent, disclosing that local Asian youths were transforming their communities into 'no-go' areas bearing the written warning 'Whites keep out' (*ibid.*).

The radio report was 'vindicated' several days later when a 76-year-old white war veteran was attacked by a group of Asian youths as he walked through an industrial estate on his way home from a rugby match.

His battered face appeared on the front of the Manchester Evening News [of 23 April], and the story then spread to all the national newspapers. In the Mail on Sunday, his story was told under the headline 'Whites beware'. In the Mirror, his face appeared under the headline 'Beaten for being white: OAP, 76, attacked in Asian no-go area'. Media pundits began to speculate on the apparent transformation of young Asian males – from the stereotype of hard-working boys, who respected their parents, to the new stereotype of angry, violent thugs. (CARF *op. cit.*: 3)

The significance attributed to the attack was unsustainable. The suggestion that the pensioner had been assaulted for trespassing into a no-go area was improbable, since it had taken place in Westwood, a district unclaimed by any teenage gangs. Indeed, the elderly man's own relatives appeared in the national press and on television to dispute that this was a racist attack (Vasagar and Ward 2001).

Nevertheless, the apparent threat posed to Oldham's Asians by the Far Right continued to amplify. On 24 April, *The Times* announced that the BNP leader aimed to contest Oldham West at the forthcoming General Election. Two days later, the *Oldham Chronicle* disclosed that the National Front intended to march through the town centre on Saturday, 5 May. Events took a sinister turn on 28 April when there was a football match between Oldham Athletic and Stoke City. In the preceding week, Asian traders had received threatening phone calls and, in the hours prior to the actual kick-off, white supporters had chanted racist slogans and intimidated non-whites in town centre pubs. With the kick-off fast approaching, the police escorted away team supporters through a predominantly Asian part of town. Sections of these supporters broke away and ran amok, vandalising business and residential properties (CARF 2001).

Once the game was in progress, members of the Asian communities contacted the police to ask them to re-route the supporters away from the area after the final whistle. The police were unresponsive to this request. Consequently, on leaving the ground, Stoke supporters were confronted by an awaiting line of Asian youths who threw stones and a petrol bomb in their direction. Dog-handlers, police with truncheons drawn and van dispersal tactics were all used to restore order (*ibid.*). Afterwards, it was firmly believed that National Front supporters had used the game as a pretext for marching through an Asian area. There was also anger that the police had provided 'de facto protection' for such people. As the Oldham Law Centre (2001: 10) stated in its submission to the Ritchie Inquiry:

> The Asian community in Westwood were going about their normal lawful business and there is no doubt that there would not have been any trouble on this day had that community not been attacked and incited by white racist youths. They were the 'victims' of this outrage and they came out onto the streets to protest and to defend their community. That was a perfectly proper thing for them to do and yet it appeared to them that the police, instead of protecting their community from an attack, turned on that community and attacked it.

One week later, on Saturday, 5 May, the National Front turned out in Oldham, with supporters carrying placards bearing the injured face of the 76-year-old pensioner. This time the police prevented marchers from encroaching on Asian areas but were criticised by the Oldham Law Centre for cordoning off and confining a rival group of demonstrators. Suspicions were aroused by the fact that some police officers wore helmets and visors, and others had fabric face masks over their noses and mouths (*ibid.*). For the next three weeks, Far Right members continued to hold meetings in town-centre pubs and to leaflet the surrounding streets. It was during one such meeting, involving members of the BNP, Combat 18 and the Fine Young Casuals in the Britannia pub on Limeside, that one of the individuals present received a fateful phone call from his sister which set off the chain of events that culminated in the Oldham riot.

The Burnley riot

The background to the riot

One month after the Oldham riot, similar disorder occurred in the Lancashire town of Burnley, that has a total population of around 91,000, of which some 5,000 (5.53 per cent) are of ethnic minority heritage. Sixty per cent of the town's ethnic minority citizenship are Pakistanis, who are mostly settled in Daneshouse. Stoneyholme, on its west, is the main location of Burnley's Bangladeshi community (roughly one-third the size of its Pakistani counterpart), while Duke Bar, to the east of Daneshouse, is home to an integrated population of ethnic minorities and whites. The main incidents leading up to the riots initially occurred in Daneshouse. However, subsequent confrontation occurred across all three localities (Clarke 2001).

The official Burnley Task Force report maintains that to label the disorder as a 'race riot' would be to do local people a 'grave disservice'. The report considers that the event should be more accurately described as 'a series of criminal acts, perpetrated by a relatively small number of people. Certainly racial intolerance played a significant role in those disturbances; the confrontations that took place were clearly identified as aggression and violence by both white people and those from the Asian Heritage communities' (*ibid.*: 8). The main source of this conclusion is the Lancashire Constabulary submission to the official inquiry (*ibid.*, Appendix 10k), which highlights the pervasiveness of drug dealing and acquisitive crime (notably burglaries) as key factors in the riot, but correspondingly de-emphasises the significance of interracial animosity and fear. King and Waddington (2004) argue that it was precisely this police misinterpretation of the context of the riot, their miscalculation of the mood of local Asian communities, and the resulting police mismanagement of racist mischief-making by Far Right groups that contributed so heavily to the Burnley riot.

The official narrative of events

The police version of the riot constitutes the only official narrative of events. Structurally, the narrative adopts a traditional 'riot curve' format of description and analysis, outlining the passage of the disorder through various predictable stages: Normality→ High Tension→ Disorder→ De-escalation→ Normality (e.g. Beckett 1992). The police characterise the pre-conflict stage of Normality in Burnley as one in which racism was not a problem, and was certainly less apparent than in nearby Oldham.

The shift to the High Tension phase (usually defined as a situation in which 'feelings are running high' and the possibility of disorder starts to present itself) was marked by a number of key incidents occurring in Daneshouse. The first of these is described as a confrontation over drugs between whites and Asians (though it is not made apparent whether these were rival ethnic groups), involving 'purely indiscriminate criminal acts', such as damage to car and house windows. Soon after, a travelling Asian taxi-cab was similarly vandalised. When the driver stepped out to inspect the damage, he was struck on the head with a hammer and eventually taken to hospital. The police submission acknowledges that 'There is no doubt that this man was simply in the wrong place at the wrong time and that he was attacked because of his ethnicity.' However, there is no attempt to link this attack with the prior incident (King and Waddington *op. cit.*: 125).

Tension continued to mount on Saturday, fuelled by rumours in Asian areas that the taxi driver had died in hospital. There was also seething resentment caused by the release without charge of the people believed responsible for his injuries. Police attempts to counter such 'misinformation' via community contacts and the local media proved ineffectual. Later on Saturday evening, armed Asian youths attacked the Duke of York on Colne Road, Duke Bar, an establishment 'frequented mainly by the white element'.

The next section of the police submission states that tension continued to rise on Sunday. Amidst fears of impending trouble, the landlord of the Duke of York closed his pub early and its customers spilled over to the nearby Baltic Fleet. There, 'something of a siege mentality' developed, as a large congregation of white males chanted racist and football slogans, and verbally abused Asian taxi drivers as a prelude to actually inflicting damage on their vehicles. Taxi-cab radios soon spread word of these events. This ease of communication, and the fact that the pub was so close to Asian areas meant that Asian youths were soon mobilised, armed with swords, machetes and clubs (*ibid.*: 126).

Before the Asian youths had time to arrive, 30 of the white males set off from the Baltic pub and headed off into Daneshouse. A second group (of unspecified size) moved off in the opposite direction, stretching the police resources. The first group was intercepted by police. However, in trying to steer them towards the town centre, the police only succeeded in bringing the whites into confrontation with a larger group of some 300 Asian males. The police submission recounts that, by forming a sandwich between the rival factions and diverting them away from each other, they effectively 'prevented a confrontation that potentially could have been a bloodbath' (*ibid.*). Nevertheless, disorder continued to escalate elsewhere as each ethnic group turned their attention to attacking rival residential areas, businesses and leisure venues. The police submission makes the implicit distinction that, while white attacks on Asian persons and property were driven by malice, corresponding Asian activities were largely retributive in nature (*ibid.*).

King and Waddington characterise the police account as dangerously misleading:

According to this standpoint, the white group involved in the initial confrontation undoubtedly harboured racist views, but their dispute was concentrated on *criminal*, rather than racial, issues. Moreover, as indicated above, whilst the submission repeatedly acknowledges that subsequent collective violence by whites was fuelled by a combination of drink and racist sentiments, it characterises corresponding Asian violence as motivated by criminal *revenge*. Virtually absent from this submission is any reference to the climate of racist hostility existing in the build-up to the Burnley riot and of how this might help us to meaningfully explain the behaviour of some of the protagonists. (*ibid.*: 127)

Police miscalculation and mismanagement

King and Waddington address this latter issue by referring to evidence contained in other submissions to the Burnley Task Force, which shows that 'anti-Asian sentiment (and the fear and defensiveness that it arouses) had been gradually stoked up and become manifest in the prelude to the disorder'. For example, local politicians and local newspapers had constantly focused on the supposedly 'preferential treatment' being allocated to predominantly Asian parts of town in the form of council investment. One Independent councillor had gone so far as to recommend the abolition of the town's Equal Opportunities Co-ordinator and its local authority Translation Unit. Burnley's increasingly right-wing sensibilities were reflected in the BNP's 21 per cent share of a recent Local Authority by-election contest. Moreover, the Burnley BNP candidate's 11.2 per cent share of the vote in the last general election represented the party's second best achievement nationwide.

Perceptions of growing threat and hostility towards Burnley's Asian communities were reinforced by the growing incidence of attacks on Asian taxi drivers and of the police's alleged indifference to their plight. The disbandment of the local Race Equality Council meant the loss of a forum for discussing policing issues of a racially sensitive nature (*ibid.*: 129–30). Even such a brief recontextualisation of the Burnley disorder suggests that police interpretations of and readiness for the disorder were fundamentally misguided. This flawed definition of the situation was the basis of an ill-chosen police policy for managing the prelude to the riot.

King and Waddington's analysis of police tactics and strategy is based on 38 witness statements signed by police officers on duty on the main day of the riot, Sunday, 24 June. Statements by the two most senior officers present reveal that police strategy and tactics for handling the build-up of white patrons outside the Baltic Fleet were consistent with customary methods for dealing with situations of 'High Tension'. Thus their overriding priority was 'to provide a highly visible police presence in the area and to reassure the community, prevent disorder and to ensure that if disorder did break out, that there was an early resolution' (ibid.: 131). These objectives were not secured. King and Waddington make the point that, had the police been more sensitive to the profound disquiet of the Asian communities and strong resolution on their part not to yield to racist intimidation, they might have dealt more forcibly and in greater number with those standing outside the Baltic Fleet.

It is evident from police statements that, by 6.30 p.m., the antics of the white males had grown increasingly disorderly: Nazi salutes were used to greet new arrivals and one youth had to be physically prevented from throwing a bottle at the police (ibid.). The Bronze commander arrived on the scene in response to a request by another police inspector who was unsure how to handle the wilfully unruly youths. By this time, two Asian taxis had already been damaged and a driver had sustained a hand injury. Bronze foresaw a danger of escalating the disorder: 'The group appeared quite agitated and, in my opinion, such a large police presence in one location was in danger of attracting even more troublemakers to the area and inflaming an already very tense situation.' (ibid.). In order to avert this possibility, he redeployed some of his officers to other locations. King and Waddington are adamant that the adoption of this policy in preference to dealing more decisively with the verbal and physical abuse of Asian taxi drivers was to tar the police strategy (in the eyes of local Asians) as illegitimate and partisan:

> To allow them to continue with impunity was to undermine police credibility and sanction a continuation of such behaviour. Perhaps more importantly, if police speculation is correct and commentaries were being fed back into Asian communities via taxi cab radios, then it was inevitable, in the current climate, that police inaction would be interpreted as 'yet more evidence' of police indifference to the plight of Burnley Asians. Given their superior numbers, it may well have been more advisable for police officers to round up, or at least contain, the rowdier section of the white racists. In the meantime serials could have been despatched into Daneshouse and Stoneyholme

where, with the help of community mediators, Asian residents could have been reassured that the situation was under control. Certainly some form of police resolve was urgently required. (*ibid.*: 132)

As it was, with their attitudes emboldened, the youths marched off towards Daneshouse. In contrast to the Lancashire Constabulary submission, individual statements emphasise that the attempted police intervention was painfully shambolic. Officers report an enduring state of fear and panic in the face of overwhelming odds. Communication between units was virtually impossible given the din of the crowd and noise of swerving traffic. An impression is given of officers acting purely on impulse, as when an armoured police personnel carrier was driven into the crowd for the sole purpose of rescuing colleagues in distress. In short, 'Officers lacking the necessary equipment, numerical strength, leadership, tactical co-ordination and any confidence that reinforcements were close to hand were panicked into hasty and hapless retreat' (*ibid.*: 135).

King and Waddington contrast this with the police's handling of an almost identical situation, on Monday, 25 June when white youths assembled once again at the front of the Baltic Fleet. This time, the police took the decisive step of dispersing the potential trouble-makers, but only after adequate numbers of officers had begun their tours of duty. The police then addressed themselves to the task of dispersing a similar group of Asian youths that had been gathering in Stoneyholme. This part of the operation was made easier by the presence of a substantial number of well-briefed officers and the ability of senior officers to reassure the crowd that the white racists no longer constituted a threat.

Conclusions

In earlier publications, I emphasised that the inner-city riots of the early 1980s resulted from particular police ways of dealing with a politically and ethnically assertive African-Caribbean youth counter-culture, fusing elements of the Jamaican-based Rastafarian and Rude Boy styles (D. Waddington 1992, 2001). Senior police, politicians and the media seized upon petty-criminal activities occurring on the fringes of this culture to brand an entire generation of black youth as morally degenerate. Such vilification was used to justify saturation policing methods, involving 'stop and search' methods which, in turn, antagonised local residents and created 'tinder box' communities.

The socio-political conditions in which the disorders of 1991 and 1992 took place were dissimilar to this in one significant respect. As Lea (2004: 190) explains,

> Whereas black youth in Brixton in 1981 could focus their attention on the police as the immediate vehicle of their oppression, white youth in the decaying industrial communities in 1991 faced the unmediated irresponsibility of global capital as it turned on its heels and went elsewhere in search of cheap labour. To this they could only react with a theatre of destruction.

Here, the persistently aggressive methods of policing black communities gave way to 'a more episodic regime' (*ibid.*) in which communities generally devoid of a police presence were suddenly subjected to massive 'crackdowns' as car crime and petty theft proliferated and public concern reached fever pitch.

Global capital also 'turned on its heels' to the obvious detriment of British Bangladeshi and Pakistani youths left unemployed and socially excluded in the former textile towns of northern England at the start of the new millennium. This kind of economic plight was closely related to other aspects of Asian experience, most notably racial harassment and the perceived indifference of the police to the safety of their communities. Such conditions became the breeding ground for a more assertive youth identity, committed to defending Asian communities against the malicious threat of white racists. Unfortunately, senior police officers helped propagate through the media a version of such communities as vice-ridden 'no-go' areas, riddled with racial hostility. Almost instantly, this attracted the mischief-making and retribution of white extremists. This process is illustrated most starkly by our example of the Oldham riot where, according to Kalra (2003: 150), 'the seeds of the riots were fertilised and watered by the release of raw racial harassment statistics in January 2001 that contained no mention of rates or analyses of different types of incident. Their release and the subsequent press coverage enabled the creation of a white victimology that was exploited by Far Right parties.'

The tendency of senior police to misconstrue Asian vigilantism as evidence of outright criminality was further evident in the build-up to the Burnley disorder. There, the police framing of events leading up to Sunday, 24 June fatally downplayed Asian concern about impending Far Right attacks on their communities. Consequently, when right-wing troublemakers gathered at a public house on the edge of an Asian area, the police were tactically under strength. The fateful decision by a Bronze commander to withdraw officers from a situation of rising hostility signalled to Asians and whites alike that police commitment to defending the ethnic minority was inadequately resolute.

The reason why this chapter has focused primarily on events in Oldham and Burnley is that details of the policing of the Bradford riot of 7–9 July remain sketchy by comparison. What we already know for sure is that the Bradford disorder also occurred in the context of heavy campaigning by the BNP, NF and Combat 18. Indeed, on the eve of the riot, the BNP national leader addressed a meeting on a predominantly white council estate. While the course of events thereafter is disputed (Pearce and Bujra 2006), it is generally agreed that trouble ignited in the city centre, where a multiracial anti-fascist rally of several hundred people had gathered amidst rumours that National Front supporters would be marching in Bradford in defiance of a ban (C. Allen 2003; Bagguley and Hussain 2003; Carling *et al.* 2004; Hussain and Bagguley 2005).

Police involvement followed an incident in which white youths (suspected of being National Front members) verbally abused and attacked an Asian man. Officers tried to restore order by pushing the crowd out of the city centre into the predominantly Asian area of Manningham. There, 400–500 Asian youths stood their ground and did battle with the police. It is possible that police were heeding the recommendations of the 1995 report and avoiding risk of damage to the city centre. Whatever their actual motives, respondents later justified their actions as a 'defence of community', predicated on the belief that the police were 'unwilling, rather than unable' to protect them (C. Allen *op. cit.*: 25).

Such perceptions of police indifference or neglect are the main distinguishing feature between the British disturbances and their American counterparts. Unlike the American riots of 1991–2001 (and, indeed the British inner-city disorders of the 1980s), the British conflicts of the past two decades were less obviously the consequences of sustained saturation policing. Rather, in 1991 and 1992, they arose when the police were pressured into recapturing communities they had long ago conceded to local youth; and in 2001, they flared up because the police wrongly branded the victims of endemic racism as its main perpetrators.

Chapter 5

Worldwide 'anti-globalisation' protest, post-Seattle

Introduction

The late 1990s saw an upsurge of 'anti-globalisation' protest. It became commonplace in this era for summit meetings of major global and regional institutions – the World Trade Organisation (WTO), the World Bank, the International Monetary Fund (IMF), the Group of 8 (G8), the United Nations (UN), the European Union (EU) and others – to be accompanied by mass street protests involving a wide range of social movements and non-governmental organisations (NGOs) (Held and McGrew 2002: 64). From 1999 onwards, such occasions were synonymous with street confrontations involving increasingly repressive forms of policing (Brooks 2004; della Porta *et al*. 2006; O'Neill 2004).

It would be disingenuous to suggest that violence accompanying anti-globalisation protest was non-existent until the turn of the twentieth century, as this would be to deny the occurrence of rioting in the 1980s during demonstrations in Third World countries against the World Bank and IMF (Walton 1987). Nevertheless, the late 1990s saw a resurgence of such activity. One well-documented example was the policing of the Asia Pacific Economic Cooperation (APEC) Summit, staged in Vancouver in November 1997, when 3,000 demonstrators gathered in condemnation of the poor human rights records of some delegate nations, notably China and Indonesia (Ericson and Doyle 1999). The Royal Canadian Mounted Police (RCMP) controversially erected a 10-foot wire-fencing perimeter to shield the motorcades transporting the 18 Internationally Protected Persons (IPPs) to and from the venue. During a sit-down protest by demonstrators, police bicycles were used as battering rams and the RCMP discharged pepper spray (*ibid.*).

Far more significant in terms of the impetus given to further worldwide anti-globalisation protest was the spectacular violence accompanying the 1999 WTO summit meeting in Seattle in November/December. This event was attended, not only by President Bill Clinton and other world dignitaries, but also by tens of thousands of anti-globalisation demonstrators from over 1,200 separate organisations. The police were unprepared for the scale and intensity of the protest. On the first day of the four-day summit (scheduled for 30 November to 3 December), a carnival-type spirit initially prevailed. However, trouble broke out at the junction of Union and 6th Streets where protesters prevented delegates from leaving their hotel:

> Apparently frustrated by their inability to guarantee delegates' access to the opening ceremony, police used tear gas to clear a path for delegates for the opening session. Anarchist groups, who had announced over protest electronic list servers their intentions to target downtown shops, did not use violence first. The authorities began the cycle of violent confrontation, which escalated into what was essentially a police riot. (Smith 2001: 13; see also Wozniak 2005)

First off, police used pepper spray and baton charges in a bid to disperse the crowd. These measures and the subsequent introduction of tear gas and rubber bullets proved escalatory. With the abandonment of the summit a growing possibility, the mayor of Seattle declared a state of emergency. A city-wide curfew was imposed involving 'no-protest zones' around the summit complex, and the Washington National Guard and US Army were brought in to relieve the beleaguered local police (Brooks 2004).

Following the 'Battle of Seattle', anti-globalisation protest grew even more pervasive and policing methods became correspondingly less permissive (Noakes and Gillham 2006: 97). Security arrangements for subsequent summit meetings in places like Washington, DC and Prague (both in 2000) and Quebec City, Gothenburg and Genoa (in 2001) were much tighter and more repressive. In Washington, this involved a strictly enforced 'no-protest zone'. In Prague, police allowed demonstrators within 200 metres of the conference centre before bombarding them with tear gas, water cannons and concussion grenades. Seven months later, similar weaponry was used in Quebec City, where police also set up a three-metre-high steel and concrete security fence. Gothenburg police went one step further in June 2001 when they opened fire on demonstrators, wounding three people in the process. Most dramatically of all, at the 2001 G8 meeting in Genoa, there were running battles between protesters and the police and *carabinieri*. During the worst violence in the history of the anti-globalisation protest, one participant, Carlo Giuliani, was shot dead by the police and run over by an armoured vehicle. Subsequently, the police carried out a retaliatory raid on a protester camp (King and Waddington 2005; O'Neill 2004).

The tragic event in Genoa appeared to induce a period of intro-spection. Within days of the confrontation, the Canadian government announced that the following year's G8 meeting would be held in Kananaskis, a remote and extremely inaccessible winter resort, high in the Rocky Mountains. Terrorist attacks on the World Trade Centre on 11 September 2001 also seemed to dampen pro-testers' appetites for confrontation but, conversely, heightened the security consciousness of the authorities (O'Neill 2004). In 2002–2003, the anti-global movement refocused its energies on opposing the war in Iraq (*ibid.*). However, there were violent clashes between protesters and police at G8 summit meetings in Evian (Switzerland) and Gleneagles (Scotland) in 2003 and 2005 respectively, and during the WTO meeting in Hong Kong, also in 2005. Table 5.1 (page 114) summarises the main forms of police–protester activities at the major anti-globalisation events from 1999–2006.

One possible explanation for the generally uncompromising police strategies and tactics employed at the international summits relates to the obvious political pressure on the police to ensure the safety of the high-ranking political delegations present on such occasions. This argument certainly applies to the 1997 APEC protest where, accord-ing to Ericson and Doyle (*op. cit.*), there were two main reasons for the RCPM's uncompromising approach. First, intense political pres-sure was exerted by the Indonesian government to ensure that its delegates were shielded from possible protest; and secondly, the travelling Indonesian police had notified the RCMP that they would not refrain from shooting demonstrators in the face of a perceived threat to their ministers.

Though undoubtedly useful, this explanation is limited in its capacity to account for variations in the levels of violence occurring at separate protest events. Thus, in the present chapter and in Chapter 6, we explore a wider range of variables capable of explain-ing continuities and discrepancies in police tactics and strategies during anti-globalisation protest, and examine their consequences for the maintenance or breakdown of public order. The focus of the *current* chapter is on theoretical insights to be gleaned from case studies running from the Battle of Seattle in 1999 to the WTO protests in Hong Kong in 2005. Chapter 6 comprises a complementary case study of the policing of the G8 meeting of Justice and Home Affairs ministers in Sheffield, England, in June 2005. The extended nature of the Sheffield study allows for a more detailed, in-depth appreciation of the factors underlying the police's tactical and strategic choices, and their implications for police–protester relations.

We begin the present chapter with a case study of the Seattle débâcle of 1999. This initial example highlights the possibility that particular forms of police engagement with protesters may well have the unintended, or 'ironic', effects of encouraging further violence. Subsequent sections then use other prominent examples of anti-globalisation protest – though not in strictly chronological order – to identify those factors responsible both for consistencies and differences of police styles. Thus, the second section will demonstrate that Western police forces have followed a general tendency to resort to tactics of 'strategic incapacitation' (involving, for example, restrictions on movement, mass arrests, the removal of ringleaders and the use of less-lethal weapons) with regard to transgressive groups of protesters. The remaining sections will then show how degrees of conformity to or departure from this norm are explicable in terms of such variables as: the nature of policing traditions within the relevant society; the salient political context and its interaction with other key institutional, cultural, contextual, situational and interactional factors; the 'lessons learned' by the police on the basis of previous confrontations; and finally, the idiosyncratic 'policing philosophies' subscribed to by individual forces.

The ironic effects of police tactics

To begin with, we explore possible ways in which police tactics employed at anti-globalisation protests may contribute to the instigation and development of disorder. This requires a brief consideration of activities during the 1999 World Trade Organisation meeting in Seattle.

Table 5.1 A selective summary of major anti-globalisation protests, 1999–2006

18 June 1999, London: Around 150 civilians are injured during a 'J18' or 'Carnival Against Capitalism' demonstration against world debt, the arms trade and other global issues. Though initially peaceful, the protest becomes violent when a minority of demonstrators set out to attack the London International Financial Futures Exchange. A McDonald's fast-food restaurant on Cannon Street is vandalised and expensive cars are overturned. Mounted police units succeed in containing the protesters in Trafalgar Square.

30 November 1999, Seattle: Tens of thousands of demonstrators from 1,200 organisations congregate to demand of the wholesale reform of the World Trade Organisation. The start of the WTO summit is delayed for six hours before the police use pepper spray and tear gas to disperse protesters blocking the highways. The local mayor declares a State of Emergency and the police impose a strict curfew, which they then enforce with the help of the National Guard.

30 November 1999, London: On the same night, demonstrators show solidarity with the Seattle protest by staging an impromptu march around central London. A crowd of around 750 congregates at Euston Station and engages in violence with police officers. Riot police with batons drawn eventually succeed in debilitating the protesters.

18 April 2000, Washington, DC: Police use billy clubs and tear gas to clear the roads of protesters attempting to prevent a meeting of the IMF and World Bank.

1 May 2000, London: Another 'Carnival Against Capitalism' descends into violence after several hours of peaceful protest. A number of monuments are defaced and a McDonald's fast-food restaurant is vandalised.

26 September 2000, Prague: Fifteen thousand people from 30 different countries attend the 'First Pan European protest against global capitalism'. Their stated objective is to form a human chain around the former communist centre of culture where the World Bank meetings are being held. However, police only allow demonstrators to within 200 yards of the centre before bombarding them with tear gas, water cannons and concussion grenades.

24 April 2001, Quebec City: Hundreds of Canadian riot police use tear gas, water cannons and rubber bullets to deter protesters against the 'Summit of the Americas' from tearing down a section of steel and concrete security fencing dubbed the 'Wall of Shame'. Four hundred people are arrested as the police strive to avoid 'another Seattle'.

1 May 2001, London: the Metropolitan Police Service apply a 'zero tolerance' policy to detain thousands of protesters in the Oxford Circus area of central London for eight hours.

15 June 2001, Gothenburg: Forty-three people are arrested and three others are wounded by police gunfire as 25,000 protesters gather at the EU summit meeting.

20 July 2001, Genoa: The worst violence in the history of anti-capitalist protest breaks out at the G8 summit meeting. An eight-hour running battle occurs in which 93 are hurt and one protester, Carlo Giuliani, is shot dead and then run over by a police armoured vehicle. Afterwards, Italian police carry out a brutal raid on a building being used by the Genoa Social Forum. Walls of the building are smeared with blood, prompting an inquiry by Amnesty International.

29-30 September 2001, Washington, DC: Less than three weeks after the occurrence of 9/11, three anti-war/anti-capitalism demonstrations are held in the American capital. Police use pepper spray and detention techniques (including metallic barriers) to contain members of the most militant group of protesters, the Anti-Capitalist Convergence (ACC), but display a more lenient attitude towards the relatively more moderate International Action Center (IAC) and Quaker-led Washington Peace Center.

1 May 2002, London: Six thousand people gather in Trafalgar Square. Notwithstanding the fact that 5,000 police are placed on standby, the event is overridingly peaceful. Around 7 p.m., police officers prevent 200 demonstrators from entering the West End. The police then adopt the containment strategy of surrounding and detaining the protesters at the junction of Dean Street and Old Compton Street in Soho in a repetition of the type of tactics used in the previous year.

26–27 June 2002, Kananaskis (Alberta, Canada): Following the previous year's violence in Genoa, the 2002 G8 summit meeting is held in an isolated holiday resort, 60 miles west of Calgary in the Rocky Mountains. Access to the meeting is further restricted by police and military blockades. The style of policing employed in protests in major cities like Calgary and Ottawa is 'soft hat' and non-confrontational, epitomised by officers riding bicycles rather than horses.

27 September 2002, Washington, DC: Police make 500 arrests as anti-IMF supporters blockade the streets. A wire perimeter fence is erected around the headquarters of IMF and World Bank. Extra police are drafted in from Chicago and buses are used to ferry prisoners to outlying detention centres.

4–10 November, 2002, Florence: Close liaison between police and demonstration organisers helps to ensure that the inaugural meeting of the European Social Forum is almost entirely devoid of the type of violence that characterised the Genoa G8.

15 February 2003, New York City: In contrast to the more permissive attitudes shown by police in major cities elsewhere in the world, the New York Police Department (NYPD) applies an uncompromising 'zero tolerance' policy to confine an anti-war demonstration by over 100,000 people to strictly designated 'protest pens'. Over 250 people are arrested in the course of this operation.

2 June, 2003, Evian, Switzerland: A third successive night of violence occurs as Swiss police (and reinforcements drafted in from Germany) use water cannons and baton charges against activists engaged in spontaneous demonstrations against the G8.

20 November 2003, Miami: A march in opposition to the establishment of a Free Trade Area of the Americas is aggressively dispersed by police.

2–6 July 2005, Edinburgh: A Make Poverty History march taking place in central Edinburgh a few days before the opening of the G8 summit meeting passes off without a single arrest. However, violent clashes between police and protesters occur during G8 week, both in the city centre itself, and on the perimeter of a fortified security zone surrounding the meeting venue at nearby Gleneagles.

17 December 2005, Hong Kong: Five days of anti-WTO protest comes to a head when hundreds of demonstrators – many of them South Korean farmers – clash with riot police. Sixty-seven police and 137 protesters are reported injured.

15–17 July 2006, St Petersburg, Russia: Police take preventative measures to turn back or detain protesters travelling to St Petersburg. Repressive measures are taken to deter street protests.

Sources: della Porta et al. 2006; Dodson 2003; copies of *The Guardian* and *Financial Times* from 1999–2006.

The Battle of Seattle

The 'Battle of Seattle' is discussed in close detail by Gillham and Marx (2000) who describe their analysis as a 'case study for better understanding the ironies that often accompany mass demonstrations' (*ibid*.: 215). The protest occurred in the week following Thanksgiving – a traditionally busy shopping period in America. Gillham and Marx explain how the initial trouble trouble was activated at around 9 a.m., outside the Sheraton Hotel, where the US Secretary of State and other important delegates were staying.

There, police in full body armour and gas marks, said to have been 'overwhelmed and frightened by the number and preparedness of protesters' (*ibid*.: 217), used batons and pepper spray to disperse hundreds of participants intent on preventing WTO delegates from leaving the hotel. Protesters who were already organised into scores of 'affinity groups' of 5–10 people immediately tightened their resistance by linking their arms and legs. Those at the front donned goggles and made vinegar-soaked face masks out of bandanas. Though the police action enabled some vehicles to leave the Sheraton, news of the violence quickly reached protesters elsewhere in the locality and 'flying squads' were hurriedly despatched to the hotel to reinforce the blockades. These included members of the anarchist 'Black Bloc', who not only used trash dumpsters to buttress barricades, but also set about spraypainting graffiti on surrounding property.

Black Bloc members had agreed beforehand with organisers that they would refrain from any 'property transformation' on condition that the police did not engage in violence (*ibid*.: 217). Events outside the Sheraton violated a prior agreement between the police and demonstrators, to their mutual indignation:

> Organizers had been assured at earlier protest management meetings with police officials that nonviolent protesters would be arrested en mass [sic], long before the use of chemical irritants and other nonlethal weapons, should that become necessary. Police, for their part, seemed surprised and angered because protest leaders had assured them that demonstrators would engage in scripted civil disobedience resulting in arrest. Thus, both police and activists believed that the other side had reneged on their promises. (*ibid*.: 217–18)

Video evidence cited by Gillham and Marx suggests that extreme forms of disorder, such as smashing windows, spraying graffiti and hurling objects at the police, were a direct consequence of the police decision to disperse, rather than arrest, the hitherto non-violent activists obstructing the streets and entrances to and from the hotel. In their view, the pivotal episode outside the Sheraton exemplifies two important ironic effects of police action, which they refer to as *reciprocal and neutralisation* and *escalation*. Included in the former category are moves by one side that produce a counter-reaction by the other. Examples of this are the defiant reactions of the affinity groups and the mobilisation of flying squads in response to police dispersal tactics. Equally in evidence outside the Sheraton were the escalatory effects of police intervention which triggered an ever-increasing spiral of confrontation. Faced with the growing defiance and hostility of those involved in the blockades, police officers fired rubber bullets, bean bags and tear gas into the crowd, many of whom responded in turn by using newspaper dispenser boxes, grates (originally used to protect trees), hammers and crowbars to smash in windows.

Gillham and Marx emphasise that the drift to widespread confrontation was undoubtedly encouraged by other ironic effects of police action. One of these was the so-called *excitement* effect, whereby protesters were attracted to the major locations of conflict by such salient stimuli as the sound of helicopters, police sirens and concussion grenades, or the sight and odour of tear gas. Arguably of greater significance was a *non-enforcement* effect where police under-enforcement of the law served to embolden crowd members and encourage further violence. One major example of this occurred when the police were forced, firstly into abandoning their attempts at crowd dispersal, and then into retreating from confrontation as stocks of chemical irritants became spent. Gillham and Marx report that officers stood by helplessly as protesters vandalised property. Afterwards, they complained that they had been too far understaffed and intimidated by the size and organisation of the crowd to risk making arrests.

The final two ironies referred to by Gillham and Marx are the so-called *role reversal* and *strange bedfellows* effects. The former involves forms of behaviour by police officers which are of questionable legality and often involve violence. Invariably related to this is the tendency for protesters – possibly harbouring differing philosophies and attitudes to violence – to unite in the face of a common enemy. The possible relevance of these ironies is encapsulated in the authors' observation that, 'As news of police behavior spread, many demonstrators felt an increased sense of solidarity and a need to stand up to police efforts at control, beyond the original goal of protesting against the WTO' (*ibid.*: 223).

Police use of strategic incapacitation

Two related articles by Noakes *et al.* (2005) and Noakes and Gillham (2006) maintain that the Seattle confrontation marked the onset of innovative and arguably more repressive police policies for the handling of major political demonstrations in North America and western Europe. In commenting, not only on police conduct at Seattle, but also at subsequent protests accompanying the IMF/WB meetings in Washington, DC (April 2000) and the Republican National Convention in Philadelphia (August 2000), they argue that US police increasingly drew on tactics and strategies evidently inspired by the 'new penology' perspective on dealing with offenders (Noakes *et al.* 2005).

The new penology approach

The new penology perspective eschews all interest in establishing the underlying causes of crime and conceiving of possible ways of rehabilitating offenders in favour of an emphasis on protecting law-abiding sections of the public from forms of risk and inconvenience posed by the criminal and unruly. Noakes *et al.* argue that, in terms of public order policing, this has involved the introduction of innovative techniques for dealing with 'transgressive' (uncooperative and potentially violent) as opposed to 'contained' (responsible and law-abiding) protesters (see Chapter 1).

These authors point out that the anti-globalisation movement's broad compositional base has created inherent divisions in terms of preferred strategic objectives and the tactical means of achieving them. The obvious problems that such characteristics pose for police planning are compounded by the 'non-hierarchical', 'leaderless' structures of the constituent groups which make it difficult for senior officers to negotiate with protesters or make them legally responsible or morally accountable for their actions (*ibid.*; see also Farnsworth 2004). In the face of such uncertainty, senior police are likely to opt for the 'insurance' of large numbers of police personnel and unyielding containment measures.

Noakes *et al.* (2005) explain how the police will still endeavour to forge pre-event agreements with national and local representatives of contained protest groups. They also tend to conduct impromptu negotiations aimed at resolving tense situations during marches, and even tolerate the activities of groups lacking protest permits. Against this, the police are apt to employ altogether more repressive measures in relation to transgressive protesters. Noakes *et al.* have coined the term *strategic incapacitation* to refer to the police use of the following techniques as an antidote to transgressive behaviour:

- the disruption of assembly or convergence centres acting as the nerve centres of specific protests;
- the use of prior and 'real time' intelligence and surveillance to predict or monitor demonstrators' behaviour and determine levels of risk or danger;
- the removal by arrest of ringleaders and other strategically important protesters;
- the establishment of 'no-protest' security zones (often defined by concrete or metal barriers);
- the mass arrest and detention of protesters without making charges against them;
- use of less-lethal weapons (e.g. pepper spray, tear gas, concussion grenades) to take or recapture public spaces. (*ibid.*: 241)

To exemplify these methods, Noakes *et al.* refer to three separate rallies on the theme of anti-militarism that took place in Washington, DC on Saturday, 29 and Sunday, 30 September 2001, less than three weeks after the 9/11 atrocity. They show how police tactics varied significantly according to the degree of transgressiveness characterising the protest groups involved.

Anti-war protests in Washington, DC

Two of the three marches occurred on the Saturday in question, the other a day later. The first of these involved members of the local Anti-Capitalist Congress (ACC), the youngest and most transgressive of the three groups of protesters. The ACC comprised an affiliation of anarchist, communist and socialist groups and was perceived by the Metropolitan Police for the District of Columbia (MPDC) as politically akin to the notorious Black Bloc. The police were steeled for possible confrontation due to the ACC's unwillingness to obtain a permit for the march. Dozens of officers in full riot gear were in position from the outset, while most of the marchers wore black clothing and sported bandanas across their faces. Noakes *et al.* point out that the MPDC eventually resorted to three forms of tactical intervention consistent with the strategic incapacitation approach – namely: use of less-lethal weapons, the partitioning of space and the rearrangement of protesters.

At the mid-point of the march, officers used pepper spray to disperse protesters who had momentarily surrounded an MPDC cruiser. A subsequent confrontation in the city park resulted in the protesters being corralled into an improvised enclosure, made out of portable metallic barriers, where they were detained for approximately two hours. Police eventually agreed to release the protesters – but only if the latter first expressed a willingness to join a second march, which had just got underway, involving the New York-based International Action Centre (IAC). As ACC members marched under strict police supervision to join the IAC protest, 'MPDC officers in full body armour lined both sides of the route, using large sticks pressed against the back of protesters to establish and maintain the boundaries of the march. Refusing exit from or entry to the body of demonstrators, they physically rebuffed any demonstrators who challenged these boundaries' (*ibid.*: 244).

The IAC march mainly comprised a mixture of young and middle-aged whites, although there was also a higher percentage of 'people of colour' than on the ACC procession. Here, too, the police maintained a large and visible presence. Faced with a less transgressive group of protesters, they were content to maintain a more respectful distance from the marchers and were visibly 'more at ease' than colleagues patrolling the ACC event (*ibid.*: 245). Noakes *et al.* make the interesting point that,

> At first glance, the merging of AAC and IAC demonstrators seems to make little sense because police risked contaminating a contained demonstration with transgressive protesters. But the MPDC was not about to let the ACC protesters out of the makeshift corral to roam the streets of Washington, potentially causing havoc for the police in numerous ways. Instead by marching the ACC demonstrators to the IAC march they concentrated the vast majority of the protesters on the streets of DC that day in one place. This served two purposes. First, it seems likely the IAC would closely monitor the behaviour Of ACC activists in order to prevent them from taking over the

rally and the march. The marshals helping to self-police IAC demonstrators would do the same with ACC members. Second, merging the ACC with the IAC police were also reuniting the majority of MPDC officers assigned to protest duty that day in one place. (*ibid.*: 250)

The police reserved their most lenient and unobtrusive control tactics for the last of the weekend's marches, which involved members of the Washington Peace Center (WPC), a pacifist organisation deeply rooted in Quakerism. These demonstrators were relatively older and more middle-class than their counterparts on the ACC and IAC protests. What is more, they boasted a long and co-operative relationship with the MPDC. Consequently, although riot police were deployed on the day, they were kept discreetly out of sight, and the accompanying police escort was extremely token in nature.

The routinisation of protest and its consequence

Noakes *et al.* justifiably maintain that methods of strategic incapacitation are likely to aggravate existing tensions between police and protesters (*ibid.*: 251). This argument has been extended by Mitchell and Staeheli (2005) who also point to violence at the post-Seattle protests in Washington, as well as the anti-war demonstration in New York in February 2003 (see below for further details), as evidence of a growing public backlash to police attempts to manage and 'incorporate' dissent.

Mitchell and Staeheli endorse the view that the police continue, wherever they can, to liaise with protest organisers according to the principles of negotiated management. Accordingly, 'Much of the groundwork for protest takes place in pre-protest meetings between protest organizers, police representatives and lawyers for both sides, as they wrangle over the ways that permits will be written, and even the plans to exceed or ignore aspects of the permit' (*ibid.*: 802). Echoing P. A. J. Waddington's (1994) observation of British public order police specialists (see Chapter 1), Mitchell and Staeheli maintain that, invariably, American police officers' 'greater expertise and knowledge of the advantages and disadvantages of protest sites' (*ibid.*: 806) allows them, not only to control demonstrations on their terms, but also to insist on containment practices (such as the use of protest pens). The danger here is that these tactics run the risk of nullifying the political effectiveness of such demonstrations and promoting an escalatory dialectic:

This routinization of protest . . . has led to protest becoming part of the 'well-oiled' system itself. And as more and more people have become dissatisfied with the workings of the system, as exemplified in growing dissent to capitalist, corporate-led globalization and the anti-war movement, protesters have broken out of the routine, and even turned against the routine itself. Dissent has become resistance. (*ibid.*: 810)

Tradition and inflexibility

Corresponding European research has highlighted several other variables, over and above police perceptions of the transgressiveness of demonstrators, to account for the discrepant styles of policing employed during anti-globalisation protest. One obvious way of accounting for such variations is to consider the effect of discrepant national traditions for the handling of public protest. The significance of this factor is illustrated with reference to the handling by Swedish police of the European Union summit meeting held in Gothenburg in June 2001.

The EU summit meeting in Gothenburg

The strategy employed by the Swedish police was consistent with their longstanding tradition of maintaining order by designating protesters to specific 'territorial spaces' or agreed routes of demonstrations. Forged in the days when dissenting groups were more easily identifiable to the police and could be reasonably relied on for their co-operation, this 'wait-and-see defensive posture' proved anachronistic in Gothenburg where

The police doggedly attempted to control territories for protest with their deployment of personnel, riot fences and shipping containers. However, protest erupted outside the police cordons in territories over which they held no or sorely inadequate control. The rigidity of their territorial strategies made them ill-prepared to deal with the flexible and mobile extraterritorial tactics of the militant activists. (*ibid.*: 47)

Compounding this problem for the police was that few of the police officers present were adequately trained or equipped for public order duties. Standard police training in Sweden was primarily designed to enable officers to work independently in the absence of close supervision, whereas public order policing necessitated styles of teamwork and discipline which were alien to most junior officers. Further difficulties also arose because police commanders had not been given the appropriate authority to respond in suitably extemporised manner to the unpredictable activities of itinerant groups of activists.

Peterson emphasises the consequences of these factors by describing events on a march by 15,000 demonstrators which culminated in the shooting of three participants. Having anticipated that all protesters would stick to a prescribed route (in customary Swedish style), the police had cordoned off all side-streets, as well as the centrally located square where the procession was due to terminate. However, senior officers had not legislated for the fact that roving groups (Peterson calls them 'packs') of the Black Bloc would attack isolated units of police based in a nearby park. Thus, when police were hastily redeployed from a side-road to go to the aid of beleaguered colleagues, patrol cars and vans left unattended were demolished by another group of anarchists. These lightning strikes by anarchists extended to attacking one police unit with torn up cobblestones. It was shortly after this incident that the police were panicked into opening fire on the activists (*ibid.*: 56).

The political context and other local contingencies

We shall soon see how national tradition of protest policing features prominently in della Porta and Reiter's (2006) account of the infamous Genoa protest, which occurred only a few weeks after the events in Gothenburg. What the Genoa case study powerfully reveals is that an emphasis on tradition can only go so far towards explaining the precise character of public order strategies and tactics and their implications for disorder. In this section, we focus on protest events in London, Genoa and Hong Kong as ways of emphasising the importance of, interrelationship between key political, institutional, cultural and contextual, situational and interactional variables.

The London May Day protests

In Chapter 2, and in the above reference to the recent work of Mitchell and Staeheli, discussion focused on the various ways in which police officers employed combinations of superior knowledge, guile and various interactional ploys to gain the co-operation and compliance of protest organisers as a prerequisite to maintaining order. It is important to emphasise, however, that on some occasions senior police may well be equally proactive in ensuring that any aggressive conduct engaged in by their officers will be perceived as reasonable and justified, and that it will take place in circumstances as advantageous as possible to the police. This point is effectively illustrated with reference to the annual May Day protests held in London from the late 1990s to 2005.

The policing of these protests became a major issue in 2000 when some 8,000 demonstrators set out with the intention of staging a mass 'Guerrilla Gardening' event, the main objective of which was to 'reclaim the streets' by inserting plants and seeds in the capital's grass verges. Fearing a possible repetition of disorders in London during the 'J18' (or 'Carnival Against Capitalism'), when thousands of people protested against world debt, the arms trade and global financial institutions on 18 June 1999, and a demonstration staged in solidarity with the Seattle protest on 30 November of the same year, the police staged their biggest public order operation for 30 years: 5,500 officers were deployed with 900 more on standby (*The Guardian*, 2 May 2000).

Both Bloom (2003) and Donson *et al.* (2004) report that a generally peaceful march suddenly became disorderly when an attack was mounted on a McDonald's fast-food restaurant close to Trafalgar Square. Bloom emphasises that, notwithstanding the fact that McDonald's outlets are regular targets for anti-globalisation protesters, this particular restaurant was closed but not shuttered and its premises virtually unguarded at the time of the attack. He and Donson *et al.* assert that police deliberately exposed the restaurant to the mercy of the crowd as part of a well-choreographed containment exercise. Once the demonstrators had responded on cue by smashing in the shop's doors and plate-glass windows, the police could confidently justify their recourse to harsher tactics.

Subsequent media coverage stridently condemned the protesters' behaviour – particularly the way that some individuals had used spray-paint to deface the Cenotaph and a statue of Winston Churchill, before finishing off the latter with a 'Mohican hairdo' made out of a slender piece of turf. Donson *et al.* are joined by Atkinson (2001) and Uitermark (2004) in showing how police spokespersons and politicians used such condemnation as the launchpad of a media campaign which portrayed protesters likely to be demonstrating on May Day 2001 as a dangerous threat to society. This advance demonisation of protesters was the basis used for justifying a subsequent policy of zero tolerance.

The strategy employed by the police for handling the 2001 May Day demonstration involved allowing protesters to gather in the busy Oxford Street, amidst strong expectations of disorder, and 'kettling' (or corralling) them in behind police cordons for a period of six hours. Only those people prepared to volunteer their names and addresses and consent to have their photographs taken were allowed to leave. A similar containment strategy was used on May Day 2002 to prevent 200 demonstrators from entering the West End during the early evening, after police had allowed a peaceful march by trade unionists and anti-globalisation protesters to proceed earlier in the day. In subsequent years, both the scale of the annual May Day protests and the levels of violence associated with them diminished substantially.

The importance of the prevailing political context is further emphasised by recent case studies of confrontations in Genoa (Italy) and Hong Kong, both of which also illustrate the interrelationship between political determinants of public order policing and other important contingent factors.

The Genoa G8 summit meeting

According to della Porta and Reiter, Genoa marked 'the culmination of the escalation of coercive strategies employed against the movement' (2006b: 19). In the course of two days, over 1,000 civilians were wounded as the Italian police and *carabinieri* launched 6,200 tear gas grenades and fired off 20 live ammunition rounds. Repeated charges were carried out by police, often spearheaded by high-speed armoured vehicles. During one such charge, a *carabinieri* Land Rover became isolated and besieged by protesters. One of the *carabinieri* on board opened fire on and killed a 23-year-old male demonstrator, Carlo Giuliani.

The Italian government used extensive border controls in advance of the G8 summit to prevent foreign activists from entering the country. From 11–21 July, they suspended the Schengen agreement on the free movement of people within the European Union and administered some 140,000 border checks. No fewer than 2,093 people were prohibited from entering the country, 298 of them allegedly belonging to the Black Bloc. The location of the summit meeting was physically isolated by closing off access roads to the city and setting up two perimeter zones: a 'yellow' (buffer) zone in which people were allowed restricted freedom to demonstrate, and a fortified, 8 km perimeter 'red' zone, surrounded by tall barriers, which demonstrators were prohibited from entering.

della Porta and Reiter highlight the explanatory significance of the Italian political context for our understanding of the overall style of policing. The hardened police response towards the protesters was greatly influenced by prevailing political opinion. Senior politicians, including the Italian Deputy Prime Minister, are said to have primed the police and public into believing 'that every street demonstration was by violent and subversive groups, and guaranteed that in the event of clashes no responsibility would on any account be allotted by the government to the forces of order' (*ibid.*: 28). This attitude reflected a longstanding refusal by the Italian government and centre-right majority (the 'law and order coalition') to recognise the legitimacy of the anti-global movement. Such a lack of political sympathy was also evident on the political centre-left (or 'civil liberties coalition'), which departed from tradition by not speaking out unequivocally in favour of the anti-global movement.

The police readiness to adopt harshly repressive strategies was further encouraged by organisational and cultural factors pre-disposing them unconditionally to obey political directives, even of questionable legality. Especially relevant here was the Italian police's enduring adherence to the traditional 'King's police' (police of the monarch) model of policing, involving unwavering loyalty to the government of the day. Following unsuccessful attempts at reform, the Italian state police remain highly paramilitarised and resolutely unaccountable.

At Genoa, special police units were deployed whose control strategies had been developed in opposition to the Mafia and football hooliganism. Paradoxically, della Porta and Reiter question the professionalism of *carabinieri* and police mobile squads at Genoa, each of which had high ratios of young (and inexperienced) auxiliary 'draftees'. They also remark on the probable effect of the 'limited transparency' of a police system of accountability in which 'identification numbers are concealed, complaint procedures are tortuous and powers of review exclusively internal' (*ibid.*: 33).

della Porta and Reiter make the point that negative police stereotypes of the demonstrators as 'troublemakers' were based on the tired images of the previous decade, rather than cool-headed assessments of their contemporary character and objectives. The novel and diverse nature of the participating groups, and unpredictability of their possible 'repertoires of action', also enhanced police readiness for a probable confrontation. Afterwards, spokespersons for different factions of protesters complained that senior police had been slow or unresponsive to their attempts at liaison, while the latter explained the difficulty they had encountered in trying to approach some 800 groups, the majority lacking formal leadership.

The presence of 'tiny but vigorous violent fringes' lent credence to dramatic assertions by the civil secret service of the demonstrators' intentions. In the week prior to the summit, police officers were informed by senior officers and read in the press that demonstrators would be armed with pistols and were likely to bombard them with burning car tyres, bladders full of infected blood and ball-bearings smeared with acid. Pre-event preparations by the security forces clearly recognised these possibilities. Commenting on the training that he and colleagues had received, one police officer revealed, 'They taught us only to repress, not to prevent; the no-global movement was presented to us as the enemy, there was no training about the various components of the movement, no distinction between violent and peaceful groups' (quoted in *ibid.*: 31).

As in the APEC summit of 1997, the state's decision to isolate the dignitaries undoubtedly enhanced the likelihood of disorder. The choice of this strategy enabled the Italian establishment to 'assert itself before international public opinion as able to display its monopoly of force on its own territory', but also had the effect of ensuring that 'Defence of the right to demonstrate [came] into tension with the objective of guaranteeing the safety of guest heads of State or government' (*ibid.*: 24). On the day of the G8 meeting, the physical as well as psychological room to manoeuvre was severely restricted by the fortification of the summit. As della Porta and Reiter maintain, such strategies are inherently dangerous in that they have the effect of 'concentrating police efforts on defending it, increasingly restricting the possibilities of protest that can be peaceful but visible, and increasing the distance between the rulers and the population' (*ibid.*).

Adding to the potential for disorder was the poor co-ordination and lack of effective communication between the five separate (and intensely rivalrous) police forces deployed on the day, and between the police and *carabinieri*. Senior police officers, ostensibly in command of units of *carabinieri*, were required by protocol to channel their orders through *carabinieri* captains. However, while *carabinieri* officers were linked up to each other via a series of throat microphones, there was no such mechanism connecting the police and *carabinieri*. The sole exceptions were a pair of police links running from their headquarters to *carabinieri* senior command. However, each of these cut out while the confrontation was in progress.

The main violence of the day appears to have been triggered by a *carabinieri* charge into a parade of demonstrators en route to the summit location. Subsequent police assertions that the security forces were reacting to attacks by demonstrators were later discredited by a video recording of the proceedings. Indeed, with the exception of minor instances of vandalism by members of the Black Bloc, the parade had been conducted in orderly fashion. The effect of the *carabinieri* intervention was to induce a commitment to 'self-defence and solidarity' on the part of the protesters. As one Italian news reporter explained, 'the *carabinieri* advance accordingly met with resistance which, apart from being active, was inevitable: either you wait for the truncheon to hit you, or you defend yourself. Thus, before my very eyes, the two or three thousand young people heading the march were converted into active, angry combatants' (quoted in *ibid*.: 20–21).

The Sixth WTO ministerial conference in Hong Kong

A similar range of political, organisational, cultural, contextual and situational variables also contributed to the violence that marred the protests against the sixth ministerial conference of the WTO in Hong Kong in December 2005. Following sporadic confrontations in the preceding four days, the worst of the disorders occurred on 17 December when police used tear gas to repel a succession of attacks by protesters to penetrate their lines. A total of 137 people were reported injured in the conflict (67 of them police). During the five-day protest period, almost 1,000 protesters were taken prisoner, of whom the vast majority (almost 900) were South Korean farmers angered by the impact of WTO decisions on their livelihoods (Lo Shiu-hing 2006).

Police preparations and planning for the event were based on 'knowledge' deriving from several different sources. Relevant 'lessons' of preceding summit meetings were influential on their approach. Eager, for example, not to be overwhelmed like their counterparts in Seattle, the Hong Kong police deployed 9,000 officers, thus outnumbering the protesters by 2,000. All efforts were also devoted to ensuring that the various participating control agencies were fully agreed on strategic policy and, therefore, un-affected by the kind of 'internal fragmentation' that had hampered the policing of Seattle (*ibid.*).

The highly distinctive culture of the Hong Kong police was another key ingredient. According to Shiu-hing, theirs is a culture 'characterised by efficiency, strong discipline, respect for hierarchy and order, distrustful attitudes towards protestors and a relatively strong disbelief in western democratic values' (*ibid.*: 153). Police tolerance of violent protest had not been too much in evidence since the communist-led riots against 'British imperialism' of 1967 in which 5,000 people were arrested and a further 59 killed. Echoing police sentiments expressed in Genoa, police branded local protesters likely to be attending the WTO as 'troublemakers', sponsored by foreign political groups. Even more suspicion was levelled at the thousands of South Korean farmers also liable to be gathering. Many of these had undertaken military training while serving as conscripts and were therefore looked upon as a realistic threat to the security of WTO delegates.

Superseding all these factors as a determinant of the police's strategic orientation was the prevailing political climate. Since the transfer of Hong Kong's sovereignty from the United Kingdom to the People's Republic of China (PCR) eight years earlier, the govern-ment of the newly formed Hong Kong Special Administrative Region (HKSAR) had been desperate to avoid any political developments that could be seized upon by the PCR's central government as grounds for reducing the island's political autonomy from the Chinese mainland. Thus,

> Against the background of minimising the likelihood of [PCR] interference, the HKSAR police were under tremendous but hidden pressure to ensure that the anti-WTO protests would by no means transform into a crisis of legitimacy for the new administration led by Chief Executive Donald Tsang . . . In short, the Hong Kong police perceived the anti-WTO protests as a test of its ability to cope with international and local protestors. (ibid.: 144)

Nevertheless, such pressure to adopt a tough stance against pro-testers was offset by a competing political priority for the HKSAR government to avoid unnecessary confrontation. Ministers were aware of the possibility that such violence would play into the hands of local pro-democracy reformists who were intent on undermining the legitimacy of their regime.

This balance of political determinants initially elicited a police strategy based on establishing rapport with the protesters and attempting to accommodate their objectives. However, police caution also dictated a parallel commitment to keeping activists under constant surveillance. Successive confrontations in the build-up to 17 December ensured that police tolerance was progressively withdrawn. Ultimately, the fact that the main protest location was imbued with such great political significance placed police officers under a powerful obligation to 'die in a ditch':

> Central Square, which is beside the Convention Centre and was occupied by some protestors, was seen as the final 'turf' or battle-line that the police could not concede. In response to the danger that protestors might flock into the Convention Centre, thus posing genuine security risks to the WTO delegates, the police decided to take strong action towards the protestors by using tear gas and arresting them. (*ibid*.: 156)

Shiu-hing speculates that the fluid nature of public opinion during the protest period may have had a considerable bearing on the events of 17 December. Initially hostile public perceptions of the South Korean demonstrators supposedly became increasingly sympathetic with each day of the protests. This was possibly related to such well-publicised instances of police over-aggression as when they turned water cannons on demonstrators during a confrontation on 16 December. As Shiu-hing explains, this growing recognition by protesters that public support was on their side increased the perceived legitimacy of their actions and encouraged them in their confrontation with the police.

Policing on the basis of 'lessons learned'

Implicit in the above analyses of Genoa and Hong Kong is the notion, first raised in Chapter 1, that public order policing methods are adaptive to the 'lessons learned' on the basis of previous encounters or the vicarious experience of confrontations involving other forces. This tendency can be illustrated with reference to two examples occurring in the wake of the Genoa tragedy: the Canadian

G8 summit meeting and the anti-war rally in Florence of June and November 2002, respectively.

The Canadian G8 summit

Two related articles by King and Waddington (2005, 2006) attempt to highlight and account for variations in the styles of policing adopted by Canadian police in their handling of transnational protests occurring from 1997 to 2002. The primary foci of their analysis are the violent demonstration coinciding with the Summit of the Americas in Quebec City in April 2001 and the relatively more peaceful protests accompanying the G8 summit meeting of one year later.

King and Waddington demonstrate how the 'exclusionary fortress-oriented' style adopted by the Royal Canadian Mounted Police (RCMP) and regional forces in Quebec City was significantly influenced by the nature and outcomes of the security arrangements implemented at earlier protest events in Canada, and activities previously transpiring in Seattle and Washington, DC. The three-metre-high, six-kilometres-long security perimeter was defiantly besieged by a crowd of 7,000 protesters (King and Waddington 2005; McNally 2001). Police reacted uncompromisingly by discharging over 5,000 tear gas canisters and firing 903 plastic bullet rounds into the crowd (King and Waddington 2006).

Following the violence in Genoa and the '9/11' terrorist attack on the World Trade Centre in September 2001, the Canadian govern-ment decided to host the June 2002 G8 summit out of reach of protesters in the remote, Rocky Mountain holiday resort of Kananaskis, Alberta. Demonstrators were forced to stage their protests in distant places like Ottawa, where two small marches of around 3–5,000 people occurred on 26 and 27 June. Only five arrests were made during the two days of protest activity (King and Waddington 2005).

Clearly, this outcome was strongly related to the fact that, unlike the situation in Quebec City, there was no gathering of IPPs to target specifically. King and Waddington (*ibid.*) also observe that the anarchist groups present in large numbers in Quebec City were not as strongly represented in Ottawa. Just as important a distinguishing feature, though, was the fact that the Ottawa Police Service (OPS) appeared to have 'learned the lesson' of a disorderly protest meeting of the previous November, after which their conduct was roundly criticised by a local civil libertarian organisation.

The event in question was the joint staging of the G20/IMF and

World Bank conferences in Ottawa from 18–20 November 2001. Following resounding complaints of police heavy-handedness, a Citizen's Panel on Policing and Community (CPPC) – subsequently renamed the Ottawa Witness Group – published a review which was critical of the intimidatory deployment of 'hard hat' police officers (some of whom were armed), the overzealous use of snatch-squads and dog-handlers, and unnecessary deployment of less-lethal weapons, such as teargas, rubber bullets and pepper spray (King and Waddington 2006). The CPPC provoked an OPS internal operations review, which then resulted in the publication of an 'Agenda for Excellence for Policing Major Events'. This document stipulated the force's commitment to: upholding the democratic rights of individuals to protest, strengthening community partnerships through communication, consultation and transparency of operation, and ensuring the safety of citizens and police personnel. In future, such objectives would be facilitated by a newly established Major Events Liaison Team (MELT) (*ibid.*).

The police were true to their words. King and Waddington (2005, 2006) use insights drawn from S. Allen (2003), as well as their interviews and other forms of documentation, to explain how, in the build-up to the Ottawa protest, a joint RCMP/OPS MELT entered into constructive pre-event dialogue with labour organisations partly responsible for organising the planned demonstration. When similar approaches to anti-globalisation groups were rebuffed, the police fell back on high-grade intelligence collated by a specially established Joint Intelligence Group (JIG), which tracked the movements of known activists and kept tabs on vehicles converging on the protest. On the day of the event, photographs of anyone with a known criminal record were fed to officers on the ground, along with similar images of anyone requiring 'special treatment'.

As part of their 'iron fist in a velvet glove' approach (S. Allen, *op. cit.*), the majority of police donned 'soft hat' uniforms with tactical squads and vehicles kept on standby but out of view of protesters. Cameras on rooftops, a helicopter and fixed-wing aircraft fed real-time surveillance footage to the police central command location. Demonstrators had already been given advance notice by the police of a temporary holding facility set up to detain protesters caught engaging in unlawful direct action. Protesters disembarking from their buses were immediately encountered by officers clad in jackets marked 'police liaison':

Although outwardly friendly, [these] officers pointedly photo-graphed each new arrival as an unmistakable statement of their intention. Finally, as part of a 'saturation' tactic, plainclothes officers infiltrated the crowd, providing tactical information while the march was in progress. Uniformed colleagues lined the route of the march, some of them openly parading cameras and their surveillance equipment. Anyone seen melting away from the march was immediately followed in order to thwart any possible intention to commit an act of vandalism. (King and Waddington 2006: 94)

The OPS's greater commitment to openness and accountability was reflected in their decisions to wear clearly visible officer identification numbers, and to co-operate with civilian observers, who were allowed to monitor their actions from close vantage positions. Determined to accommodate the crowd's objectives, police officers also dealt leniently with a van capable of broadcasting amplified sound which merged unexpectedly into one of the two marches. The police were concerned about the safety implications of the vehicle. However, rather than insisting on its outright removal, they successfully persuaded protesters to relocate the van within a safer section of the march (King and Waddington 2005).

The anti-war protest in Florence

For the demonstration in opposition to the war in Iraq, held in Florence in November 2002, Italian police managed to cultivate a far more harmonious relationship with the estimated 500,000 protesters than the one which had prevailed in Genoa a year earlier. della Porta and Reiter (2006b) acknowledge that this relatively peaceful outcome was partly due to the nature and objectives of the participants: in addition to having an underlying anti-war rationale, the march was organised by 'mainstream' sections of the European left and trade union movement. Police fears of possible violence were further assuaged when 'disobedient' groups signalled a more conciliatory stance by not wearing their usual protective garments. However, della Porta and Reiter also maintain that various aspects of the authorities' control strategy, based on the lessons learned from Genoa, helped to ensure a violence-free event.

In contrast to Genoa, negotiations between the demonstration organisers and the authorities were established several months prior to the event, with a trusted local politician acting as intermediary.

These discussions helped to override the potentially destructive effects of a 'virulent' centre-right and media campaign against the protest. Moreover, in order to offset the 'alarmist' secret service prognoses already circulating the press, police officers on duty in Florence were required to attend a month-long preparatory course run by sociologists and psychologists. On the day of the march, operations were directed by a local police chief (whereas a national vice-chief of police had been present in Genoa) and officers assigned to the march kept themselves a respectful distance from participants. These tactics were consistent with the notice given by senior police to the demonstrators' legal team of their 'intention to wipe out the image of Genoa' (*ibid.*: 39).

The evolution of policing philosophies

The final case study to be examined in this chapter – the New York anti-war protest of February 2003 – illustrates the important point that force principles of public order policing may be tied, not merely to lessons learned on the basis of recent protest encounters, but to wider force philosophies prescribing a general approach to everyday policing. As we shall see from this example, such philosophies are often the result of crises of police legitimacy which oblige the relevant police force to re-orientate its particular styles of operation.

The anti-war protest in New York City

Called in opposition to the impending war in Iraq, the New York demonstration was one of many protests taking place on 15 and 16 February in major international locations like London, Rome, Paris, Sydney and Montreal, as well as in other large American cities, such as Los Angeles and San Francisco. Yet, of all these large demonstrations, typically in excess of 100,000 people, only the one taking place in New York City was notably confrontational, with the police persistently resorting to force (NYCLU 2003). Vitale (2005b) argues that the exceptional nature of the violence occurring in New York was due, primarily, to the New York City Police Department's (NYPD) singular commitment to a *zero tolerance* approach to crowd management (and for dealing with criminal activity more generally), based on the 'broken windows' philosophy of policing.

In a slightly earlier study, Vitale (2005a) explains how the NYPD's growing adherence in the 1980s and 1990s to the zero tolerance approach could be traced back to a 'crisis of legitimacy' induced by a number of civilian-led campaigns for police action against drug dealers, street beggars and the 'squeegee men' who leaped out to wash the windscreens of vehicles temporarily halted at traffic lights. Such lobbying, and the endorsement it received from city politicians, produced a shift in police philosophy towards the broken windows approach:

> The broken windows theory argues that low-level crime and disorder, if left unchecked, can lead to a climate of lawlessness, which in turn can result in higher levels of serious crime and economic downturn for local communities. The solution is increased police attention to these minor crimes and disorders as a way of restoring a sense of safety and order, which will allow residents to reassert control over their neighbourhoods. (*ibid.*: 101)

The pseudonym 'quality of life policing' is also applied to this approach to denote its fundamental concern with the elimination of visible disorders and the eradication of everyday nuisance. In New York City, the philosophy is manifested in such tactics as: enhanced stop and frisk procedures; the greater use of civil enforcement (e.g. closing down businesses associated with drug dealing); the creation and implementation of new laws, rules and regulations (e.g. to clamp down on 'panhandling' near ATM machines); and proactive policing methods – such as saturating a known prostitution area. As Vitale makes clear, 'It is only when a crisis of legitimacy emerges in combination with calls for doing things in a new way that the police will respond. The depth and length of that response will depend in part on the level of crisis and the pressure they receive from elected officials' (*ibid.*: 122).

The implications of this for public order policing are that the NYPD now routinely assumes that all protesters will:

- not be allowed to 'disrupt' the life of the community;
- stay confined to protest enclosures with fixed points of entry and dispersal;
- be subdivided into smaller, more manageable units;
- be outnumbered by police officers;
- find themselves harshly dealt with should they depart from strictly permitted activities.

This basic strategic orientation requires officers to respond, un-compromisingly and as forcibly as is necessary, to minor violations of the prescribed police rules for the conduct of the demonstration:

> Use of force in this style of policing is under the direct command of high-ranking officers, leaving little room for discretion at lower levels of supervision. Individual officers are kept in line through training and the presence of large numbers of supervisors at all mass mobilizations . . . Nothing is left to chance as police develop deployment plans. The timing and course of all movements of demonstrators are carefully orchestrated by police; there is very little negotiation with demonstrators, especially at the last minute. This includes the flow of people into and out of demonstration areas through the use of elaborate systems of road and sidewalk closures. (Vitale 2005b: 292)

Vitale explains that the five characteristic components of this approach, listed above, were evident in the policing of the New York demonstration. The first of these – *an aversion to disruption* – was visible in the authorities' refusal to agree to the organisers' request to allow the march to proceed through Manhattan, past the UN building. The second component, *controlled access*, was apparent in the police use of wooden and metal barriers to form protest pens which separated the protesters from the public. This tactic facilitated the third principle – *divide and conquer* – involving the subdivision of the crowd into smaller, more easily managed (and closely surveyed) units. The fourth component, *shock and awe*, involved overwhelming numerical superiority. The NYPD's deployment of 4,000 officers far exceeded the few hundred typically called upon in other major US cities. Finally, there was an accent on *zero tolerance*, with the police coming down hard on anyone found overstepping the mark.

Vitale emphasises that the vast size of the crowd made the com-plicated system of controlled access unworkable. People prevented by the sheer scale of the protest from entering the pens found themselves treated harshly for unwittingly defying the permit conditions. Evidence contained in a report by the New York Civil Liberties Union (NYCLU 2003) shows how the police's strict enforcement of their rules created chaos, confusion and disorder. During one incident, for example,

> A police officer with a bullhorn made announcements for people to move west on 51st Street, but those announcements could

only be heard by those close to the officer. Videotape shows that a line of police officers then started forcing themselves forward with batons outstretched, with the mounted officers coming behind the advancing line of officers. Because of the intense overcrowding and the speed with which the police officers moved, many people were knocked down, and in some instances were trampled by the police horses. Many people who fell were arrested. In certain locations, people who had been pushed out of the street onto the sidewalk and who then stopped retreating were pepper sprayed. (*ibid*.: 9)

The NYCLU received scores of complaints of police misconduct occurring even after the rally had ended. Due to indignation resulting from the fact that they had not been allowed to voice their opposition to the war, groups of protesters decided to stage an impromptu protest in Times Square. However, on reaching 42nd Street between Broadway and Seventh Avenue, they found their path blocked by a line of waiting police officers. According to one protester, the police 'were obviously very tense and frightened – they seemed overwhelmed and unsure of what to do' (quoted in *ibid*.: 20). The police's immediate reaction was to make 'examples' of people through arbitrary arrests. An already tense situation further escalated when the crowd surged forward in reaction to the rough arrest of a young woman by four or five officers. The police responded by using temporary barricades to hem in the crowd close to surrounding buildings. More arrests and minor injuries were then sustained as the police eventually cleared the sidewalk. Such actions clearly lend credence to Mitchell and Staeheli's (2005) assertion that overbearing police tactics that seek to restrict or 'routinise' dissent have an inherent potential to backfire.

Conclusions

The growth of anti-globalisation protest since the late 1990s has been accompanied by sporadic confrontations between demonstrators and police forces seemingly committed to more repressive forms of crowd control. This tendency is undoubtedly due, in part, to the enhanced sense of obligation acting on the police to guarantee the safety and protection both of prestigious summit venues and the internationally significant dignitaries attending them. Variations in the amount of violence are inevitably related to the particular nature of the police tactics and strategy employed. The study of the policing of the Seattle protest undertaken by Gillham and Marx clearly illustrates how police tactics are often ironic in their consequences. In other words, they can unwittingly serve to escalate the conflict, not least by unifying and emboldening previously disparate groups of protesters.

Case studies undertaken by Noakes *et al.* (*op. cit.*) and Noakes and Gillham (*op. cit.*) suggest that there has been a consistent trend, post-Seattle, for police in Western democracies to embrace strategic and tactical approaches consistent with the 'new penology' philosophy of order management. Specifically, this has involved a commitment to applying tenets of negotiated management in relation to contained protesters, alongside techniques of strategic incapacitation designed to undermine the objectives and activities of transgressive groups of protesters. Mitchell and Staeheli contend that mass protests have become so 'routinised' and 'neutralised' by the police as to render them virtually ineffectual. Protest activists have become correspondingly resentful and defiant – hence the increased potential for further violence.

The relish and severity with which particular police forces have applied the principles of strategic incapacitation is usually a function of the presence or absence of other significant variables. Prominent among these are: longstanding policing traditions that may moderate or enhance tendencies toward more proactive and/or aggressive modes of police intervention, the 'lessons' absorbed on the basis of previous public order events, the enduring 'missions' or 'philosophies' adhered to by individual forces, the prevailing political context, and the way that senior police officers strategically 'manage' both the public order environment and public impressions of the protesters. Our case studies suggest that these variables tend to fuse and interact with numerous cultural, contextual, situational and interactional factors to produce disorderly or non-violent outcomes. This relationship is explored in greater depth in the following chapter, which comprises a case study of the protest accompanying the meeting of the G8 Justice and Home Affairs ministers in the major English city of Sheffield, South Yorkshire, in June 2005.

Chapter 6

The G8 Justice and Home Affairs Ministers' meeting in Sheffield, June 2005

Introduction

Aside from the annual May Day protests referred to in the previous chapter, the most significant examples of anti-globalisation protests occurring in the United Kingdom in the post-Seattle era were those accompanying the G8 ministerial meetings held in Derby, Sheffield and Gleneagles in March, June and July 2005, respectively. This chapter is chiefly dedicated to outlining and analysing the various institutional, cultural, practical, professional and political considerations affecting South Yorkshire Police's (SYP's) tactics and strategy for managing the Sheffield meeting, codenamed 'Operation Octagon'. The primary aim of the chapter is to further underline the significance and interrelationship of ideas introduced earlier by viewing them in the context of one particular instance of police public order management.

We saw in the introduction to this book how the kinds of fortification and exclusion strategies employed at previous transnational protests were similarly deployed at the English and Scottish G8 meetings of 2005. At Derby, for the forum of G8 Environment and Development Ministers, held on 15–19 March, Derbyshire Police invoked Section 14 of the Public Order Act 1986 to limit a demonstration on 17 March to a confined area of Derby Market Place and restrict the number of people attending to a maximum of 3,000. The actual protest by some 100 people occurred well out of reach of the international delegation, which convened at the Marriott Breadsall Priory Hotel two miles north-east of the city. The venue was encircled by steel barricades that 'cut across the [golf] fairways' and a protective cordon of 2,000 officers (Black 2005).

South Yorkshire Police forged a similar 'ring of steel' (Waple 2005) and drew a two-mile 'exclusion zone' around the suburban hotel used as the main venue for the meeting of the G8 Justice and Home Affairs Ministers in Sheffield on 15–17 June. However, the police also sanctioned a series of city-centre protests variously organised by Sheffield Dissent (a network of resistance to the G8) and the Sheffield Stop the War Coalition. This included a city-centre march of 1,000 people on the Saturday before the meeting (11 June) and a pair of small, static demonstrations coinciding with civic receptions for the G8 delegations on Wednesday, 15 June, and Thursday, 16 June, at the downtown locations of the Winter Gardens and Cutlers' Hall, respectively. The Public Order Act 1986 was invoked to limit the size of the static assemblies to no more than 150 people and to ban all marches for the duration of the meeting. A controversial feature of Wednesday's demonstration was the playing of the Stocksbridge Brass Band – positioned midway between the demonstrators and the dropping-off point for the visiting VIPs – which drowned out the protest chanting.

Other forms of protest, including a 'Rice for Dinner' meal – organised by Make Poverty History to coincide with the 'official' meal inside the Cutlers' Hall and highlight the dietary deficiencies of the world's poor – were allowed to proceed with minimal police supervision. Indeed, the tone of police methods for controlling the event from start to finish was markedly low-key. The three arrests of Wednesday evening and the seven of the following night all occurred some distance away from the scheduled protests. Wednesday's arrests followed an attempt by a small group of anarchists to break through a line of police patrolling an access road. On the following evening, police reacted to an impromptu march by a section of people attending the Rice for Dinner meal by corralling them into a side-street for 2–3 hours, during which time 'snatch-squads' made occasional arrests.

We also learned from the Introduction how the police management of the Scottish G8 summit meeting in and around Edinburgh in early July incorporated diverse tactical approaches. The rock star, Bob Geldof, had called on one million people to descend on Edinburgh in the G8 week to campaign against global poverty. The Make Poverty History march through Edinburgh by 250,000 people was notable for the *absence* of disorder – save for a heated moment in which 60 anarchists were corralled into a side-street, though no-one was arrested. Confrontations did occur, however, on two sub-sequent, unscheduled marches through the centre of the Scottish capital: first, a 'Carnival for Full Enjoyment', involving protesters perceived to be threatening the city's financial institutions; and secondly, an impromptu march by protesters exasperated on learning that police were not allowing them to travel by coach from Edinburgh to Gleneagles. In the first instance, the police brought in 'iron horse' portable steel barriers to corral-in the crowd for several hours; and in the second, they briefly halted the march and threw a police cordon round the participants before allowing it to continue around the city. Major disorder also broke out when protesters at Gleneagles encountered the main perimeter fence and a breakaway section of the march was repelled by riot police arriving by helicopter to prevent a breach from occurring.

The policing of the Sheffield event was subjected to rigorous scrutiny by me and four colleagues acting as participant observers. Thirty-two in-depth interviews were also undertaken with various respondents, including senior police, media personnel, a representative of Sheffield City Council, protest organisers and a wide cross-section of demonstrators (see Table 6.1 for a full list of respondents). This data forms the basis of the following analysis of the policing of this event.

The analysis initially picks up on the important theme highlighted by Vitale (2005b) in the previous chapter. Thus the first section of the chapter uses the conclusions drawn in a previous study (Mawby 2002) in explication of the singular everyday philosophy subscribed to by SYP. Only by appreciating the significance and pervasiveness of this philosophy can we fully understand the force's preferred style of managing the Sheffield G8. The second section provides a brief overview of the forward planning engaged in by the city council, and the processes of deliberation and liaison operating between the council, the police and protest organisers. This is followed, in the third section, by a consideration of the police's preparations for the event. Two further sections then discuss the implications of SYP's strategy and tactics for police–protester interaction during the main public protests of the Wednesday and Thursday evenings. Thus far, academic analysis of the Edinburgh protests has been limited to a single study of the Make Poverty History march (Gorringe and Rosie 2006), making it difficult to arrive at authoritative conclusions about the policing of the event. Nevertheless, the final section of this chapter contains a speculative analysis of corresponding police tactics and strategy in Scotland.

Table 6.1 List of interview respondents

Type of respondent(s)	Male	Female	Total
(a) *Official agencies*			
Senior police officers	2	–	2
Journalists	3	–	3
Sheffield City Councillor (Elected)	–	1	1
City Centre Manager, Sheffield City Council	1	–	1
(b) *Protest organisers*			
Sheffield Stop the War Coalition	–	2	2
Rice for Dinner/Make Poverty History	2	–	2
(c) *Protesters**			
Students' Union officers	1	1	2
Anarchists	3	–	3
Socialist Workers' Party	1	1	2
Sheffield Rhythms of Resistance	1	–	1
Clandestine Insurgent Rebel Clown Army	–	1	1
Others	8	4	12
TOTALS	22	10	32

Note: *Includes three people who were arrested during the protests

South Yorkshire Police: force purpose and values

Just as the New York Police Department of the 1990s underwent a crisis of legitimacy in its relations with the local citizenry, South Yorkshire Police also experienced a loss of public confidence following its controversial involvement in the 1984–5 miners' strike and its role in the infamous Hillsborough tragedy of 1989, in which local officers were held responsible for creating the 'crush' which resulted in the deaths of dozens of football supporters. The way in which the force responded to this crisis, and formulated a new statement of purpose and values in the process, is fundamental to our understanding of its handling of the protests accompanying the Sheffield G8.

As Mawby (2002) explains, South Yorkshire was one of the key battlegrounds of the miners' strike: bitter confrontations occurred at miners' rallies in Sheffield; there were set-piece battles between hundreds of pickets and police drawn from 11 forces at Orgreave coke works on the edge of the city; and residents of South Yorkshire mining communities like Maltby and Grimethorpe reacted violently to incursions by mobile police units. The sense of alienation felt across the county was accentuated by the then Chief Constable, Peter Wright's, outright resistance to attempts by his civilian Police Committee to have him soften force policy towards the striking miners. Following the strike, the police's critics saw themselves vindicated by the acquittal at Sheffield Crown Court of 15 men charged with rioting at Orgreave.

The Hillsborough tragedy has had an equally enduring and traumatic effect on the force's image and morale. This happened on 15 April 1989, when Sheffield Wednesday's Hillsborough stadium was the venue for an FA Cup semi-final between Liverpool and Nottingham Forest. Liverpool supporters had been allocated the Leppings Lane end-terraces but, with the kick-off only 10 minutes away, a large number of their supporters had still not entered that part of the ground. At this point, the senior officer present tried to relieve the build-up of pressure by ordering the opening of a gate. The sudden influx of 2,000 people into the stadium resulted in a massive crush of bodies which caused 96 deaths and hundreds more injuries.

A subsequent judicial inquiry attributed the tragedy to a failure of police control. It accused the main commanding officer, Chief Superintendent David Duckenfield, not only of having 'frozen' on the day, but of also having falsely reported to the Secretary of the Football

Association that the catastrophe occurred because Liverpool fans had forced the gate open. Duckenfield was instantly suspended. His Chief Constable apologised on behalf of SYP and offered his resignation, though this was not accepted. Despite such tacit acceptance of blame, various legal bodies refrained from taking action, either against the force or individual officers, leaving relatives of the Hillsborough victims to continue their ceaseless campaign for justice.

A major turning point was reached with the resignation of Peter Wright in May 1990 and the appointment as his successor of Richard Wells, an Oxford-educated former deputy assistant commissioner of the Metropolitan Police with varied experience in media and community relations, training and operational command. There is no doubt that 'Wells took over a force which was beleaguered and dispirited. The force was demoralized as a result of a series of events which had damaged its reputation, confidence and integrity' (ibid.: 117). The Chairperson of the South Yorkshire Police Authority stated that their main purpose in appointing Mr Wells was to 'win back public support and to restore confidence in the police' (quoted in ibid.).

Wells soon set about the task of transforming the force image and identity. Following a widespread consultation exercise involving 250 community groups and all South Yorkshire Police employees, he produced a document called *Statement of Force Purpose and Values*. As Mawby explains,

> The Statement concerns what the force will do and how it will conduct itself in the discharge of its duties. It exhorts staff to strive to act with 'integrity' to be 'honest, courteous and tactful' and to 'use persuasion, common sense and good humour'. It emphasizes also that staff should display honesty, humanity and compassion, be willing to listen, to try new ways of working and to admit failings. It is, in sum, a statement which both provides guidance to members of SYP and also gives people expectations concerning how they will be treated in their dealings with the force. (ibid.: 119)

This and similar documents provided the keynotes for a new philosophy of policing. Mawby illustrates how this philosophy was manifested in the local policing of public order. One example he provides focuses on a demonstration called by Reclaim the Streets (a coalition of environmentalist and anarchist groups) in May 1997. According to him, this involved low-key and tactful policing, the consequence of which was that only one demonstrator was arrested. Most notably, in his briefing of the 60 officers deployed, the Gold commander had urged them to act *'in a professional manner in accordance with our statement of purpose and values'* (quoted in *ibid.*: 160, emphasis added). This example provides a useful foundation for understanding the relatively liberal force attitude to the policing of public order. As we shall see from the subsequent comments of senior officers, the philosophy was evident in attitudes to the management of the G8 meeting. This will become evident as we continue our analysis of the event, starting with the political context in which it occurred.

The political context of the event

In September 2004, Sheffield City Council gratefully accepted a Home Office invitation to host the meeting of the G8 Justice and Home Affairs Ministers, due to be staged in June 2005. A subsequent council press release of 24 January 2005 emphasised how this was a heaven-sent opportunity for the city to promote itself to a wide international audience:

> Hosting the JHA G8 summit will give Sheffield the opportunity to showcase itself to a global audience. Ministers, their aides and the world's media will be able to see for themselves that Sheffield is a city on the up that is at home on the international stage.

As the council's City Centre Manager explained in interview, right from the outset, he and his department explored every possible means of 'selling Sheffield internationally' as a world-class conference, commercial and tourist destination. The council's eventual decision to employ protest compounds reflected their attempt to strike a balance between allowing a safe and orderly expression of protest while safeguarding the city's world-wide reputation. Suggestions that the hiring of a brass band was a cynical ploy to drown out the noise of protesters gathered in Tudor Square on Wednesday, 15 June, were repudiated by the council on the grounds that this aspect of the evening's entertainment had been booked well before they had known where the protesters would be assembling.

Due to fears that both South Yorkshire Police and Sheffield City Council might well sacrifice the local right to protest in order to guarantee the security of international delegates, both Sheffield Dissent and the Sheffield Stop the War Coalition lobbied and campaigned assiduously to ensure that the protest would ultimately be allowed. It was with this objective in mind that one member of Dissent – an elected council representative of the Green Party – submitted a motion to a full council meeting of 1 June, opposing the staging of the G8 in Sheffield. The resulting debate in the council chambers was witnessed by members of the Stop the War Coalition, some of whom submitted an anti-G8 petition comprising 500 signatures. Prior to the debate, a coalition committee member was allowed to deliver a five-minute speech deploring Sheffield's decision to host the meeting:

> The discussion the speech generated in the council chambers lasted for two hours, if not more. But also, we got such good media coverage on ITV, Channel Four and local press and radio that we were able to exert subsequent leverage on the police. (Sheffield Stop the War Coalition member, female)

Representatives of the two primary protest groups continued to employ the media with a view to pressurising the police and city council into allowing as open and extensive a form of protest as possible. On one occasion, the Chairperson of the Stop the War Coalition appeared in the *Yorkshire Post* of 7 June 2004 ('Protests Row as Summit Comes to City') to object that police plans to forbid protesters from gathering within close proximity of the ministerial entourages: 'would be an abuse of our civil liberties, and a great shame in a city that has a proud record of standing up for peace and justice'. She and her colleagues were convinced that, but for their campaigning, the protests would either have been banned outright – or, at least, subjected to a more repressive form of policing:

> At first, I think the police were concerned about allowing any demonstrations at all. But as a result of the petitioning, 'the G8 isn't welcome here' got a lot of press and public support and we were able to apply that pressure against the police. Plus, it was supported by such a wide range of groups of people, like the Greens, the Muslim Association of Great Britain, CND, ourselves and several others, so it was very difficult for the police to refuse the demonstration. (Sheffield Stop the War Coalition member, female)

Despite this public pressure, the police kept both the organisers and larger general public hanging on until the last minute before finally sanctioning limited protests on the Wednesday and Thursday evenings of 15 and 16 June. The police's seemingly dilatory attitude was widely interpreted as a deliberate – albeit uncharacteristic – strategy to deter people from attending and undermine the protest's effectiveness. Positive relations between senior members of the Stop the War Coalition and police liaison officers had been very much in evidence in preceding negotiations regarding anti-war marches in the wake of the 9/11 atrocity. On this latest occasion, the police expressed very few objections to the idea of a march being staged on the Saturday prior to the ministerial meeting (11 June). It was in relation to the planned protests *of the following week* that they were reluctant to give their approval.

This was apparent on Friday, 10 June, when the chairperson visited Sheffield's West Bar police station to hand in a requisite pro-forma affirming the coalition's intention to stage a succession of protests. She had simply intended leaving the document at the front reception desk.

> However, two officers came down from another floor and insisted on having a 'quiet' discussion with me in the corridor, where they told me 'off the record' that, whilst they'd very much like to support our application, they were pessimistic about its chances of being approved of because the demonstration was likely to be 'hijacked' by 'outside elements' that the police were particularly concerned about. (Chairperson, Sheffield Stop the War Coalition, female)

At the eleventh hour, she received confirmation from the police that the protests could go ahead, as requested, but that they would be limited to a maximum of 100 participants. Coalition representatives urgently appealed to the police to lift the stipulation that the protests be designated to fixed locations and to withdraw their restrictions on the amount of people they had said they would allow in. They were especially worried about the possibility that trouble might arise due to protesters being refused access to the pens and having their 'right to protest' denied. In order to understand the police's apparent reluctance to heed the Coalition's advice and grant them the kind of co-operation they had received on earlier occasions, it is necessary to examine the former's strategic thinking and preparation regarding the event.

Police planning and preparation

Police preparations for 'Operation Octagon' took the form of monthly meetings involving a senior Strategic Group, concerned with overall policy, and of a separate group of Bronze commanders responsible for planning the security of specific venues. Home Office intervention was minimal but SYP's final plans for securing the event were subject to the approval both of the Metropolitan Police Service's Special Branch and the international security services relevant to each of the summit delegates.

Police intelligence in the build-up to the G8 was largely prepared on the basis of scanning the internet sites of radical organisations. By the police's own admission, this proved a relatively fruitless activity:

> The only thing that we knew for sure was that there were going to be some anarchists coming to Sheffield en route to Edinburgh. But after the Saturday, people seemed to be bypassing Sheffield and going straight up to Edinburgh. We made it quite clear on the Saturday that anyone arrested would be prohibited from going up to Scotland. (Bronze commander, SYP, male)

In his determination to balance the competing and often con-tradictory needs and objectives of parties, like the summit delegates, Sheffield City Council, discrepant groups of protesters and their non-protesting fellow citizens, Meredydd Hughes, the Chief Constable of South Yorkshire, decided to invoke Sections 13, 14 and 14A of the Public Order Act 1986. These sections authorised Mr Hughes, not only to ban marches for the duration of the summit meeting, but also to restrict static assemblies to prescribed venues, subject them to certain conditions of occurrence, and take appro-priate action against anyone trespassing on private property. Underlying the Chief Constable's decision was a perceived need to exercise caution in the face of great uncertainty:

> I did take the opportunity to prevent marches at a certain time and place because I couldn't separate sheep from goats in terms of those who were intent on demonstrating lawfully. I mean we were going to get people demonstrating who were Quakers, who wanted to demonstrate in groups of four or five, lighting candles and holding banners up. We didn't want to see anyone

stopping them from doing that. I come from that background of protest tradition. But what I didn't want was the opportunity for a march to go so close to the venue that people within that march could then start throwing rocks. I set out very clearly in the Gold strategy for Sheffield that we would facilitate the lawful business of the summit – they were entitled to be here and entitled to have their meeting in peace and quiet; we would facilitate the lawful protest, with the emphasis on *lawful*; we would try and locate venues where people could make their feelings known so that they were close enough to let people know they were there and protesting, but not so they could commit any act of violence. (Chief Constable of South Yorkshire, male)

To achieve the preferred 'tone' for the policing of the Sheffield G8, the Chief Constable instigated 'cascade briefings' with local and visiting commanding officers, underlining the need to extend a huge welcome to anyone intent on peacefully protesting. All commanders were then required to watch a DVD on which Mr Hughes emphasised precisely how he wanted the protests to be policed.

This is why, in fact, I don't believe in having a national public order police. I take the decisions about public order in the G8 in the light of the fact that I'm still going to be here the day after. I've been here the year before, so I've had time to meet the community, talk to leaders, get to know the MPs a bit, get to know the councillors, appear in front of them and tell them what I'm gonna do, and make my decisions on the basis of very firm local roots. *Because we do remember the legends of the NUM dispute and the stories of the Metropolitan Police and we are all very anxious to put those legends to bed.* (Chief Constable of South Yorkshire, male, emphasis added)

Cultural influences on police strategy and tactics

Cultural differences – between the police and protesters, and within each of the two parties – further help to explain aspects of the police planning, briefing and behaviour. Operation Octagon drew on approximately 350 public order personnel from the South Yorkshire, West Yorkshire, Greater Manchester, Lancashire, Northumbria and Durham constabularies. As a rule, SYP officers were positioned at the direct interface with the public, while other forces assumed responsibility for policing the more peripheral activities.

The Bronze commander acknowledged in interview that public order units often worked according to a 'football mentality' because controlling events on match days was their staple activity. In the course of his briefings to SYP's own officers, he emphasised the need for a subtler approach, which was sensitive to the fact that these were primarily local people who the officers might be dealing with in future, and exhibited due respect for the protest's central theme of anti-poverty.

> So that was the tenor of the brief: only respond and react if you have to and that will be dictated to by the PSU commanders, the sergeants and the inspectors; no unilateral, sort of 'I'm going to arrest him because he's upset me.' In any case, they were the more professional of my public order units; they can stand around and take that sort of stuff all day. (Bronze commander SYP, male)

Police stereotyping of particular groups of protesters inevitably influenced their tactical orientation. Senior officers were wary of the intentions of anarchist groups likely to be present but were especially concerned by the possible antics of a group known as the Clandestine Insurgent Rebel Clown Army (CIRCA), whose tendency to non-violently lampoon those in positions of authority was perceived as a potentially embarrassing for such prominent parties as the meeting delegates, the Home Secretary, Sheffield City Council and the police themselves. Actual members of these groups were scornful of the characterisations and assumed motives attributed to them by police and media. One CIRCA member confided that she and several colleagues, had only 'joined the army' one month previously and had since received a mere two days' training in relevant techniques. Far from striving to provoke or incite people into violence, the clowns' objectives were to employ humour to subversive effect while *de-fusing* the potential for violence:

> Once you've got your clown uniform on, it gives you that kind of freedom that you wouldn't have normally – to go up to police and dust down their truncheons and generally interact in that way. It helps you, hopefully, to turn tense situations into something a bit lighter. It's a bit like saying, 'Look, they might well be police and they've got their tear gas and truncheons

upon them; we might well be no match physically, but they're only human and we've got to find disarming ways of challenging their authority and their function for the state. (CIRCA member, female)

Respondents emphasised that one major reason why the demonstration was largely free of incident was that participants generally subscribed to principles of non-violence:

They're not, the majority of them, looking for a fight. They are desperately angry about the way in which the world is being run and how the consequences of that are being played down, ignored or manipulated out of sight. There isn't really the appetite for playing up to the role of the antagonistic, violent anarchists of the tabloid stereotyping. (Organiser, Rice for Dinner, male)

As we shall now see, these cultural ingredients interacted with the institutional, political and communicative variables also referred to above to encourage particular forms of police–protester interaction. Such interaction was underpinned by a generally good-natured rapport between both sides. This aspect of the Sheffield demonstrations is now analysed with particular emphasis on the two main nights of protest activity – Wednesday and Thursday, 15 and 16 June, respectively.

Activities prior to and during the Tudor Square demonstration

The Saturday before the two main demonstrations (11 June), the Stop the War march took place in Sheffield city centre. The march set off as planned from Devonshire Green (see Figure 6.1). Initially, there were around 400–500 participants, increasing to 1,000 as it developed. The Stop the War Coalition had arranged for 25 of its own members to act as stewards. Those present commended the police on their attitude, albeit with one minor reservation:

The notable thing was the amount of videoing by the police. That was very invasive compared to most marches I've been on. They did it in pairs. There was usually a bloke with a blue tabard accompanied by another in a red tabard whose job, I

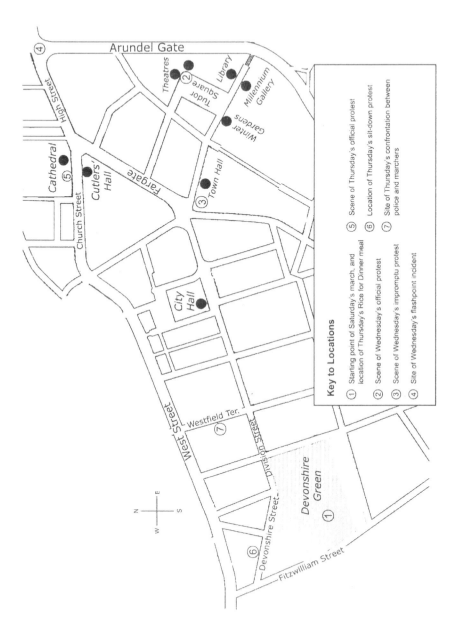

Figure 6.1 Map of Sheffield city centre, showing locations of main protests

suppose, was to look after him. And they did that right the way through, I would say every hundred yards of the march. Despite that, I saw people chatting and smiling with the police. It was all very good-natured. (Protester, male)

In the early morning of Wednesday, 15 June, members of Rhythms of Resistance performed their 'banner drop' from a bridge over-looking the busy Sheffield Parkway. Police looked on amiably as some participants loudly beat their drums while others distributed leaflets among slow-moving rush-hour traffic. At the outset of a Critical Mass bicycle protest, staged later in the afternoon, police used Section 12 of the Public Order Act 1986 to prevent protesters on foot from joining in the procession. Officers explained to the individuals concerned that this was to prevent the possibility of accidents and subsequently released them without charge. Other-wise, here, too, police kept a benign eye on the proceedings while leaflets were handed round.

Feedback on the remainder of the day's activities suggests that, by and large, the police remained tolerant and restrained. Leaflets circulated prior to Wednesday night's demonstration by Dissent and the Stop the War Coalition had asked protesters to assemble *en masse* at 5.30 p.m. on Devonshire Green. However, the air of uncertainty and discouragement generated by the police stipulation that only 100 people were to be allowed in the protest compound meant that people arrived in random fashion and gravitated to the front of the Town Hall, just off from Tudor Square (Figure 6.1).

Included in this spontaneous gathering were members of the Sheffield Socialist Choir, Rhythms of Resistance and CIRCA. Opposite them, a line of police spread out across Surrey Street. Behind them were dogs and horses; further back still were riot vans. The 200–300 demonstrators outside the Town Hall were double the size of the protest in the official compound, where an organised chant was drowned out by the Stocksbridge Brass Band. The police were considered by respondents to have been generally impassive or 'stony-faced' in their determination not to be goaded by protesters or allow themselves to be fazed by the mild ridicule directed at them by the half-dozen members of CIRCA (protester, female).

As predicted by the organisers, the evening's main violence occurred outside of the prescribed protest areas and involved people frustrated at being denied the right to protest. The first major incident occurred when the police arrested two members of a group of 15–20 anarchists who had unsuccessfully tried to pierce an outer ring of officers on Arundel Gate to the north of the official protest (Figure 6.1). As one of them (a 31-year-old man) explained, 'We never went there to confront the police. It was simply that the police were stopping us from getting where we wanted to be!' It was not his arrest, however, but that of his 16-year-old colleague that triggered wider disorder.

Eye witnesses of this event referred to the unnecessary 'brutality' shown by one of the four arresting officers as he and his colleagues (all allegedly from Greater Manchester) roughly overpowered their prisoner.

> I saw 'em get him. His misfortune was to get caught by the wrong copper. He was literally twisting his arm. It could have been any of us really. Everyone was saying, 'Get your hands off him! He's only sixteen! What are you doing to him? What's he done?' I think people were extra pissed off because he's only a kid and looks every inch like a kid! They had him pinned against this wall and that's when the copper pulled out his baton. He just *went mad*, you could see it in his eyes. It was a complete abuse of power. Even his police colleagues had to drag him away. He hit me on my arm and cracked a few other people with his baton; one guy got smashed in his face; another got thrown down some stairs. (Anarchist, male)

By this time, the anarchist group had just been joined on Arundel Gate by many of the 200–300 demonstrators who had originally gathered outside the Town Hall. The latter were responding to a bogus rumour that police had relented and were now allowing far more than 100 people into the protest compound. These relatively new arrivals regarded this latest incident as a marked change from the grudging tolerance previously shown by the police:

> It was one of those incidents like a spark which produced a really noticeable change of atmosphere. I noticed that one of the policemen who were arresting him had him in a hold and he was actually told to leave it – he was actually pulled away from the arrest by another policeman. They then formed a police line to stop the protesters from getting to this boy. (Student union officer, male)

The situation escalated when the policeman who had just been restrained by colleagues hit out, once again, at a 'slightly drunken elderly man' who had approached him to remonstrate about the arrest:

> I saw him take the baton out and hit him straight in the face with no warning or anything. It was brutal, it really was. And as soon as he'd done that, his colleagues next to him presumed there was a reason for it and pulled their batons out. But they didn't actually use them. They had them poised on their shoulders, which I've seen police do before on demonstrations. Then, of course, it was pandemonium because we rushed in to help this guy back to his feet and the same policeman just started *hitting people*. And once he started that, it created a vicious circle with people running in and getting hit. There were protesters kicking back at the police at that point. It was the kind of masked punks who were doing it. But within five seconds, the riot police came in. More importantly, that aggressive copper had his baton taken off him by one of his superiors while he was being taken out of the firing line. The police then put their lines across Arundel Gate and used them to stop any protesters from going further forward. Once they retreated back, things cooled down a lot. (Student union officer, male)

A stand-off briefly ensued, after which the demonstrators back-tracked towards the Town Hall. The attitudes of some protesters remained tetchy. However, there was only one further incident of note, when a local activist of some notoriety spat at police officers from what he wrongly presumed to be the security of the crowd.

> It was the only spitting incident but it was particularly disgusting. I've not got much time for this guy anyway. Every time I go on a demonstration he seems to be the guy that gets stuck in or causes trouble. He's an anarchist guy. I saw a police sergeant, or whatever, point him out to another policeman and they documented it and took a photo. I remember seeing him leaving about 8 or 9 o'clock with a couple of friends and, from what I've read, he was arrested on the way home. They got him on his own rather than arresting him at the time, which was probably the most sensible thing to do. (Protester, male)

The Cutlers' Hall protest and afterwards

Those people intending to gather in the accredited protest compound, opposite the Cutlers' Hall on the Sheffield Cathedral
forecourt (Figure 6.1), found that the majority of obvious access roads
were cordoned off by police. Security measures dictated that the
main pedestrian thoroughfare, Fargate, was barred from public use.
Individuals knowledgeable or fortunate enough to locate the official
entry point to the rear of the Cathedral were allowed in on a
first-come-first-served basis until the police-imposed limit of 100
people had been reached. In the compound, an equal number of
police officers awaited the protesters, forming two cordons between
them and the Cutlers' Hall.

Back outside the compound, 60–70 disgruntled late arrivals tried
their hardest to draw those officers monitoring the exclusion zone
into an argument about the way they felt the police were deliberately
undermining the protest's effectiveness. The officers good-naturedly
fended off this criticism and, eventually, these protesters moved off
to the Rice for Dinner event at Devonshire Green. The prevailing
mood at the green was carnivalesque. The 500 or so people present
lazed around on grass verges, eating their rice meals and listening to
speeches and music, the latter provided by the Sheffield Socialist
Choir and Rhythms of Resistance. A handful of local youths performed skateboarding stunts for the entertainment of onlookers. For
much of the event's duration, police officers maintained a low-key
presence. A small number of police vans were parked up discreetly
on the periphery, and pairs of police officers maintained a casual
indifference to the proceedings. However, just before dusk, a group
of 20–30 young anarchists moved from where they were sitting and
formed a circle in the middle of the road. A gas stove was hastily
assembled and they started to cook a meal.

Police numbers increased substantially at this point. Officers began
diverting traffic and, although they made no attempt to disperse
the group, their video surveillance team commenced recording.
Onlookers then started to join the anarchists in the road,
encountering no opposition by from the police. A few minutes later,
the sit-down protesters rose back to their feet and set off, marching
as a group:

> The reason we started marching and even went into the road is
> because we were sat on Devonshire Green and there was like a
> choir and this guy going on in his speech about how Bob Geldof

had inspired him, and we were scratching our heads. I mean, they were shouting all these messages to, like, a bunch of *skaters* and people who had already made their minds up. So what was the point? You've got to tell the average person who doesn't have a clue what the G8 is all about. That's when we went into the road and on up West Street. (Anarchist, male)

The group of marchers numbered between 150 and 200. Although they initially seemed destined for the Cutlers' Hall, they suddenly tried to give accompanying officers the slip by turning off right down Westfield Terrace, a side-street linking West Street to Division Street (Figure 6.1). A police cordon was already lying in wait. Police officers charged the protesters from the front and rear of the march and tightly hemmed them in. Among those now held captive were a handful of press and radio journalists, and several unwitting by-standers, including two local university lecturers – a male English tutor and a female History professor – who were both treated roughly by the police:

We got pushed quite brutally. No consideration for who you were or what you were doing. We were just standing there. I mean, *I* was a middle-aged lady professor in a suit. *They* were big, heavy, burly, like rugby players, and they just pushed us over this low wall so that we were flat out in these flower beds. The most terrifying thing, though, was that, having done this, they wouldn't let us go past them. I don't usually pull rank but I said, 'Now, look here, I'm a professor of history,' to the little bastards. 'Please let me out!' I said, 'This is absolutely ludicrous! Have you seen the type of people you're imprisoning in here? I mean, most of them are *school pupils*. And have you thought about who you're protecting? A corrupt bunch of worthless poseurs who are busy munching on some freebie!' After about two minutes, they stepped aside to let [my colleague] and I out. And as I walked past these two Chinese people, I said, 'What do you think about our democracy? I've just been beaten to the floor by *our* police!' It really is so violating when people just treat you with such contempt. (Professor of History, female)

This assortment of bona fide protesters, journalists and those unfortunate to have been in the wrong place at the wrong time was detained for well over two hours. Their prevailing mood was buoyantly defiant, as emphasised by the constant rhythms of the drums. However, police snatch-squads tore in, without warning, on several occasions to remove a total of seven prisoners (four men and three women) from the crowd. Independent observers, including an on-the-spot BBC Radio Sheffield reporter, maintained in interview that none of those concerned was doing anything sufficiently criminal to warrant being arrested. The police Bronze commander insisted that officers had acted on the basis of Special Branch intelligence in removing the arrestees, all of whom were known anarchist ringleaders. Anarchist respondents counter-argued that each arrest had been randomly executed: 'They were just clutching at straws, arresting anyone they could. Nobody did anything violent. We were literally just shouting, "Whose streets? Our streets!", "Get a real job!" and "Go back to Manchester!" The age range was about 15 to 40. It was a right good atmosphere. Everybody was dancing, laughing and cheering – except the fucking police!' (Anarchist, male).

According to a senior member of Rhythms of Resistance, the conciliatory approach adopted by South Yorkshire Police was crucial to ensuring an orderly termination of the evening's events:

> A copper, a South Yorkshire inspector, came over and apologised and said the heavy-handedness had been un-necessary and asked us if we would be willing to lead the crowd back to Devonshire Green. We told people behind us that that was happening and they just cheered and tagged along behind us. Had they done that in the first place . . . You see, most people in the pen were just pissed off from being in there. The reason we decided to co-operate was that it was totally out of character because my sense of the whole week was that they'd decided not to harass us, so long as we didn't break through their lines.

Police officers subsequently adopted an unequivocally co-operative manner during a Friday-morning demonstration outside the Marriott Hotel. Here, a few members of CIRCA and Rhythms of Resistance unexpectedly assembled on a small roundabout opposite the hotel's entrance gates. Following a brief burst of drumming, protesters cheekily approached the police line (CIRCA members 'hiding' behind their feather dusters), where they were received with smiles and welcoming conversation. Protesters were surprised by the extent to which they were permitted to stop people and talk to them – including delegates and their staff – as they were entering the hotel. As traffic started to build up, the protesters were politely asked to return to the roundabout, a request which they obeyed, content in the knowledge that they had been allowed to make their point.

Later that morning, some of these protesters joined colleagues outside the South Yorkshire Police headquarters to demonstrate their solidarity with people arrested in the course of the week's protest. A handful of participants donned 'Guantanamo Bay' boiler suits and taped over their mouths in protest at the restrictions that had been imposed on their 'rights' to demonstrate. These activities were videotaped by police. Otherwise, as one individual explained, 'It was all quite benign. One of the officers I was chatting to was perfectly pleasant. Insofar as we told them what we were there to do, and kept to that objective, they were very, very tolerant' (protester, male).

The policing of the Scottish G8

There are obvious similarities between the police measures adopted in Sheffield and the tactics used by Scottish police in corralling-in demonstrators embarked on the two unscheduled marches in Edinburgh city centre. Police tactics in Edinburgh undoubtedly reflected a perceived need to 'take out insurance' in circumstances where the intentions of protesters were either deliberately withheld (as in the Carnival for Full Employment) or too weakly formulated for even its participants to be sure of (as in the impromptu protest down Princess Street following the cancellation of coaches to Auchterarder). As the Chief Constable of South Yorkshire explained in interview, similarities between these tactics and those employed to thwart the spontaneous march by anarchists in Sheffield city centre was not due to prior strategic planning. Rather,

> It comes in because we now have a national public order tactics manual. Wherever you are trained, you are trained to the same tactics and standards; your equipment should look the same and so on . . . It' s a training function of the last 20 years in which we've tried to standardise training. The greatest emphasis, the greatest reason, is nothing sophisticated. It' s actually that, once you establish a set training level, if you don't train to that standard and someone gets injured, you'll get a claim against you! There are more reasons than just operational efficiency for training in a particular way. (Chief Constable of South Yorkshire, male)

One decidedly more unusual feature of the Scottish operation was the obvious determination shown by senior officers from the Lothian and Borders constabulary not to allow their strategy for the Make Poverty History march to be swayed by outlandish media forecasts of Aanarchist-inspired mayhem. Gorringe and Rosie's (2006) interviews with high-ranking force personnel show how the police became exasperated by media forecasts of trouble on the march. As in Sheffield, senior officers recognised that it was part of their responsibility to help to showcase their city in as favourable a light as possible to an onlooking world audience. They also knew that it was down to them to set an appropriate tone for the policing of the entire summit. These were key factors in helping to ensure the orderly nature of the march.

In the absence of interview material with senior officers, it is only possible to speculate on the thinking behind the police tactics for dealing with the breakaway Gleneagles marchers who tried to penetrate the so-called ring of steel. It is possible, of course, that the sudden arrival of mounted police, short-shield units and mobile reinforcements in Chinook helicopters represented a hastily improvised measure to compensate for a lack of police preparation. Given the pinpoint nature of the remaining police tactics, it seems inconceivable that this was ever the case. An alternative possibility is that, as with the siege of the McDonald's restaurant during the May Day protest of 2000, Tayside police deliberately presented the protesters with an apparently vulnerable focal point around which resulting violence could be easily contained.

Contributions by participants in the march to the *UK Indymedia* web site reflected a widespread feeling that the police had, indeed, used a policy of entrapment, designed to lure protesters away from local housing and into a an open field where they could be more effectively controlled (*UK Indymedia* 2005). Early evening news reports also talked of the surprising ease with which demonstrators made their way across the field to the perimeter fence:

> Without a single police officer to stop them, hundreds of protesters strode off the march route, across a cornfield, and right up to the perimeter fence of Gleneagles. The majority stood, bewildered they'd made it this far. (Martin Geisler, *ITN early evening news*)

> Police are doing remarkably little to try and stop the protesters who've broken into this field to try and get closer to Gleneagles

Hotel, secure in the knowledge they probably can't do much damage to anything other than the crops here. (Sarah Smith, *Channel Four early evening news*)

Other reporters emphasised that the police action was a justifiable *counter response* to having been overrun by protesters:

This is exactly what the police feared – that they wouldn't be able to hold the line. They've had to break out of Gleneagles, not just with dogs, but with batons and with horses. (Gavin Hewitt, *BBC late evening news*)

We have no guaranteed way of knowing for sure whether police tactics at Gleneagles were part of a pre-determined strategy. Nevertheless, it is surely not being too fanciful to suggest that, as in the May Day protest of 2000, when the Metropolitan Police appeared deliberately to expose a fast-food restaurant to possible crowd vandalism, here too was a case of the police setting out to 'win by appearing to lose'.

Conclusions

The policing of the Sheffield G8 lends credence to the claims of P. A. J. Waddington (1998) that senior commanders are genuinely committed to protecting, and, even, facilitating, protest activities of a law-abiding nature. The strategy and tactics employed by South Yorkshire Police in this instance were tightly underpinned by a permissive force philosophy reflecting an enduring desire to recapture public confidence and re-establish their legitimacy after the setbacks of Hillsborough and the miners' strike. The undoubted preference among senior officers to sanction a slightly less regulated expression of local dissent was stymied by countervailing political and pragmatic considerations.

The primary political imperative was that of ensuring the safety of visiting dignitaries. In this respect, the situation was essentially no different to scores of previous similar situations obliging the police to 'die in a ditch' (Ericson and Doyle 1999; King and Waddington 2005). Adding to this obligation, here, was the police's civic responsibility to ensure that Sheffield's reputation and commercial potential were not undermined by collective violence. In anticipating the appearance of transgressive groups, including local anarchists and

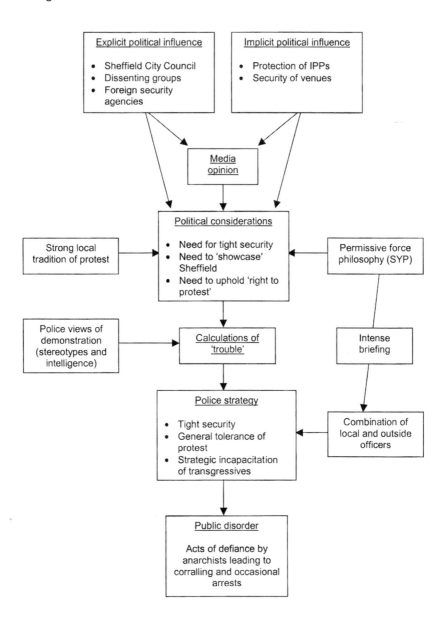

Figure 6.2 Interpreting South Yorkshire Police's handling of the G8 Justice and Home Affairs ministerial meeting in Sheffield

CIRCA, the police invoked the Public Order Act 1986 as a means of restricting the less co-operative demonstrators' activities and sanctioning the possible use of techniques of strategic incapacitation. The customary co-operation between police liaison officers and protest organisers was correspondingly circumscribed.

It is entirely conceivable that the police ceded greater latitude to the protesters due to the primacy of a 'civil libertarian' discourse (della Porta and Reiter 1998). A broad spectrum of local democratic audiences (Jefferson and Grimshaw 1984) affiliated to the Stop the War Coalition was able to lobby and generate media publicity in such a way as to legitimise the protest as a genuine humanitarian gesture, in keeping with the longstanding 'traditions of the city'. The local dimension to the protest was given prominence in the briefings of all ranks carried out by the Chief Constable and his Bronze commander. Due emphasis was placed on the negative consequences for long-term police–community relations of any conflict that might occur. The police's perceived commitment to facilitating lawful protest was rewarded when members of the samba band responded positively to a request for their co-operation in helping officers to escort those protesters being detained on Westfield Terrace back on to Devonshire Green.

Confrontation was therefore limited to two instances of note: first, when police officers activated a contingency plan, involving the corralling-in of protesters and use of snatch-squads, to stifle transgressive behaviour; and secondly, when visiting Greater Manchester officers responded over-zealously when a handful of local anarchists attempted to breach their lines. Three factors may each have had some relevance here: (i) negative police stereotyping of the anarchists may well have produced a misreading of their intentions and resulted in tactical overkill; (ii) it seems that the anarchists were reacting to frustration and indignation arising from perceptions that the police were deliberately 'neutralising' the protest's effectiveness (Mitchell and Staeheli 2005); and (iii) the police officers involved were drafted in from outside forces and may, therefore, have lacked commitment to maintaining positive long-term relations with the Sheffield public. Other forms of police behaviour suggest an overriding commitment to SYP's prevailing force strategy. In both instances of disorder, police officers made pacificatory gestures to emphasise that certain aspects of their conduct were considered regrettable. Elsewhere in the proceedings the police also delayed making arrests in order to avoid creating flashpoints for the wider occurrence of violence. A diagrammatic interpretation of the nature and consequences of SYP's policy for the policing of the event is given in Figure 6.2.

One month later, in and around Edinburgh, officers from the Lothian and Borders and Tayside constabularies used a similar range of incapacitation techniques to contain unscheduled activities by groups of transgressive and/or disaffected protesters. These tactics were taken to extreme at Gleneagles where the police apparently resorted to a ploy reminiscent of that used by the Metropolitan Police during the 2000 May Day march in London. This involved 'encouraging' misbehaviour by groups of protesters in order to justify aggressive police intervention. By and large, however, Scottish police were committed to a low-key, tolerant *modus operandi*, seemingly intent on avoiding any form of confrontation which might portray either themselves or their capital city in a negative light. The peaceful outcome of the Make Poverty History march, in particular, is related to an unusual example of the police's resolution *not* to allow themselves to be swayed by media prognoses of mayhem and violence.

Chapter 7

English football fans abroad, 1990–2006

Introduction

At the 2006 football World Cup tournament in Germany, a total of 711 travelling English football supporters were arrested, 510 of them during a confrontation with rival German followers in downtown Stuttgart on 24 June. The incident occurred as supporters of the host nation were dispersing from a city-centre square, having seen their team defeat Sweden, 2–0, on a specially erected giant television screen. English fans had already gathered nearby in readiness for their team's match against Ecuador the following day. Trouble broke out when a group of Germans assembled outside a bar containing English supporters. Chairs and bottles were thrown by rival fans before riot police moved in to separate them (BBC News 2006; Ingle 2006).

During the 1990s and the early years of the new millennium, supporters of the English national team had gained worldwide notoriety for their hooligan behaviour. Well-publicised clashes had occurred between England fans and the police and/or rival supporters during the preliminary or final stages of major international knockout competitions between 1990 and 2004, in Italy (twice), Sweden, Holland, France, Belgium and Portugal (Dunning *et al.* 2002; Pennant and Nicholls 2006; Perryman 2002). Additionally, a 'friendly' international between the Republic of Ireland and England at Dublin's Landsdowne Road in February 1995 had been abandoned after 22 minutes when away fans 'rioted' shortly after the Irish had taken a 1–0 lead (Lacey and Bowcott 1995).

At first sight, the incident in Stuttgart may well have looked like 'yet another instance' of the large-scale disorders involving followers of the national team. Yet this was far from the actual truth. What made the Stuttgart incident different from those of the previous decade was that most of those arrested were detained as a *precautionary* measure, with the intention of preventing wider disorder, and released without charge on the following morning. Moreover, events in Stuttgart were grossly untypical of the otherwise harmonious and mutually tolerant relationship existing between English fans and the German police (BBC News 2006).

This view was endorsed in the wake of the competition by the English Football Association's Chief Executive, Brian Barwick, who wholeheartedly commended the behaviour of the estimated 315,000 of his compatriots who had made the trip to Germany (Rumsby 2006). Mr Barwick reflected that this was the third international tournament in a row (following the 2002 World Cup in Japan and Korea, and Euro 2004 in Portugal) where England fans had earned such plaudits – a marked improvement in behaviour which he attributed to the implementation of banning orders preventing known hooligans from attending such competitions (*ibid.*).

This chapter outlines the markedly contrasting argument – that variations in the behaviour of travelling England fans are more effectively explained in terms of the changing contexts and dynamics of the relevant policing arrangements. The chapter begins by highlighting the possible utility of explanations of football hooliganism *per se* (as opposed to police-related approaches). Particular attention is given to pertinent anthropological and structural/dispositional approaches. Subsequent sections then focus, in turn, on case studies of confrontations between England fans and the police during the Italian World Cup of 1990, and the European Football Championships of 2000 and 2004, to emphasise the importance of such key variables as police culture and knowledge, the role of media and political discourse, and the quality of police–fan interaction in the genesis of disorder. The final section constitutes a slight departure from our main focus on the policing of matches between competing footballing nations. Here, concentration is shifted on to a European *club* cup tie between the Turkish Galatasaray and England's Manchester United. The purpose of this discussion is to further underline the importance of the interplay between key contextual and interactional variables.

Relevant theories of football hooliganism

We begin our analysis of this area by considering two contrasting types of explanation of football hooliganism that are each capable of improving our understanding of confrontations between the police and English fans abroad. These may be conveniently referred to as the *anthropological* and *structural/dispositional* approaches.

Anthropological approaches

The main anthropological perspective, Marsh *et al.*'s 'ethogenic' approach, is predicated on the idea that disorder is rule-governed and ritualised. Based on direct observation of crowd behaviour at Oxford United's ground in the mid-1970s, these authors contend that much of the aggressive behaviour that occurs is largely symbolic – a repertoire of obscene chants and threatening or denigratory language or non-verbal behaviour. Regular football hooligans tend to abide by a set of 'unwritten rules' determining when it is legitimate to confront an individual or group and when it is appropriate to desist. Ironically, it is in those situations in which activities of major protagonists (including the police) go beyond the norms of acceptability that violence is most prevalent.

These general conclusions are supported by Armstrong's two-year participant observation study of a core group of 40–50 'ardent' Sheffield United hooligan supporters, the 'Blades Business Crew' (BBC) (Armstrong 1998; Armstrong and Harris 1991). Like Marsh, Armstrong and Harris contend that the violence associated with football matches is considerably exaggerated, both by journalists and academics:

> The worst that can be said was that most of these fans were willing on occasions to get into relatively minor physical conflict with rivals . . . Unfortunately, once started, minor physical conflict could escalate. For the most part, however, it was only relatively harmless conflict in which individuals engaged, and that only occasionally. (Armstrong and Harris 1991: 455)

Of particular relevance to the present study is Marsh *et al.*'s observation that police intervention at football grounds is usually tolerated – and sometimes even welcomed – by hooligan supporters, since their presence can often prevent a confrontation from going too far (*op. cit.*: 60 and 104). 'Real violence' (as opposed to the more symbolic and relatively harmless 'aggro') is only likely to occur on the rare occasions when rival fans or police officers deliberately or unwittingly transgress the rules of disorder. As part of their research, Marsh and his colleagues showed a group of Oxford fans a video-recording of an encounter between police and the 'away' supporters of Plymouth Argyle during the half-time break in their match against Crystal Palace.

What began as a mischievous decision by two Argyle fans to run on to the pitch and start kicking a ball around in front of Palace followers soon developed into a confrontation between away supporters and the police. The first Argyle fan was stopped in his tracks when a police officer performed a flying rugby tackle. The second proved more elusive and succeeded in making it back into the cheering ranks of away fans gathered on the terrace. Determined not to be outdone, a group of roughly 20 police officers surged on to the terrace in a bid to retrieve the fan who had just eluded them. However, they were driven back by other supporters. The police regrouped and, with the help of reinforcements, drove back into the crowd. This time, they succeeded in arresting a number of fans and they maintained their presence (and authority) for the remainder of the game (*ibid.*: 112).

When proffering their own interpretation of this incident, Oxford fans pointed out that, even though they understood that the police had an obligation to remove the Argyle supporters who were kicking a ball around, they were nonetheless convinced that the police had 'totally mismanaged the whole affair. They had made unwarranted charges into the Argyle crowd and were seen as provoking fans beyond reasonable endurance' (*ibid.*: 113). Marsh *et al.* can see how the police might well have justified their actions in terms of their legal obligation to apprehend such obvious offenders. However,

> The point which arises out of all this is that fans have a clear idea of how they think police and other officials at football games should act – in other words, they have rules for the actions of others as well as themselves and they are able to interpret some of the actions on the part of officials as being in breach of propriety. In the same way that kids in classrooms have a clear idea of what are the limits of legitimate action on the part of teachers, football fans appeal to the fact that the police 'went too far' or were 'making people a bit mad for no reason' in their explanation of certain events. One might argue that these imposed limits are unreasonable, but in the

explanation of social action they figure very prominently and must therefore be given very serious attention. (*ibid.*)

Implicit support for this approach is evident in the accounts of Manchester United fans following their team to the away ties of European competitions. Such accounts emphasise the arousing effect of perceptions that police and stewards are 'taking liberties' against United supporters (King 2001). In a slight variation on the ideas of Marsh and his co-workers, King maintains that there are tacitly agreed 'rules' determining how 'status honour' can be won or lost in the context of football hooliganism. There is no honour to be gained by, for example, attacking a rival hooligan group that is significantly outnumbered, or police or stewards who are reasonably conducting their duties. Conversely, honour is conferred on hooligan groups who stand up for themselves whenever authority is exercised in an unsuitably disrespectful or unreasonable manner.

Further implicit support is contained in recent work by Frosdick (2005), a police officer turned academic, who used a participant observation approach to study the policing of three 'derby' matches (local rivalries) involving two teams from the south coast of England, Southampton ('The Saints') and neighbouring Portsmouth ('Pompey'), during the 2003–4 season. Frosdick refers to several incidents in which unnecessarily aggressive behaviour by the police heightened the possibility of confrontation. An example of this occurred at the first of the three matches, a cup tie in December 2003, at St Mary's Stadium, Southampton, where Frosdick saw reason to be critical of the police. The relevant incident happened when Southampton scored the opening goal in a 2–0 win. Portsmouth supporters rushed towards a 'segregation net', spread across eight rows of seating, which separated the away supporters from the rest. At this,

> The stewards responded well, spreading their arms wide to make themselves big and to try and preserve their cordon. The police were less effective. Some just stood there and did nothing. However, one police officer pushed a Southampton fan backwards, sending him and a number of other fans sprawling. This was an inappropriate response by a frightened young police officer. (*ibid.*: 153)

Structural/dispositional approaches

Williams (2002) is critical of anthropologists like Marsh and Armstrong on account of their failure to explain why it is only some men (and not women) who engage in violent behaviour, why such conduct should be more commonplace among some sections of society and not others, and why it varies in nature and prevalence from one era to the next. Williams acknowledges that there is considerable disagreement regarding the demography of football hooliganism.

> However, despite bitter disputes over the issue of the social make-up of core hooligans, most of the evidence on hooligan offenders in England . . . still seems to suggest that they are aged from their late teens through to their 30s (though some hooligan 'leaders' can be older); that they are mainly in manual or lower clerical occupations (or, to a lesser extent, are unemployed or working in the informal or illegal 'grey' economy) and that they come mainly from working-class backgrounds. Some of those involved, certainly, are street sharp, have perhaps 'settled down' and are in 'good' jobs. (*ibid.*: 46)

The fact that most hooligans come from the working class is acknowledged by structural (or 'dispositional') explanations, the two most influential of which are the 'magical recovery of community' and 'ordered segmentation' approaches (see D. Waddington 1992, Chapter 6). The former is predicated on the assumption that the post-war disintegration of working-class communities and accompanying loss of their erstwhile industrial base has involved a loss of identity and communality for young, lower-working-class males. The solution adopted by these youths has been to 'renegotiate their relationship with the parent culture via a nostalgic attachment to a hooligan group' (Hobbs and Robins 1991: 570). Seen from this perspective, hooligan groups serve the functions of 'surrogate communities' in which the traditional male working-class values of toughness, parochialism and solidarity can be 'magically recovered', demonstrated and endorsed (Robins and Cohen 1978: 137).

The *ordered segmentation approach*, developed by Eric Dunning and his colleagues at Leicester University, argues that football hooligans are predominantly drawn from lower-working-class housing estates with particularly tough and violent reputations. This explanation highlights the tendency for working-class gangs to combine against common enemies. Thus, it is assumed that gangs ('segments') of working-class communities which are usually in conflict with each other will nonetheless combine in the name of their local football team to confront the threat posed by opposition supporters. At the next level up, 'rival' northern fans (of, say, Liverpool and Manchester United) will join forces against the visiting supporters of a London team, such as Chelsea. The logical conclusion of this process is that, ultimately, football hooligans from all over England will forget any prior animosities and fight, side by side, 'on behalf of' the national team (Williams *et al.* 1990).

According to Dunning *et al.*, the aggressive tendencies of such youths stem from the characteristic form of socialisation they are exposed to as young boys, a process which they refer to as the *sociogenesis of masculine aggression*. Here it is assumed that in contrast to their middle-class peers, lower-working-class males are rarely exposed to a parental emphasis on self-control, but are more regularly subjected to physical punishment and therefore see violence as more normative. Play tends to be rougher and un-supervised, providing a further opportunity for unrestrained aggression. Dunning points out that lower-working-class males

(C)ome regularly into conflict with similar groupings from neighbouring communities and this reinforces both their internal solidarity and the aggressiveness of their dominant males. Further reinforcement of aggressiveness comes from the adult role models available in a lower working class community, above all from the fact that prestige is accorded locally to males who can fight. Because it involves the conferral of prestige, fighting becomes associated with the arousal of self-love and pleasurable feelings, in that way leading such males to develop a love of physical confrontations and actively to seek them out. (Dunning 1990: 76)

The idea that football hooliganism is a predominantly working-class activity is emphatically repudiated by Armstrong (1998). He is adamant that the hooligan behaviour of BBC members suggested 'no conscious notion of creating "resistance" (real or semiotic) to some vision of hegemonic morality or lost community' (*ibid.*: 169). Despite this assertion, Armstrong informs us that the majority of the Blades were employed in manual occupations and that the middle class and highly educated did not feature significantly among their ranks (*ibid.*: 150 and 151). Indeed, Armstrong hints at a possible structural explanation of the BBC's violence towards rival fans by raising the possibility that, 'With the deskilling of the workforce and the ending of exclusively male occupations the one surviving facet of masculine credibility that has come down to the current group of young men is the ability to fight, and via that ability to hold a reputation' (ibid.: 156).

With the exception of the ordered segmentation approach, the above explanations exhibit a common failure to account for the intensely nationalistic and chauvinistic conduct of English supporters abroad. Indeed, as Perryman (2002: 15) has observed, 'The curious bi-polarity of England fans' culture is rarely commented on. They are huge in number, highly committed, yet contain within their ranks a brand of thuggery that few other national teams' support can match.' This issue is dealt with specifically by Taylor (1989: 105–6) who maintains that the main perpetrators of such violence are an 'upwardly mobile, individualistic fraction of the (male) British working class', which was virtually unique among manual workers in prospering amidst the Thatcherite restructuring of British industry:

> This fraction of the working class (first sighted, perhaps, in the lump workers in the building industry and in London's Docklands) has done well because of its ability to master particular crafts and to move between work sites. It has a certain sense of residual solidarity, born of neighbourhood and gender, but it is generally individualistic, chauvinistic and racist . . . It is this particular fraction of the class, according to many different accounts, that is most deeply attached to its reading of the *Sun* newspaper and the *Sunday Sport*, and which was most enthusiastically carried along by the jingoistic nationalism that accompanied the Falklands Malvinas war.

Whatever the origins of this behaviour, there is a danger of wrongfully assuming a universal predisposition among travelling English fans to engage in violence. Weed (2001) infers from press reports of the hooligan activities of English fans in Belgium during Euro 2000 that there were at least three categories of supporters: a small minority (around 10 per cent) who were outright troublemakers or 'thugs'; a second core group of respectable, law-abiding fans; and a third group of good-humoured but occasionally obnoxious others who were likely to pile in during aggressive encounters. Such press characterisations identify a loud and, allegedly, unappealing culture, based on patriotism and pride in the country's achievements, and manifested in racial hatred, anti-Irish Republican Army (IRA) sentiments and insults harking back to the Second World War.

A more benign interpretation of such behaviour is set out by Parry and Malcolm (2004), who remark on similarities in the conduct of travelling English football supporters and the behaviour of the self-styled 'Barmy Army' of fans accompanying the national cricket team to places like Australia and the West Indies. Parry and Malcolm subscribe to an explanation of the exuberant (but fundamentally non-violent) behaviour of the majority of England football fans which emphasises the causal effect of the recent shift towards a more affluent, middle-class spectatorship. Hence, it is assumed that

> Football fans who see themselves as 'traditional' or 'long-standing' supporters increasingly define themselves in contradistinction to the so-called 'cardboard cut-out' spectators (those supporters perceived as new-comers and largely middle class) whose relatively pacified support has led to accusations of them not 'getting behind' the team. Barmy Army members also define themselves in opposition to the more reserved spectators, though in this context it is they (the Barmy Army) who are the newcomers, and the 'traditional' supporters who characteristically exhibit lower levels of emotional display. (*ibid*.: 85)

Parry and Malcolm suggest that, in order to distinguish themselves from their less committed middle-class counterparts, these traditional football supporters have embraced an array of carnivalesque devices, such as the use of face paints, fancy dress and inflatable toys. This tendency has coalesced with other cultural developments to help shape the characteristic conduct of travelling English fans. Among these innovations are: the growth of organised football supporters' clubs and organisations, which not only facilitate travel abroad, but also actively promote liberal agendas, such as anti-racism; and the rise of a 'New Laddism', which promotes an 'aspirational' lifestyle incorporating travel and consumption, while embracing a 'cheeky, irreverent humour, in which sexist and coded-racist remarks are rationalised as "excusable"' (*ibid*.: 87). All of these tendencies have combined to produce the characteristically boisterous, consumerist and fundamentally irreverent behaviour synonymous with supporters of the national teams.

The distinction between the culture of non-violent England supporters and that of the hardened hooligan minority is crucially important. Stott and Pearson (2006: 245) make the point that the majority of fans arrested at major overseas competitions invariably have had no prior involvement in football-related disorder.

> This fact alone makes it difficult to sustain the rather circular argument that these individuals are involved in 'disorder' because they are 'hooligans'. Conversely, there have also been a number of large crowd events involving English fans abroad where 'known hooligans' have been present but 'disorder' has not occurred. Moreover, when 'disorder' has occurred, the idea that it has been caused by 'hooligans' offers little theoretical basis for understanding the targets of collective violence. (*ibid.*)

Stott and Pearson are correct to emphasise that what is also required is a complementary approach, addressing variations in the context and dynamics of disorder. It is to explanations of this type that we therefore turn our attention.

The Italia 90 football World Cup tournament

The Elaborated Social Identity Model (ESIM) referred to in Chapter 2 has been extensively applied in the study of football hooliganism involving England supporters travelling abroad (Stott 2003; Stott *et al.* 2006; Stott *et al.* 2001; Stott and Reicher 1998b). These authors have repeatedly acknowledged the importance of 'structural/ dispositional' approaches addressing the reasons why particular individuals travel to football matches with the intention of fighting with similarly inclined opposition supporters (e.g. Stott *et al.* 2001: 361; Stott and Reicher 1998b: 354–55). However, they sensibly insist that, in situations where conflict escalates to involve far greater numbers of supporters, the utility of explaining aggressive conduct in terms of the violent predispositions of those involved is significantly weakened. They argue that what is required instead is a focus on the *inter-group dynamics* relevant to a particular situation (Stott and Reicher *op. cit.*: 354–355).

Stott and Reicher apply the ESIM approach in a participant observation study of events occurring on the day of a match between England and Holland during the 1990 World Cup football championships in Italy in June 1990. In the build-up to this competition, the British media had predictably focused on the strong likelihood of travelling English fans engaging in public disorder. Two weeks prior to the competition, the British Channel Four television station had dedicated a 10-minute news item to the subject of England fans travelling to Italy with the intention of committing violence. This expectation was reinforced in briefings of the Italian police by Scotland Yard's National Football Intelligence Unit, while the British Minister for Sport urged his Italian counterpart to take un-compromising action against British offenders. As it turned out, there was sporadic violence involving English fans during the first two weeks comprising the first round of the competition. The most serious confrontation took place in the immediate build-up to the Holland game.

This trouble occurred in the course of a march by 2,000–3,000 English fans from the centre of the host city, Cagliari, up the main street towards the stadium where the game was scheduled to be played. When the supporters had travelled two-thirds of the distance to the ground, there was a brief stand-off between them and around 40 rival Dutch fans. Soon afterwards, the marchers were confronted by 25 Italian riot police with batons drawn who had spread them-selves and two personnel carriers across the road, blocking further progress to the stadium. The marchers initially pushed against the police line, forcing them back several metres. A can of soft drink was thrown in the process. This proved to be an important turning point as, almost instantaneously, officers started striking out at anyone within reach (*ibid.*: 363–364).

Those at the front of the march scattered onto areas of un-developed land which yielded a handy supply of ready-made missiles (e.g. bricks and stones) for throwing at the police. A 'substantial proportion' of these fans then charged the police, throwing projectiles as they ran. Police officers were forced to take refuge behind their vehicles, from where they fired off tear gas canisters, affecting *all* the spectators present. After a two- to three-minute lull, a police vehicle drove into the crowd, but hurriedly retreated on finding itself bombarded on all sides. Even the non-active majority within the crowd cheered loudly at this development.

Three hundred or so of the marchers then set off again for the stadium. However, they had not travelled more than 150 metres when they were confronted by a second group of 20 riot police. Following a charge by 50 or so fans, the police once again fired rounds of tear gas. Police reinforcements then arrived and proceeded to encircle the entire crowd. Marchers were individually searched. Those with tickets were escorted into the stadium, while those with-out were taken back to the city centre and dispersed.

Early in their analysis, Stott and Reicher point out that, on arriving in Sardinia, the majority of supporters had declared themselves opposed to violence and antithetical to the small minority of fans likely to be responsible for any trouble that should occur. The Italian authorities did not seem capable of distinguishing the potential troublemakers from the 'ordinary' travelling fans. In the weeks prior to the event, 'the Italian media was portraying them as violent and uniformly dangerous', such that, even from the outset, 'a framing of the English fans as hostile and dangerous was in place' (*ibid*.: 366). English fans touching down on Italian soil were thoroughly searched in an atmosphere of suspicion and hostility. Day-to-day activity was closely monitored and fans were often subjected to harassment:

> This included gathering together in bars, drinking, singing and shouting – behaviours rooted in a vision of masculinity through which the social identity of the 'England fan' was defined and hence behaviours that were seen as legitimate if not normative in terms of that identity. Of course, in relating the fans' perspective it is important to avoid reifying or even romanticising it. What the English supporters characterise as mere high spirits may well be experienced by others as offensive and intimidatory. Certainly, the fans' perspective was not shared by the police and they were liable to intervene with force. (*ibid*.)

On one occasion, following England's earlier game against the Republic of Ireland, England fans were taunted and attacked by local youths, whom they chased off in self-defence. Consequently, the Italian police aggressively baton-charged the English, indiscriminately beating and injuring several of them, while those responsible for starting the incident managed to escape, scot-free (*ibid*.: 367). As Stott and Reicher explain, accounts of such incidents were soon widely circulated. 'Thus, through a series of interactions experienced either directly or vicariously, wider and wider sections of England supporters came to view the police as predisposed to unprovoked acts of aggression towards them' (*ibid*.: 368).

This history of interaction between the police and English supporters helped to frame their contrasting interpretations of each other's conduct during the march. Thus, the police officer in command of operations in Sardinia was adamant that the reason why the march had suddenly come to a halt was because of the fans' intention to commit violence. However, from the competing perspective of the England fans, the construction of a police cordon was seen as 'unwarranted and hence exemplifying the illegitimate nature of police action' (*ibid.*: 371). Thus, as Stott (2003: 642) points out in a subsequent, though related, article,

> Conflict was not seen as hooliganism but as a reassertion of rights. Moreover, the (actual or perceived) indiscriminate nature of police hostility towards England supporters created an inclusive social identity that incorporated rather than rejected hooligan fans (i.e. those prepared to initiate conflict). This incorporation led to increased expectations of support that empowered hooligan fans enabling them, and indeed 'ordinary' England fans, to act aggressively towards the police during a crowd event.

Stott and Reicher (*op. cit.*: 373) conclude their article by declaring that it would be just as unhelpful to dismiss 'predispositional' (or structural) explanations as it would be to focus on the inter-group dynamics of football-related disorder. In their view, 'The challenge is to articulate issues of prior normative commitment and of inter-group dynamics in a common explanation rather than to counter-pose them.'

The European Football Championships of 2000 in Belgium and the Netherlands (Euro 2000)

During the Euro 2000 football tournament, staged jointly by the Dutch and Belgian football authorities in the June of that year, 965 British fans were arrested for their part in hooligan behaviour and 474 of those deported (Stott 2003). In the most notorious of the incidents involved, over 200 English fans were arrested during a confrontation with Belgian police in the central square of Charleroi (Weed 2001). Afterwards, the British press universally condemned the English fans (Bishop and Jaworski 2003). The *Sunday Express* of 18 June 2000 was typical in highlighting how 'Charleroi's main square, the Place Charles II, which should have been the centre of celebration, resembled a battleground. More than 200 English yobs attacked German rivals, hurling chairs and sticks as they charged' (quoted by Weed 2001: 412). The British Prime Minister, Tony Blair, publicly apologised to his Belgian counterpart for the behaviour of his fellow countrymen, and there was even talk for a while of UEFA expelling England from the competition (*ibid.*).

However, in the aftermath of the confrontation, a rival media view soon emerged, insisting that there had been no pitched battle of the kind portrayed by the media and that the level of actual violence had been considerably overstated (Poulson 2005: 34; Weed 2001: 413). Indeed, subsequently shown television pictures suggested that the violence was largely perpetrated by the police, who later conceded that many of the arrests had been undertaken on a purely preventative basis (Weed 2001: 413). Several authors have since speculated that the violence occurring in Charleroi was due to a combination of factors – notably, the attitudes and tactics of the Belgian police, and a general attitude of disrespect for the culture of travelling English football fans (Crabbe 2003; Weed 2001).

Stott (2003) employed a questionnaire survey to explore the attitudes towards English and other groups of supporters harboured by some of the 8,000 Belgian Gendarmerie officers on duty at Euro 2000. Thirty-six officers completed the questionnaire following England's first-round matches against Portugal, Germany and Romania. The study was ostensibly designed to ascertain the expectations that police officers had of English fans prior to the tournament. Stott concedes that the fact that the questionnaires were administered *post hoc* does raise the possibility that 'Responses to some items could clearly have been influenced by events and may actually have been more representative of post event justifications' (*ibid.*: 647). However, even allowing for these limitations, the results show interesting variations in police perceptions.

Generally speaking, of the fan groups of all the 16 nations participating in the competition, England's fans were perceived as posing the highest threat to public order. Mean scores on relevant rating scales also revealed that officers calculated around half of England's travelling fans to be hooligans, expected a similar proportion to be actively looking to incite violence, and some two-thirds of all England fans to be violent at some time in the competition. Officers had further anticipated that games involving England were more likely to result in disorder than games involving other nations in their group. There was a 'clear consensual expectation' on the part of the Gendarmerie that trouble would occur in the build-up to, during or after England's game against Germany in Charleroi. Finally, in regard to interpretations of normative behaviour, heavy consumption of alcohol and 'boisterous' activity on the part of English fans were far more likely to be perceived as a threat to public order than were similar forms of conduct engaged in by Germans or Romanians. As Stott (*ibid.*: 653) points out, 'Such responses are certainly consistent with methods of policing in which the relatively indiscriminate dispersal and/or arrests of large groups of boisterous England fans would be seen as a rational tactical decision.'

The significance of policing style is illustrated by the fact that England's opening game, a 3–2 defeat by Portugal in Holland, was trouble-free. The attitude of the Dutch police was exemplified by the pre-tournament comments of their Director of Police Intelligence who indicated: 'We want to make a positive contribution to the festive nature of such an event. You don't do that by policing too firmly. So it's balancing between maintenance of public order and being a real host to the fans' (quoted by Weed 2001: 411). The contrast between this attitude and the corresponding stance of the Belgian police can be discerned by briefly recounting the main events in Charleroi.

According to Crabbe (2003: 415), the immediate build-up to the England versus Germany match involved confrontations on the streets of Brussels between English supporters and local youths. One day prior to the game, the Belgian police resorted to indiscriminate mass arrests to tidy up this problem. 'Hooligan' stories made the front pages of local and international newspapers, and a rumour spread that an English fan had been stabbed by a German. For all the heightened anticipation of violence, events on the day of the match were surprisingly sedate. England fans sunbathed, played football and sought relief from the intense sunshine by dancing in a fountain. All was peaceful until two German fans were arrested in a cafe/bar, situated on the main street connecting the town square to the stadium.

England fans, press journalists and photographers immediately gravitated towards the incident:

They were quickly followed by an increasingly animated voyeuristic crowd which added to the sense of danger as a plastic garden chair was thrown into the air. A mêlée ensued, with more chairs flying back and forth, which appeared to last for no more than one minute and result in no visible injuries, but which provided some highly photogenic images around which the wider discourse of football violence could be deployed. The drama, which it has been alleged was itself something of a set up by the Belgian police . . . soon enabled those same forces to mobilize their armoury in the shape of mobile water cannons, sirens and tear gas which sent crowds of people scattering across the streets and central square, adding to the spectacle. (*ibid*.: 416)

Complaints by many of those caught up in the confrontation that they were non-hooligan fans unwittingly drawn in by the indiscriminate tactics of the Belgian police were later given credence by a Home Office statement which emphasised that scores of those arrested and subsequently deported were known to have been 'entirely innocent'. This included a pair of American tourists with no connection to the tournament (*ibid*.: 413). Such injustices were a consequence of the Belgian police's policy of 'administrative detention', which allowed them indiscriminately to arrest people in the absence of any criminal offence (Poulton 2005: 29).

Crabbe sees this development as proof that 'England supporters' reputation is such that upon arriving on foreign soil they are often treated with suspicion and intolerance, itself whipped up by local media scare stories' (2003: 419). A similar 'amplification spiral' was evident in the media pre-coverage of the 2002 World Cup tournament in Japan and Korea where attention was concentrated on the Japanese police's commitment to using martial arts, water cannons and 'Spiderman net guns' to round up misbehaving fans (Poulton 2003: 24).

Ultimately, though, only a mere 13 of the estimated 8,000 English fans attending the World Cup were arrested. Crabbe (2003: 420) attributes this outcome to an 'important cultural dimension'.

In Japan the absence of obvious central gathering points and bars with the capacity to cater for large groups in most of the host cities, as well as the widespread local celebration of the pageantry and national symbolism of the fans themselves, left little space for the forms of cultural practice associated with the discourse through which 'hooliganism' is constituted. Indeed, in a country often seen as isolated from the West, here was a fascination with the exoticism of those football fans that had travelled to the tournament which seemed to be most intensely and warmly directed towards England supporters and the perceived exuberance of their style of support.

The European Football Championships of 2004 in Portugal (Euro 2004)

More recent work by Stott and his colleagues (Stott *et al*. 2006) provides further evidence to suggest that, where overseas police officers are sufficiently tolerant of the fan culture of travelling English supporters (notwithstanding its frequently boisterous and jingoistic nature), the possibility of violence will greatly be reduced. As part of their liaison work with Portuguese police, Stott *et al*. were able to recommend a 'model of good practice' to the Polícia de Segurança Pública (PSP) to guide them in their handling of England supporters at Euro 2000. The PSP has jurisdiction over Portugal's city areas and, as such, was responsible for supervising all of England's games. The policing of rural areas and small towns – including Albufeira, which played host to English supporters for a couple of nights in June – was the responsibility of the Guarda Nacional Republicana (GNR). The GNR did not incorporate Stott *et al*.'s policy recommendations. Indeed, theirs was a much more 'high profile' style of crowd management. Stott *et al*. use participant observation data to highlight the differences of police style and their implications for hooligan activity.

The study shows how the PSP's generally tolerant attitude towards English fans was manifested in an overall reluctance to intervene unless absolutely necessary. Police tactics were implemented according to the principle of minimum force and with adequate differentiation between innocent and guilty. Senior PSP officers regularly consulted with their English counterparts and often heeded their advice to reduce the numbers of officers deployed to avoid appearing too provocative. Far from automatically siding against the English, the PSP frequently shielded them from attack. Feedback from English fans revealed that the PSP's actions were widely regarded as legitimate. Interviewees commended the way that PSP tactics had seemed designed to *facilitate*, rather than stifle, their admittedly boisterous behaviour. Furthermore, such tactics gave rise to a culture of self-policing which played a key role in suppressing potential disorder during three incidents which failed to escalate.

This was in stark contrast to events in Albufeira on 15–16 June 2004. A first major incident of disorder occurred on 15 June when police instructed the owner of a bar on the town's main entertainment strip to prematurely close his premises. Following the closure, scores of English fans were forced out on to a dangerously busy roadway and, in the ensuing commotion, they became embroiled in sporadic confrontations with GNR 'intervention squads'. This incident framed the following night's activities.

These started at around 2 a.m. when English fans congregating at the same bar attacked four non-English males who had been observed videotaping them. The English aggressors then threw beer at other customers and spat upon the owner before starting to vandalise the property. Two groups of police charged the fans with their batons drawn. Among those beaten to the ground by intervention squads were innocent bystanders who had been appealing to their fellow countrymen to end their violent behaviour.

Some 20 minutes later, police in riot gear threw a cordon around 150 fans in an adjacent bar and made several arrests. Fans who had been involved in the earlier violent incident stood outside the police cordon where they threw missiles and shouted abuse until a police cavalry charge dispersed them. The situation then stabilised and the cordon was relaxed. Just before 3 a.m., though, 20 GNR officers walked towards stationary fans and started to strike them with their batons. Fans continued to shout abuse and throw missiles at the police while in the process of being dispersed.

In contrast to the tactics of the PSP, the GNR's actions were perceived by England fans as having prevented them from engaging in their customary exuberant activities. This latter policing style encouraged mutual feelings of disrespect lying at the root of confrontation. The intervention of police squads on the first night in Albufeira was widely considered to have been excessive and unjustified. These interventions also set off rumours that England fans had been abused by police (one of them going so far as to allege that one of the fans had been beaten to death). Fans therefore re-gathered defiantly and,

> As conflict escalated on the second evening, 'violent' actions against the police came to be described by some previously non-confrontational England fans as appropriate. One England fan interviewed during the 'riot' argued that he had thrown a glass and a table at the GNR in order to protect himself from a baton charge. (*ibid.*: 16)

King's multivariate approach

The above case studies implicitly highlight the significance of ideological, cultural and interactional factors in the causation of football-related disorder. The way in which these features tend to fuse and interact is better illustrated by the work of King (1995) which focuses, not on England fans *per se*, but on the events surrounding a match in a European *club* competition.

In the first week of November, 1993, Manchester United were due to play the Turkish club, Galatasaray, in the away leg of a European Cup tie. On the eve of the match, disturbances broke out at the Hotel Tamsa, in downtown Istanbul. These involved local Turks and sections of the 160-strong contingent of United supporters staying at the hotel. King was present and witnessed these events. He uses an adapted version of the Flashpoints Model of Public Disorder, discussed in Chapter 2, to analyse and explain the episode. Rather than employing the six levels of the model, he condenses them into three levels of analysis, referred to as 'historical background', 'level of actualization' and 'level of interaction'.

At the first of these levels, King focuses on two important contributory factors: the 'nationalist and masculinist' culture of the Manchester United fans, and the role of the Turkish state and media in encouraging an anti-Western climate in the build-up to the match. King commences his analysis by highlighting the way in which English fans abroad have committed themselves to an 'imagined national community' or culture of fellow travellers. This has been constructed and sustained via the use of numerous social devices, such as marking out their allocated section of the stadia with Union Jacks and Cross of St George flags, chanting patriotic and xenophobic slogans, and propagating particular conceptions of masculinity in football songs, both to emphasise their own potency and to highlight the sexual inadequacy and depravity of the opposition.

A second important component of the relevant historical background was the anti-Western fervour whipped up by the state and media. Pre-match Turkish newspaper editorials depicting English supporters as 'hooligans' helped reinforce existing political bitterness resulting from the recent rejection of Turkey's application to join the European Union, from European criticism of the country's treatment of the Kurds, and from 'the putative favouritism of the West towards the Muslim Iraqi Kurds in contrast to their neglect of the Bosnian Muslims' (*ibid.*: 644). The domestic credibility of the Turkish government had also been undermined by its apparent inability to curb a spate of recent attacks on Turkish guest workers by German Neo-Fascists. King therefore speculates that the negative labelling of United fans by the media and their aggressive treatment at the hands of the police 'can be seen as an attempt by the state to regain credibility by whipping up nationalist populist support behind its actions' (ibid.).

The transformation of the historical background into violence occurred via the intermediate process of 'actualization', in which the nationalistically masculine behaviour of the United fans surfaced alongside the hostile sentiments of rival Turkish and their police force. This was played out in a bar situated only half a mile away from the Hotel Tamsa. There, some 50 or so Mancunians started to sing a repertoire of songs, commonly identified with the national team. These included the national anthem ('God Save The Queen'), 'No Surrender to the IRA' and 'Eng-ger-land'. Though ostensibly an expression of Englishness, they nonetheless 'encouraged a hostile attitude to foreigners generally' (ibid.: 645). King concedes that it is impossible to tell exactly how rival Turkish fans interpreted the United fans' singing. However, he interprets the fact that they gathered outside the bar in such numbers as an indication that they had been primed by hostile state and media discourses to regard the singing by United fans as an affront to their national character.

The interactional level was reached when, following 'intimidation' by the Turks, some fans became involved in fighting. King confesses to being unsure as to precisely when violence actually broke out. However, he is confident that, 'In that moment of aggression and retaliation, where every action of the other group was over-invested with meaning, the level of interaction was reached and a new self-propelling dynamic was initiated' (ibid.: 647). As part of this dynamic, police intervened to break up the fighting before escorting the United fans back to their hotel. En route, the English supporters engaged in repeated skirmishes with Turkish rivals and, at one point, were bombarded with plastic and glass bottles from surrounding flats. Any United fans found lagging behind were batoned by the police.

With the United fans back in their hotel, there was a half-hour lull in the proceedings. Hostilities then resumed when Turkish fans regrouped outside the building and started to bombard English supporters with bricks and bottles. Two attempts to chase off the Turks were thwarted by other barrages of missiles. It was only after an hour and a half of confrontation that the riot police eventually arrived, not only to disperse Turkish fans, but also to arrest United followers – for, as King puts it, 'politically symbolic purposes' (*ibid.*: 649).

Conclusions

Academics generally agree that football-related disorder is largely a working-class phenomenon. Different theorists assert that the type of hooligan behaviour manifested in the English football leagues is either the product of working-class socialisation practices, or represents an attempt to magically recover a long-lost sense of community. Complementary explanations have been developed to account for the hooligan propensities of English fans travelling in support of their club or national teams in overseas competition. One such example proposes that the violent conduct of hooligan fans reflects the Thatcherite hedonism and chauvinistic tendencies of the 1980s and early 1990s. Another theory interprets these international rivalries as a higher order manifestation of the propensity of working-class lads to unite in the face of a common enemy. Despite some discrepancies of perspective, academic and journalistic commentators nonetheless concur that it is only a small minority of the overall travelling support that is inclined to pursue violence. The boisterous and high-spirited behaviour of other fans may seem obnoxious, insulting and provocative to residents of the host country. However, it is seldom ill-intentioned.

Statistical evidence shows that the majority of those arrested at major international competitions tend not to be known hooligans. Conversely, there have been competitions at which hundreds of 'regular' hooligans have been present which have not degenerated into violence. Studies reviewed in this chapter strongly indicate that, in order to understand why hooligan behaviour occurs, it is necessary to refer again to the type of contingencies referred to earlier in the book. One obvious example is the presence or absence of political and media discourse encouraging a political/ideological climate of negativity towards the supporters. Additionally, 'police knowledge' based on the unsavoury stereotyping of travelling fans may operate in conjunction with contextual factors, such as a recent history of police–hooligan confrontation or media sensitisation, and situational variables (e.g. the overt and confrontational deployment of officers) to raise the potential for violence.

Previous research suggests that, while most 'ordinary' fans (and even many of their hooligan counterparts) often welcome the police's presence at or around football matches, tactical interventions deemed unnecessary or unwarranted are likely to be responded to aggressively. Even where fans not predisposed to violence are involved, the unjustifiable use of force may enhance the crowd's in-group solidarity and generate widespread opposition to the police. Social psychological research has demonstrated that, where foreign police have been primed to show a tolerant attitude to the boisterous and irreverent culture of England supporters, violence has been minimised and a tendency towards self-policing has emerged. We shall soon return to the implications of these findings in our final chapter, which includes a series of recommendations for best practice.

Chapter 8

Conclusions

Public disorder – sans frontières

This book began by focusing on the violence that broke out during the anti-G8 march at Gleneagles in July 2005. Later that year, we saw ample evidence that public disorder is not constrained by cultural or international boundaries when urban rioting flared up, firstly, in neighbouring France, and then in faraway Australia. As a prelude to reviewing the contents of previous chapters and bringing together their policy implications, the following conclusions are preceded by brief summaries of the French and Australian riots which help to reiterate this book's abiding theme: that police methods implemented, not only during but also in the build-up to disorder, are pivotal to its instigation and development.

The French riots

The first of numerous French riots occupying a three-week period in October/November 2005 took place on 27 October in the north Parisian *banlieue* (suburb) of Clichy-sous-Bois when two teenage Muslim boys of north African heritage were fatally electrocuted in a substation while fleeing from the police. The two youths had become unwittingly involved in a police investigation of a break-in. It is not clear whether they were actually being *chased* by police officers at the times of their deaths. Nevertheless, rumours that they had been pursued and left to die soon circulated the locality, provoking violent confrontation between youths and police (Duvall Smith 2005). More rioting then followed in neighbouring Parisian suburbs and other major French cities with similar concentrations of Muslim youth:

thousands of young men battled with police, set fire to local buildings and ignited hundreds of motor vehicles (Sage 2005).

The underlying causes of the French riots seem similar in character to those of the British urban disorders of 2001 – *as well as* their predecessors of 1981. Like the British Asians arriving in the textile areas of the north of England, thousands of Arabs and north Africans from France's foreign colonies were recruited in the post-war period into menial factory jobs. Since then, the wholesale relocation of French industry abroad has bequeathed a legacy of high youth unemployment and an uncompromising policing of the social margins, which has gradually intensified since the mid-1970s in parallel with the stereotyping of Muslim youth as a possible terrorist threat (Bonelli 2005). As Murray (2006: 31–32) explains,

> Just as the notorious 'sus' laws and stop and search methods of the British police outraged Britain's black communities in the 1980s, repetitive identity checks of France's ethnic minority youths have only served to further alienate and antagonise the very poor people whose *assimilation* the authorities claim to desire. Verbal interaction between the police and non-white youths is often initiated by the inevitable 'show me your papers, please'. But while 'sus' was eventually discredited due to the flimsy pretexts being used to apply it, an identity check is just another identity check. Another specifically French issue concerns the language employed by the police. Even the authorities are now acknowledging that the not uncommon police practice of addressing non-white youths with the condescending *'tu'* rather than the more respectful *'vous'* under-mines police–community relations.

In April 2005, an Amnesty International report had spoken of the 'generalized impunity' with which French police carried out identity checks on the youths in question (Bouteldja 2005). French and British commentators linked the extent and intensity of the riots to a recent police crackdown on crime in the *banlieues*, and on provocative comments by the French Minister for the Interior, Mr Nicolas Sarkozy (Bonelli 2006; Fassin 2006; Harding 2005).

One of Sarkozy's first initiatives as minister had been to disband a special police unit set up in 1997 to forge better relations between themselves and the youth of the *banlieues* (Godoy 2005). On Monday, 20 June, Sarkozy visited an estate to the north of Paris where, one day previously, an 11-year-old boy had been accidentally shot dead in cross-fire between rival youth gangs. Speaking in response, Sarkozy had pledged that: 'The louts will disappear. We will clean this estate with a Karcher' (*ibid.*). This was a reference to a high-pressure hose, used for cleaning grime off cars or buildings. Sarkozy then visited a similar estate in Argenteuil on 25 October, where he was bombarded with small missiles by local youths. The minister responded to this ordeal by promising to rid such estates of the *'racaille'*, or rabble, inhabiting them (Henley 2005). The semantic importance of these words appeared not to have been lost on Muslim youths when rioting broke out two days later (Ireland 2005). Sarkozy's prime ministerial colleague responded by invoking a 1955 curfew law, originally passed to quell unrest by Algerians at the height of struggle for independence. This policy rebounded on the authorities by provoking further hostilities (Freedland 2005; Henley 2005).

The Cronulla beach riot

Race relations involving Muslim youths were also a central feature of the Cronulla riot in south Sydney, Australia, on 11 December. As Poynting (2006: 85) explains, this disorder involved a violent attack by 5,000 white Australians on youths of Lebanese heritage who were in the vicinity of the local beach. On the following day, youths from the victimised ethnic minority retaliated by smashing cars and beating up white passers-by. The initial attacks by whites had followed an incident occurring several days earlier when four Lebanese-Australians allegedly laid into three surf lifesavers. In the week-long hiatus, tabloid newspapers and local 'talk back' radio had whipped up an anti-'Middle-Eastern' hysteria, while a local 'shock jock' radio presenter had given his on-air endorsement to a text-messaging campaign calling for a huge 'reclaim the beach' rally the following weekend.

Poynting (2006) echoes Hartley and Green (2006) in emphasising the symbolic significance of the beach and its life guards for white Australians. He also identifies the importance of the gradual construction since the mid-1990s of a Muslim 'folk devil', depicted as 'backward, uncivilised, irrational, violent, criminally inclined, misogynistic and a terrorist threat' (*ibid.*: 88–89). Kabir (2006: 194) similarly maintains that calls for Muslim women to be banned from wearing the *chaddor* (head-to-toe cloak) in public, and for Muslim girls to be forbidden from wearing the *hijab* (head scarf) in public schools, each helped to foster a 'climate of alienation and enmity'.

Police spokespersons undoubtedly contributed to such negativity by perennially complaining about the misbehaviour on Sydney beaches by youths of 'Middle Eastern appearance' (Poynton *op. cit.*: 87–88). The sentiments of local commanders in the build-up to the riot were exemplified by a local assistant commissioner who, 'remarking that he grew up surfing in Cronulla, instructed [*Daily Telegraph*] readers on what was the "Australian way" at the beach; something the front-page headline said he vowed to defend' (*ibid.*: 86). Ten months after the riot, a report by a retired assistant police commissioner of New South Wales not only criticised the roles of the print media and talk show hosts in stirring up local resentment but also blamed the police for underestimating the degree of racial tension existing in the build-up to the riots and of responding inadequately to the eventual crisis.

Despite the clear risk of major disorder indicated by media commentaries and the violent atmosphere promoted by 270,000 subscriptions to the text-messaging campaign (Maynard 2006), police planning was superficial and only 47 riot-trained officers were eventually deployed with an extra 52 on standby. The police command centre set up at Cronulla Surf Life Saving Club was inadequately resourced for the purpose and even lacked a functioning telephone line. The report further criticised senior police for leaving operational decisions to local and regional commanders, rather than treating the event as a national issue requiring the supervision of specialist commanders. According to its author, the police failed to institute a 'major incident management system'. The resulting chains of command were blurred and uncertain and specialist response teams were never actually deployed (Clennell and Davis 2006).

The French and Australian riots are potent reminders to Western societies in general, and to policy makers especially, of the need for an adequate understanding of the underlying causes of disorder and the police's role in subduing or enhancing its potential. Bearing these imperatives in mind, the contents of previous chapters are now reviewed as a basis for advocating a number of policy recommendations.

Theoretical foundations

We saw in Chapter 1 how, in recent decades, police forces in Western democracies have abandoned their commitment to a relatively coercive and confrontational *escalated force* conception of public order policing in preference of a softer *negotiated management* approach, designed to restore and enhance their perceived legitimacy. The resulting emphasis on preventative techniques – of liaison and negotiation and the use of intelligence and tension indicators to predict and hopefully offset disorder – has been complemented by a generally more tolerant style of policing public order. Wherever possible, the rights of civilians are upheld, minor law-breaking is tolerated, and fewer arrests occur. This is not to pretend that the police coercive capacity has been abandoned entirely. The iron fist is still likely to be revealed – and used, if need be – in situations involving transgressive (as opposed to contained) protesters and within political climates of opinion which vilify culturally or politically dissenting groups, their goals and their means of achieving them.

Generally speaking, the police will 'die in a ditch' to protect the integrity of persons, locations, buildings or monuments, and ceremonial occasions where, for them to do otherwise, would run the risk of incurring severe in-the-job trouble. Police policy will be subjected to the more explicit influence exerted by relevant legal, democratic and occupational audiences. The power to induce particular forms of police strategy and tactics is, of course, unequally distributed and tends to reside with government and other state-sponsored institutions. That said, the mass media plays a highly influential role in assessing – if not always dispassionately – the relative merits of competing shades of ideological opinion.

The 'human element' inherent in public order policing provides a further basis for understanding police behaviour and its con-sequences. Studies of police rank-and-file emphasise that officers tend to subscribe to a 'pathological' view of crowd behaviour which sees the respectable majority as prone to 'manipulation' by a deviant and sinister minority, intent on 'hijacking' police–community or police–protester relations. Logic therefore dictates that all crowds must be strictly marshalled to prevent the spread of contagiously impulsive and hostile behaviour. Theorists maintain that practical problems confronting police lower ranks (the inability to see perfectly well through a visored helmet and shield, and the im-possibility of determining with infallible accuracy which ones within the crowd were responsible for throwing stones) can unintentionally promote disorder.

Research by the American sociologist, Gary Marx, on the American urban disorders of the 1960s highlights the possible contribution of police tactics to the instigation and development of rioting.

According to Marx, rioting is often the outcome of ill-chosen or ineffectual police tactics, such as: drawing large, hostile crowds on to the scene because of the ostentatious and over-dramatic manner of their arrival; showing initial reticence in the face of overwhelming opposition; making premature attempts at dispersal;, and failing to enter into pre-emptive negotiations, even where the crowd has a well-founded grievance and credible community representatives are available.

Marx's study is of additional utility in helping to isolate other policing variables conducive to public disorder. In some cases, these are institutional (such as bureaucratic malfunction within police forces, the presence of decentralised units lacking requisite organisation, and an absence of formal accountability), or cultural (the fact that officers brought in from outside the area may be unfamiliar with local mores and sensibilities, or are more used to working in ones and twos than in riot squads). In addition, technical problems such as breakdowns of radio communication can hamper tactical co-ordination. Finally, the fact that officers are only human means that aspects of judgement and motivation are affected by such conditions as hunger, tiredness or exhaustion, or the desire to avoid a loss of face, exact revenge or simply to demonstrate their efficacy.

The adoption of increasingly paramilitarised tactics and strategies by Western police forces since the late twentieth century has brought with it ways of ensuring that officers are adequately disciplined and well co-ordinated, and that the macho and action-oriented culture of junior ranks is held in check. In certain circumstances, though, such methods can prove intensely provocative and also bring out the worst excesses of the police occupational culture. This militarisation of the police is one of an array of factors incorporated by della Porta's model of protest policing.

This model is unique in emphasising the significance of numerous institutional factors, notably the overarching legal framework (including, for example, the permissiveness of public order legislation) and the police organisational structure (i.e. the extent of its centralisation, accountability and militarisation). Aspects of culture are incorporated in the model. This includes the police occupational culture and the particular policing culture of the host society (e.g. whether liberal or authoritarian). The model shares with the concept of police audiences an emphasis on ideological forces, highlighting the possible significance of the current configuration of power (the nature and extent of government influence) and the opinions of other parties (notably, sections of the 'civil rights' and 'law and order' coalitions). The model has a further historical dimension, insofar as it assumes that previous encounters between police and protesters may well have left a legacy of scores to be settled. Finally, there are the interactional dynamics of the situation: whether local or unfamiliar officers are involved; the extent to which police tactics adequately differentiate between guilty and innocent; and the degree to which lines of communication and command function effectively.

Ideas featuring in the policing literature are occasionally duplicated and, sometimes, complemented and enhanced by more general theories and models of public disorder. In Chapter 2, we saw how 'naïve', single-factor explanations, based on the Group Mind approach of LeBon or the 'agitator view' of conflict, have largely been discredited in favour of multivariate models of rioting. The earliest and most influential of these is Smelser's Theory of Collective Behaviour which establishes the importance of a triggering or precipitating incident in crystallising collectively held grievances (elements of social strain). This and subsequent approaches based on analyses of the 1960s American urban riots (by Hundley and Spiegel) emphasise the importance of such contextual factors as the presence or absence of channels for expressing grievances and the facilitating effect of the presence and convergence of large numbers of people. They also focus on the role of leadership and interactive communication in the mobilisation of riotous behaviour.

Where these models do vary is in the degree to which they regard particular forms of policing as responsible for the instigation and escalation of conflict. Thus, according to Smelser, rioting is less likely to develop in situations where the police act decisively to prevent communication and interaction, refrain from bluffing or vacillating and avoid becoming embroiled in any discussion of underlying grievances. Hundley emphasises that, as long as police interventions are widely seen as legitimate and are devoid of rudeness, impoliteness or brutality, they are unlikely to cause a riot. Like Smelser, he advocates that the police divide up the crowd and prevent communication, and recommends that withdrawal tactics should only occur in situations where the police have already contacted credible community leaders. Spiegel calls for an intermediate approach between under- and over-enforcement. Tactics of under-control are likely to have a liberating and empowering effect on those present, leading to an 'efflorescence' of looting, while over-the-top interventions that are out of all proportion to the seriousness of the initial flashpoint will prove escalatory unless entered into with an overwhelming show of force.

The Flashpoints Model of Public Disorder sees police activities contributing to disorder at five of its six stipulated levels of analysis. This can potentially happen, for example, where senior officers contribute to a negative climate of opinion (political/ideological level); where the culture of lower-ranks predisposes them to conflict (cultural); where there has been no liaison or negotiation with protest organisers or community leaders, or there is a negative history of police–civilian encounters (contextual); where they perceive territory as turf to be won back or retained, and are deployed in threatening or provocative formations (situational); and when they make especially rough or degrading arrests that emphasise their unwillingness to accommodate the values and interests of the policed (interactional).

Otten *et al.* reiterate many of the features of policing highlighted in the flashpoints model. They emphasise the significance of an incuba-tion phase involving a festering social problem such as deteriorating relations between the police and youths from an ethnic minority. They also appreciate the significance of a concentrated rise in tension (e.g. where the possibility of conflict reaches boiling point due to an increase in emotive incidents or growth in complaints. These authors further underline how conflict will escalate when police mobilisation beyond the triggering incident is hurried, uncoordinated and un-restrained, and when their departure is sudden and leaves no place for explaining their tactics to the community through accredited representatives.

A further insight into the way in which police tactics may prove escalatory is provided by the Elaborated Social Identity Model (ESIM). This model maintains that any police action perceived as unjustified and illegitimate will have the effect of inducing solidarity and opposition based on a renewed sense of shared social identity. Such opposition will be all the more resolute in situations were the police are perceived as numerically or tactically vulnerable.

Theoretical approaches – both to public order policing and to crowd disorder, *per se* – undoubtedly provide a solid basis for under-standing the nature and consequences of police actions. Chapters 3–7 of the book outlined a succession of case studies with the objectives of unearthing insights capable of endorsing, complementing and enhancing existing theory. The following section reiterates the main lessons yielded by these chapters.

The case studies

Urban disorder

In Chapter 3, we saw how public order policing in the United States is inseparable from wider class and ethnic conflicts. This was made apparent by our two examples of American commodity riots. In the Mount Pleasant (Washington, DC) riot of 1991, police were reacting to pressure imposed on them by 'yuppies' and local traders to 'clean up' the streets of out-of-work Salvadorans engaged in beer-drinking on street corners and public parks. Police policy was carried out amidst claims of harassment, discrimination and incivilities allegedly perpetrated by non-Spanish-speaking officers. The shooting of a resident Hispanic by an inexperienced officer proved to be the final straw. The local mayor was later criticised for ordering the police to hold off in the early stages of the riot and telling community representatives that their grievances were well-founded. Official investigators noted that there was no mechanism for monitoring police misconduct.

Ten years later, in Cincinnati, Ohio, drug trading and the presence of growing numbers of downtrodden African-Americans in the recently gentrified Over-the-Rhine area provoked complaints to the police by white residents and business owners and night club proprietors. Enhanced police presence (both officially, and in the form of officers doubling up as private security guards) created intense hostility within the local community. A Draconian local ordnance effectively excluding drug offenders from the area was zealously enforced by police officers also committed to achieving arrest quotas. Processes of racial profiling and police harassment were rife, with police tactics predicated on the assumption that anyone running away from a screeching patrol car was bound to be hiding something.

Drug use among black residents was a problem in Brooklyn's Crown Heights area, where local African-Americans and African-Caribbeans not only objected to the repressive policing of their community, but also felt that the police and other authorities were guilty of giving preferential treatment to local Jews. As in Mount Pleasant, the police were accused of not having acted with sufficient resolve in their attempts to quell the conflict. Although a Rapid Mobilisation procedure was already established for prioritising police calls for assistance, this was never activated due to fears that too few officers understood the relevant codes. Field commanders rued the absence of a tangible force philosophy for handling large-scale disorder and were forced, either into looking on passively and waiting for the rioting to blow itself out, or into concocting an improvised and haphazard response. Recent new appointments and personnel changes had meant that many senior officers were placed in unfamiliar roles and environments. Such commanders were tentative and indecisive, to the detriment of communication and co-ordination.

The most momentous American disorder of the last century, the Los Angeles riot of 1992, occurred on the heels of a police crackdown induced by a moral panic concerning 'drug wars' between rival gangs. Weak formal accountability structures allowed the chief of police a relatively free hand with which to steer the tough-minded brand of policing traditionally championed by his force. This had generated an intensely hostile and mistrustful relationship between the police and ethnic minority youths, for whom the acquittal of police officers seen on tape beating the black man Rodney King was the final straw.

The eruption of violence consequent on the King verdict soon showed the LAPD to be ill-equipped, outnumbered and ill-prepared for the riot's initial flashpoint in South Central. Their hapless retreat from a hostile crowd emboldened the initial miscreants and set the tone for the remainder of the riot. Much of the blame for this has been attributed to the fact that, following official criticism of the chief by an official report on the King beating, LAPD's senior officer had broken off contact and consultation with senior staff. There was also a widespread feeling that, as the defendants were bound to be sent down, it would have been wasteful of resources to have prepared too meticulously and expensively for a riot.

The acclaimed LAPD Metropolitan Division fast-response units were exceptional in having been put through pre-riot refresher training in anticipation of a possible riot. An LAPD technical manual actually provided a plan for responding to an incident of this kind. A Metro senior commander had specifically requested that his units be deployed throughout South Central to project a well-disciplined but high-profile deterrent to disorder. He had also wanted his officers to be supplied with protective clothing and visible weaponry as symbolic deterrents to rioting. These requests were turned down. In the prevailing atmosphere of confusion, field commanders had good reason to bemoan their lack of training or preparation.

Community alienation, in conjunction with the ideological vilification of ethnic minority youth, was also at the root of the British urban disorders of the 1990s and 2001, and of the French and Australian riots of 2005. In 1991 and 1992, car-related crimes among disaffected youths on white, working-class British housing estates eventually attracted the attention of riot police responding, at last, to rising crime statistics and howls of protest by local residents. Prior to intervening, the police had been conspicuous by their absence in these wastelands of industrial decline and local authority indifference. Their sudden involvement proved incendiary – a classic case of 'too little policing followed by too much'.

The 1995 Bradford riot was the earliest product of the growing impoverishment and marginalisation of Asian youth. In addition to the growing tide of Islamaphobia threatening their security, Asian communities in cities like Bradford were being stigmatised by senior police as hotbeds of drug trading where youths were beyond the control of elders and hostile to white society. The rising tendency for Asian youths to respond to racist attacks was being mistakenly construed as Asian racism towards whites. In an atmosphere of mutual mistrust and contempt, police reacted to alleged verbal abuse by some Asian youths playing football in the street without duly distinguishing between the actual offenders and casual bystanders. An official report found that officers treated all concerned with equal measures of contempt and incivility, as if residents were incapable of understanding what was going on before them. Even the hurried nature of their exit was considered inherently provocative, while the escalation of the riot seemed tied to the police's failure to convince community representatives that their concerns had been noted and understood.

The 2001 riots resulted from similar police misinterpretations of the motives and behaviour of Asian youth. In Oldham, senior police sponsored a particular interpretation of statistics on racist attacks which unjustifiably accused local Asians of wanton aggression towards whites, aimed at deliberately creating 'no-go areas' in which drug-dealing could flourish unchecked. The resulting attention and mischief-making devoted to Asian communities by elements of the Far Right provided the immediate backdrop to the riots. A similar miscalculation occurred in Burnley where *defensive* activities by Asian youth were similarly castigated as evidence of criminal activity ('turf wars' connected to drug trading). In this context, police hesitancy in dealing appropriately with white racists menacingly gathered on the edge of the Asian communities provoked a determined counter-reaction by Asian youth. Police inability to appreciate the dimension of the perceived threat posed by the BNP led to them being numerically under-strength and incapable of coming between the rival factions. The shambolic nature of their eventual intervention was marked by poor communication, panic and eventual retreat.

These events resonate with those of the Cronulla beach riot, referred to above. There, too, negative police interpretations of the character and alleged behaviours of local Muslim youth formed part of the process of ideological 'demonisation' which resulted in white vigilantism on a mass scale, for which the police were strategically and tactically unprepared. The French riots of one month earlier were likewise presaged by the longstanding vilification and criminalisation of Muslim youth. A corresponding intensification of police stop and search tactics, incorporating blatant displays of disrespect, then brought the suburbs to boiling point. In this respect, the disorders arguably had more in common with the British disorders of 1981 and the American 'communal riots' addressed in Chapter 3 than the English 'textile town' riots of 2001.

Anti-globalisation protest

The character of public order policing in Western democratic societies has been radically transformed by the recent proliferation of anti-globalisation protest. World summit meetings place a huge political onus on the police to 'die in a ditch' in order to guarantee the security, not only of the venues in which they are taking place, but also the Internationally Protected Persons attending them. Senior officers are now forced to contend with the possibilities that the non-hierarchical and 'leaderless' structures of protest movements will make liaison a practical impossibility, while the sheer diversity of their protest repertoires will make it exceedingly difficult to predict their tactical intentions.

As part of a general response to these changes, the police have continued to operate according to the tenets of negotiated management – endeavouring to liaise and co-operate with 'contained' sections of the protest movement which have retained a willingness to share information and co-operate. This approach is invariably complemented by tactics and strategies of strategic incapacitation (e.g. blocking protesters' movements; enforcing bans, curfews and no-protest zones; making pre-emptive arrests and deploying less-lethal weapons) in relation to transgressive groups of protesters. The greater the perceived transgressiveness of the protesters, the less compromising is the police's response. While the police have become increasingly adept at preventing the 'hijacking' of demonstrations via direct action, the long-term effect of their 'routinisation' strategies has been to arouse anger and frustration among activists knowing that the effectiveness of their protest has been undermined.

The emphasis on strategic incapacitation is exemplified by the case of the infamous Genoa G8 summit meeting of 2001, when Italian police applied strict border controls and, more locally, perimeter zones as restrictive control measures. Extensive fortification structures became a symbolic as well as physical target for the protesters. The uncompromising attitudes of the police and *carabinieri* are partly explicable in terms of a prevailing political climate of opinion in which senior Italian politicians and the 'law and order' coalition refused to endorse the values and objectives of the protest movement and urged the police to deal resolutely with any misconduct. Such messages reinforced the police commitment to their traditional 'King's police' *modus operandi*, predicated on intense loyalty to the presiding government.

A similar obligation to deal resolutely with demonstrators was placed on Hong Kong police in advance of the 2005 WTO ministerial conference. In this instance, senior police were aware that the perceived inability of their officers to cope with large-scale domestic and international dissidence would attract criticism of their regime by the onlooking Chinese mainland government. Such an outcome might well be the precursor to a disinvestment of local political autonomy and control. Initially, police reactions to public displays of unruliness were softened by a competing priority not to lend credence to the claims of pro-reform activists by behaving too aggressively. However, as protesters adopted an increasingly con-frontational orientation, the superseding political imperative – of capably suppressing the dissidents – immediately held sway.

Another major problem encountered by protesters in Genoa was that there were few formal restraints acting on the police. For one thing, most officers had their personal identification numbers concealed and could not, therefore, be made accountable for their actions. Likewise, the police and public were equally aware that, given the toothless nature of civilian complaints procedures, officers were unlikely to be disciplined, or even reprimanded, for un-acceptable conduct on their part. Police culture also created a predisposition to violence, insofar as public disorder units were heavily paramilitarised, and more used to dealing with Mafia gangs and football hooligans. Negative stereotypes of the protesters and feelings of hostility and suspicion towards them were reinforced by the police's inability to predict what sort of tactics demonstrators were likely to employ.

Poor police liaison with protesters was attributed by the former to the fact that organisers were too elusive to be contacted. In the absence of concrete information regarding the protesters' intentions, state intelligence agencies predicted that demonstrators would engage in unrestrained atrocities. Police training was thus predicated on the prospect of violent confrontation. The highly contrasting organisation and command structures of police and *carabinieri* created poor communication and coordination between them. The random, indiscriminate and aggressive tactics employed on the ground produced intense resistance and solidarity.

The bitter confrontation occurring during the infamous battle of Seattle further elucidates the various ways in which police tactics can produce a number of unintended consequences (or 'ironies') in their dealings with protesters. What happened at Seattle underlines the implicit message of other case studies, like Genoa – that police actions often draw together 'strange bedfellows' (i.e. unify ideologically discrepant sections of the crowd). Other police tactics at the Seattle protest served only to induce retaliatory or escalatory responses by protesters. Conversely, instances of police hesitancy and indecisiveness had the effect of empowering and encouraging their adversaries.

Other case studies referred to in Chapter 5 show how patterns of tradition and change are fundamental to explaining police tactical and strategic orientation. At Gothenburg in 2001, the ineffectual nature of police tactics and strategy was due to the police's adherence to traditional methods based on the containment of static forms of protest, which were certainly no match for the 'hit and run' tactics adopted by anarchist groups unwilling to follow the prescribed route of the march and assemble in designated protest areas. Two other examples from the following year further emphasise that police styles often evolve as a result of lessons learned on the basis of previous encounters. The relatively 'soft hat' approach adopted by the Canadian police at the G8 rally in Ottawa highlighted their sensitivity to public criticism of their tactics during previous summit meetings – in Ottawa, months earlier, and Quebec City in 2001. The Italian police also displayed a more tolerant and co-operative orientation towards anti-war protesters in Florence, following public outrage regarding their tactics at Genoa.

Featured case studies of the New York anti-war protest of 2003 and the Sheffield G8 Home Affairs and Justice Ministers' meeting of two years later suggest that the general philosophies of policing subscribed to by individual forces will have an important influence

on their strategies and tactics. In the former case, the force commitment to a 'Broken windows'/'zero tolerance' mode of policing led
to the extreme confusion and provocation of demonstrators who
violently expressed their corresponding indignation. By contrast,
the adoption of a more benign and tolerant philosophy by South
Yorkshire Police had a moderating effect on police–protester
relations during the Sheffield G8.

In Sheffield, the police commitment to eradicating the unwanted
legacies of the miners' strike and Hillsborough tragedy was a key
determinant of their approach. The police's hands were tied, to a
large extent, by the need to protect the visiting IPPs and the overriding political objective of 'showcasing' Sheffield to a world-wide
audience. However, senior officers were equally responsive to the
objectives of local protesters perceived to be dedicated to a worthy
and unselfish political cause. In the final analysis, the police were
guilty of overdramatising their impressions of the transgressive
groups involved. Containment procedures were therefore brought in
to restrict the size and location of the main protests. However,
pre-briefings ensured that PSUs were committed to tolerant interaction with protesters. The two relatively minor incidents that did
occur were the result of police over-caution and the involvement of
outside officers.

Other British case studies of transnational protest describe a
dialectical relationship between the police and public opinion. In the
build-up to the May Day protest of 2001, senior police proactively
generated negative characterisations of the protesters and their
supposed intentions as justificatory rationales for repressive policing
measures. It has also been suggested that, at the May Day protest of
one year earlier, the Metropolitan Police Service pulled off an equally
proactive ploy – by deliberately exposing a local McDonald's
fast-food restaurant to vandalism by protesters in order to: (a)
concentrate the violence to a small and manageable area; and
(b) ensure that public sympathy was right behind the police.

Events at the Gleneagles G8 summit meeting also suggest that the
relationship between the media-led vilification of protesters and
the corresponding police tactics and strategy is highly negotiated.
Both for the Make Poverty History march and the main march in
Auchterarder, police were sceptical of alarmist media predictions
and, indeed, sought to assuage public anxiety by appointing
specialist communications personnel to the task. That said, there
are grounds for speculating that the apparent vulnerability of the
protective fencing around Gleneagles may have represented a

reimplementation of the 'winning by appearing to lose' scenario previously deployed at the 2000 May Day rally.

Football hooliganism

Research on football hooliganism involving English supporters abroad suggests that police perceptions of, and corresponding reactions to, the fans are key to explaining the occurrence of large-scale disorder. There is growing academic agreement that, in addition to hardened hooligans and 'ordinary supporters', the fan-base also includes a substantial contingent which embraces a nationalistic and laddish/masculine culture, stereotyped by foreign police as offensive, threatening and aggressively volatile. In situations where negative police impressions of the fans are hardened by hostile media and political discourse, and further re-inforced by a build-up of negative incidents along the way, violence almost inevitably arises.

Police transgressions of the 'unwritten rules' governing per-missible or legitimate intervention on their part not only serve to solidify the self-confessed hooligans, but also enhance the collective outrage and sense of 'common fate' of those bystanders offended by the apparently indiscriminate nature of the chosen crowd control manoeuvres. By contrast, crowd disorder has been less prevalent during competitions where the police have been permissive of the cultural norms of travelling English supporters, and when their interventions have been more judiciously implemented.

By combining the main conclusions of the theory-based and case study chapters of this book, it is possible to arrive at the list of police-relevant factors associated with the instigation and develop-ment of disorder appearing in Table 8.1. Such factors provide correspondingly useful pointers to the type of police tactics and strategies required to ensure the preservation and maintenance of public order. It is on these matters of policy that we lastly focus our attention.

Policy implications

The theoretical and case study chapters of this book suggest that certain policy interventions are required on the part of the police and other important societal institutions in order to offset the possibility of future examples of major public disorder. As I pointed out in an earlier publication,

> Politicians need to be responsive to the material and cultural deprivations experienced by specific sections of society, notably working-class youths. Society needs to ensure adequate representation to those currently excluded or alienated from its political institutions. Media practitioners must recognize that, in vilifying dissenting groups and systematically ignoring or misrepresenting their grievances, they are promoting the potential for disorder. (D Waddington 1992: 215)

Senior police officers can also play a central part in ensuring that macro sociological variables of this nature are geared towards the achievement of public harmony. One of the major lessons of the Make Poverty History march through Edinburgh in July 2005 is that it can undoubtedly be in everyone's interests for the police to keep the alarmist predictions of local and national media in sensible proportion. Given what we have also learned about the ways in which statements by police spokespersons contributed to the subsequent disorders in places like Oldham and Sydney, it would seem advisable for high-ranking officers to refrain from publicly castigating dissenting groups and their objectives. Rather than patronising or repressing the alienated, impoverished and disaffected, senior police should be acting as advocates on their behalf – giving credence to the theoretical link between poverty, social exclusion, crime and disorder. Otten *et al.* (2001) are among other academics advocating a more socially sensitive role for the police. They recommend, for example, that Dutch police officers should strive to reduce the alienation and disaffection of Dutch-Moroccan youths by lobbying on their behalf for greater political representation, special youth employment programmes and wider leisure facilities.

One of the principal lessons of our main empirical case study, concerning the policing of the meeting in Sheffield of the G8 Ministers of Justice and Home Affairs, is that operations of this magnitude are more likely to remain peaceful where local (rather than central) control is exercised with due regard for the wishes and sensibilities of the local population. The relative tranquillity of this occasion, compared to (say) the conflict occurring at the 2003 anti-war protest in New York, or in the 1992 Los Angeles riot, shows the obvious benefits of tolerant everyday policing philosophies

Table 8.1 Policing public order: factors conducive to violent confrontation

Political/ideological
1 A hard-line government willing to sanction police repression
2 Explicit pressure on the police (from government and other politicians, interest groups, general public, the media, police personnel) to apply uncompromising tactics and strategies
3 An absence of countervailing appeals for restraint from the 'civil rights coalition'
4 Implicit political pressure on the police to 'die in a ditch' in defence of important symbolic targets (e.g. IPPs, national monuments) or occasions of national significance (e.g. royal ceremonials)
5 Police implementation of non-permissive public order legislation

Institutional
1 Centralised rather than local control over police operations
2 Weak or non-existent formal accountability mechanisms restraining police behaviour
3 Disorganised and/or malfunctioning police bureaucracy and decision-making procedures
4 An absence, or lack of knowledge of, force plans of action for dealing with public order
5 A general police mission or 'philosophy' of 'zero tolerance'
6 A police tradition of servitude to local or national government (the 'King's police' model)
7 A lack of up-to-date training in tolerant crowd control methods

Cultural
1 Officers from outside the locality who are unfamiliar with local customs and sensibilities, and do not have a full commitment to maintaining good long-term relations with the public
2 Special units subscribing to norms of confrontation
3 Novice, inexperienced or untrained officers
4 Predominantly male personnel whose core values of machismo, solidarity, action and control are given free rein in paramilitary units
5 Mistrust and stereotyping of sections of the public due to their age, class, transgressiveness and organisation (e.g. heterogeneous, non-hierarchical, leaderless, non-institutionalised, having violent or unpredictable 'repertoires of action')
6 An unwillingness to accommodate the values and objectives of relevant sections of the public
7 A regional or national political tradition of intolerance and repression

Contextual
1 A history of previous incidents or negative encounters (with possible scores to settle)
2 A history of routinising and neutralising protest in such a way as to enhance political resentment and indignation
3 Non-existent, partial or bogus negotiation, liaison and co-operation with public representatives
4 A recent build-up of police activity (e.g. a 'crackdown' on local crime)
5 An absence of (or lack of faith in) any prior agreements or contingency plans formulated with public representatives

6 Prior intelligence suggesting the need for a resolute police response or the 'insurance' of 'tooled-up' reinforcements
7 Pre-event training in readiness for confrontation rather than peace
8 Provocative or threatening statements by senior officers in the build-up to a public order event
9 Overreaction to provocative messages by public representatives and media sensitisation in the build-up to an event
10 Inadequate pre-briefing of officers, directing them to avoid confrontation and facilitate the objectives of the public

Situational

1 Difficulties in dictating the layout of the event, limiting the crowd's movements and maintaining effective surveillance
2 Officers deployed in high-profile and provocative formations (with reinforcements, weaponry, dogs, horses, etc. all on public display)
3 Deployment of officers from a variety of different forces, leading to poor coordination and blurred lines of command
4 No 'situational adjustment' involving newly arrived officers
5 An absence of trusted and reliable self-stewarding
6 Police definitions of public behaviour as sinister, illegitimate or ill-intentioned
7 Public perceptions of the police role as illegitimate and/or impartial
8 A strategic intention by the police to engage in confrontation (e.g. to clear an area or 'win by appearing to lose')
9 A symbolically significant location (e.g. a 'front line' to be defended by a community or subculture, or 'no-go area' to be retaken by the police)

Interactional

1 Sudden or overdramatic police interventions which suggest 'overkill' and/or draw other people to the scene
2 Insufficient police tolerance and respect for public behaviour and objectives (non-facilitative policing)
3 Unclear communication to public of police instructions or warnings
4 Police tactics that depart from normative expectations or prior agreements, and which prevent protesters from achieving their objectives
5 Police tactics which are indiscriminate, brutal or otherwise unfair, and which have the effect of inducing crowd solidarity against them
6 Dispersal tactics by the police that serve only to spread the crowd geographically and make its activities more unpredictable and less easy to control
7 Police involvement in incidents involving intensifiers (e.g. a particularly prominent or vulnerable person, or an especially rough or degrading arrest)
8 A failure to engage in (or a rejection of) opportunities to arbitrate or negotiate a reduction of hostilities, especially when credible representatives are present and issues do not seem intractable
9 Police interventions that look weak, ineffectual or under-staffed, and which therefore serve to empower and encourage the crowd
10 Police affected by poor physical condition (e.g. tiredness) or psychological state (e.g. fear, panic, determination to exact revenge, not to lose face or defend reputation)
11 Police judgement impaired by defective equipment (e.g. scratched helmet visor) or inability to pick miscreants out of large crowd

or 'missions', clearly prescribed decision-making procedures and plans of action, and the up-to-date training of officers. Chief police officers should devote themselves to ensuring that such procedures and mechanisms are firmly in place and systematically refreshed. Western societies also need to consider whether formal systems of police monitoring and accountability are currently adequate for their purposes (see D. Waddington [1992] for a fuller discussion of this debate). Numerous of our case studies, ranging from Genoa to Los Angeles, indicate a positive correlation between public disorder and an absence of civilian direction or formal restraint on police behaviour.

In addition to proposed changes at the political and institutional levels, police should also consider ways of changing their attitudes and behaviour to sections of the general public in such a way as to lessen the likelihood of disorder. For example, Otten *et al.* maintain that training schemes should be instigated with a view to sensitising rank-and-file officers to relevant cultural differences between themselves and ethnic minorities. The need for such preparation is exemplified by the 'wastebasket incident' involving the police and Moroccan youths, referred to in Chapter 2. Otten *et al.* reckon that, in this case, the police were too insensitive to cultural diversity: 'The fathers of Moroccan youths, for instance, did not understand why the police failed to negotiate with them when their children violated the law, as is [the] custom in Morocco' (*ibid.*: 33).

According to Otten and his co-workers, this raising of cultural awareness should be undertaken in conjunction with training to ensure that police tactical interventions do not backfire in escalatory manner. They criticise the Dutch police in the example just referred to for having adopted a 'no-nonsense' policy of stopping *all* youths on suspicion of traffic violations in the build-up to the confrontation that occurred. This crude, indiscriminate practice was one of the main causes of police–community tension. Otten *et al.* maintain that senior officers would have been better advised to have consulted well-informed community members to target specific groups or individuals, rather than resorting to such provocative saturation measures.

Further training might also have ensured that the 'flashpoint' incident was handled more sympathetically. As Otten *et al.* explain,

When police personnel are not taught to recognize the differences between simple routine situations and potential inflammable flashpoints, mistakes are quickly made. The 'wastebasket' incident could have been defused by the police at every step of the escalation process: the initial approach by the police (demanding answers, being accusative), the sending off, the immediate threat of a booking and the actual booking and arrest of the kid. A controversial arrest by the police should be followed by an explanation of the rationale for police behavior. In Moroccan culture, it is it is custom for parents to be consulted by the police on the nature of the arrest and the punishment needed . . . Instead of explaining behavior, every police officer went back to their station. (*ibid.*: 34)

The blatant insensitivity underpinning the entire police response was critical to what followed. Their tactical mobilisation was 'quick, massive [and] uncoordinated', while their departure was all too sudden (*ibid.*: 42). Afterwards, the police made the equally crucial mistake of failing to contact and de-brief community leaders. For Otten *et al.*, the lessons of the incident are clear: ideally, police interventions should appear composed and avoid impressions of overkill. Once the intervention is over, the police should maintain a precautionary presence while senior officers seek out community representatives in order to explain and justify their actions. Trained police negotiators should also liaise with local authorities in a bid to pacify and appease the community. Should all else fail, use of force should be measured and controlled.

Similar recommendations have been proffered by two other Dutch academics, Stol and Bervoets (2002), who collaborated with police departments in Amsterdam, Utrecht and Gouda in a joint effort to improve relations between police and Dutch-Moroccan youths. Based primarily on interviews with those officers considered most adept in their handling of youths, Stol and Bervoets emphasise the need for individual officers to get to know local youths personally on the basis of regular interaction. However, they also emphasise that it is imperative for the police to develop social networks around the youths which utilise family, youth workers and members of local mosques as ways of influencing the young men's behaviour.

Stol and Bervoets stress the need for appropriate standards of 'decency' during police–youth interactions. In particular, they advocate that youths should be approached politely and without unnecessary abruptness or obvious presumption of guilt. Such encounters should also be adequately cognisant of cultural differences between the police and Moroccan youths:

Dutch people are rather direct in their way of communicating. Without any introduction they reveal the reason for coming ('What's going on here?'). Moroccans, on the other hand, are less direct. They prefer some small talk before getting to the actual subject. Therefore, in the eyes of Moroccans, the direct Dutch approach is rather blunt and rude. Good policemen bear this in mind, and are successful in their approach. (*ibid.*: 198)

Taken together, these studies advocate a general style of policing based on regular contact and communication with the community. This view is certainly endorsed by Power and Tunstall whose work showed how sudden, high-profile police interventions resulted in the head-on confrontations with white youths on council estates, referred to in Chapter 4. As Power and Tunstall (1997: 57–58) explain,

It is cheaper to have regular policing at the front line that cuts crime and disorder than continuous and inadequate interventions to quell disorder. Extreme suppression such as curfews is costly, short term and unequal, though it may be effective in extreme conditions. A complete reappraisal of core policing methods is needed stressing visibility, contact, clarity and proactive policing. The division between 'community policing' and 'normal policing' should go.

The type of recommendations deemed most appropriate for avoiding community disorders are arguably just as applicable to the policing of crowds attending protest or sporting events. Such principles have recently been explored by Reicher *et al.* (2004) who urge the police to follow a general approach which avoids treating 'the crowd' as an undifferentiated whole and to refrain from tactical interventions that fail to differentiate between 'guilty' and 'innocent'. They maintain that police actions undertaken without sensitivity to the *aims of the crowd* run the risk of alienating participants and increasing their readiness to retaliate: 'What is more, in this context, it makes sense to group together with the strongest, the meanest, the most experienced people. Those who one would ordinarily do most to avoid become the most valuable allies once crowd members perceive their situation as one of "self-defence"' (*ibid.*: 564).

As a general strategy for counteracting this possibility, Reicher *et al.* advocate an *interactive* approach to crowd management which not only helps to promote rapport, but which also enables the police to distinguish between those harbouring malicious intent and those not. They outline a number of prescriptions for effective policing. Such guidelines pinpoint the need for the police to engage in appropriate *education, facilitation, communication* and *differentiation*.

In terms of education, Reicher *et al.* make the point that, in recent years, police preparation for public order events has primarily been concerned with amassing criminal intelligence, pinpointing violent individuals and second-guessing their sinister intentions. The authors recommend that relevant police departments should devote similar levels of energy to educating themselves in terms of the social identities of groups they are likely to come into contact with. By probing into such issues as the group's prior history of interaction with the police, their likely stereotypes of police officers and any- thing of particular symbolic significance (e.g. dates or places), it improves the police's chances of predicting important matters like 'what the aims of the groups are, whether and how to support them, the forms of police action that might antagonise them and make them more sympathetic to violent elements in the crowd' (*ibid.*: 566).

Closely related to this is the need for police planning and organisa- tion to strive to facilitate the crowd's legitimate objectives:

> If there is some reason why they cannot be met in the way that organisers request it is essential not simply to give a negative response, but to be positive and creative in finding alternative ways of meeting (and being seen to meet) the underlying aims. If the danger of violence or the actual occurrence of violence forces the police to impose limits on the crowd, it is especially important to make clear why it has been necessary to impose these limits and to provide alternative means by which legitimate aims can be met. (*ibid.*: 567)

The achievement of this objective may require effective communication between the police and 'credible' (i.e. trusted and respected, as opposed to merely 'self-appointed') representatives of the crowd (*ibid.*). Instead of approaching such individuals to play the traditional role of 'community mediators' once violence has broken out, the emphasis should be on contacting them proactively to explore ways of facilitating legitimate aims and working out possible contingency plans for any unscheduled occurrence of disorder (*ibid.*: 567–568). Correspondingly, the police could employ the print and broadcast media, web sites or leaflets as ways of communicating, not only essential information about arrangements for an event, but also of their respect for the aims of the crowd. There is also a wide range of visual and sound technologies (e.g. large LED screens mounted on trucks or helicopters, and mobile loudspeakers) that can potentially be employed to keep crowd members informed of police activities in ways that prevent misinterpretation and enhance their perceived legitimacy (*ibid.*: 568).

Finally, the police should reject the traditional notion that, once violence is under way, *everyone* is fair game by striving to differentiate between those who are culpable and those who are not. Reicher *et al.* caution that: 'It is precisely when some crowd members start to become hostile that it becomes important to treat the generality of crowd members in a friendly way. It is precisely in order to stop the violence of the few that one must be permissive towards the many' (*ibid.*: 568). This principle is especially applicable to police tactics involving 'sweeping the street' or 'containing' (corralling-in) sections of the crowd. Here the challenge for the police is to determine 'How then can one use communication, selective filters and staggered dispersal to make the tactic more selective?' (*ibid.*: 569).

A notable exemplar of this type of policing approach is outlined by Veno and Veno (1993). Their case study is concerned with the annual Australian motorcycle Grand Prix held at Bathurst, New South Wales, from 1939 to 1987, which had constantly been marred by tensions between motorcycle enthusiasts and the police, manifested in vandalism and occasional riots. By the mid-1980s, police were resorting to rigid control measures including increased numbers of uniformed officers and the presence of riot squads. Motorcyclists en route to the Grand Prix were frequently intercepted by police, searched by officers with batons drawn and given traffic citations. This emphasis on tighter security led to drastically reduced attendances at the meeting and an eventual decision in 1988 to relocate the race to Phillip Island, Victoria.

Based on advice offered to them by Veno and Veno, Victoria Police adopted a strategy of co-operation and facilitation with the motorcycle fraternity. Central to this approach was a motorcycle rally enabling 10,000 bikers to proceed, under police escort, from central Melbourne into their camping areas at Phillip Island. Along the way, the police blocked off intersections, giving the motorcyclists priority, in an attempt to generate trust and respect. Police then drew back from controlling the camp-sites, preferring to help set up a marshal system whereby the riders policed themselves. Finally, police public relations personnel and event organisers used specialist media publications to promote the Grand Prix as a peaceful, family-oriented event in the hope of attracting a wider demographic spectrum of spectators and generating a non-violent ethos. Veno and Veno report a corresponding decline in tension between the police and bikers, and absence of public disorder.

Our own policy suggestions (e.g. D. Waddington and Critcher 2000: 116–117) are equally consistent with the principles outlined by Reicher and his colleagues. We also advocate a need for police training to address (and hopefully moderate) the macho orientation to action, challenge, confrontation and control inherent in the police occupational culture. In selecting the officers for duty at demonstrations or on picket lines, senior commanders should veer towards local personnel who are likely to be more attuned to the cultural sensibilities of the crowd, and be more concerned about the long-term implications of police conduct for police–community relations. Similar thought should also be devoted to deploying female officers whose presence has been shown to have a calming effect on the situation (Heidensohn 1994).

Reicher *et al.*'s emphasis on facilitation and communication is mirrored in our recommendation that police officers engage, as helpfully and co-operatively as possible, in negotiation and liaison with event organisers in order to formulate a tacit 'contract with the crowd'. This process is bound to affect what we refer to as the *situational level*. Thus, as we have emphasised elsewhere:

> If mutual objectives are established beforehand, suspicion of each other's motives is less likely. The police should actively encourage the use of stewards, formal speeches and entertainment and permit non-violent symbolic expressions of grievance. It is also preferable to police demonstrations and picket lines by deploying small groups of 'traditionally' dressed police officers in a low-key manner with reinforcements kept out of sight. Clear lines of police communication and command are imperative. 'Situationally adjusted' officers, familiar with the mood of the crowd, are less volatile than loosely briefed Police Support Units arriving cold at the scene. Necessary police surveillance should be as low-key as possible. Traditionally uniformed officers communicating on two-way radios are less threatening than helicopters flying loudly overhead. (D. Waddington and Critcher 2000: 117)

Such, then, are the recommendations of 'ivory tower academics'. The public order police are entitled to maintain that theirs is a generally thankless and unenviable task, demanding quick thinking and great courage all the while. They might further object – with similar justification – that their efforts only typically get noticed when, in their parlance, 'the wheel comes off' (P. A. J. Waddington 1994) and their control strategies and tactics are brought into disrepute. This book has indicated the variety of ways in which forms of police rhetoric and conduct have the potential to rupture the public order they have a moral obligation to uphold. It has also recommended a range of policies designed to reduce the abrasiveness of police–public interaction and gain legitimacy and consent for the police's role and objectives. The standards of professionalism and impartiality implicitly being asked of police commanders and their rank-and-file colleagues may strike them as unreasonably high and over-demanding. However, it is unquestionably in the interests of public peace and wider social harmony that the police must strive so assiduously to achieve them.

References

Ahmed, N. M., Bodi, F., Kazim, R. and Shadjareh, M. (2001) *The Oldham Riots: Discrimination, Deprivation and Communal Tension in the North of England*. Media Monitors Network. http://www.mediamonitors.net/mosaddeq6.html.

Alexander, C. (2004) 'Imagining the Asian gang: ethnicity, masculinity and youth after the "riots"', *Critical Social Policy*, 24 (4): 526–549.

Alexander, M. (2005) 'Running battles fought in field', *The Courier*, 7 July 2005.
http://www.nadir.org/nadir/initiativ/agp/resistg8/media/0707running_battles.htm.

Allen, C. (2003) *Fair Justice: The Bradford Disturbances, the Sentencing and the Impact*. London: Forum Against Islamaphobia and Racism.

Allen, S. (2003) 'Velvet gloves and iron fist: taking the violence out of major international protests', *The Police Chief*, 70 (2): 50–55.

Amin, A. (2002) 'Ethnicity and the multicultural city: living with diversity', *Environment and Planning A*, 34: 959–980.

Amin, A. (2003) 'Unruly strangers? The 2001 urban riots in Britain', *International Journal of Urban and Regional Research*, 27 (2): 460–463.

Armstrong, G. (1998) *Football Hooligans: Knowing the Score*. London: Berg.

Armstrong, G. and Harris, R. (1991) 'Football hooligans: theory and evidence', *The Sociological Review*, 39 (3): 427–458.

Association of Chief Police Officers (ACPO) (2000) *Manual of Guidance on Keeping the Peace*. Bramshill: National Police Training Centre.

Atkinson, I. (2001) 'May Day 2001 in the UK, the news media and public order', *Environmental Politics*, 10 (3): 145–150.

Bagguley, P. (2000) 'The petrol blockade of September 2000: the emergence of a petit bourgeois countermovement'. Paper presented to International Sociological Association Research Committee 48 (Social Movements, Social Change and Collective Action) and British Sociological Study Group on Protest and Social Movements Conference, 3–5 November 2000.

Bagguley, P. and Hussain, Y. (2003) 'The Bradford riot of 2001: a preliminary analysis'. Paper presented to the Ninth Alternative Futures and Popular Protest Conference, Manchester Metropolitan University, 22–24 April 2003.

Baker, D. (2001) 'The fusion of picketing, policing and public order theory within the industrial relations context of the 1992 APPM dispute at Burnie', *Australian Bulletin of Labour*, 27 (1): 61–77.

BBC News (2006) 'England fans held by riot police', Sporting Life, 4 July 2006.
http://worldcup.sportinglife.com/football/teams/story_get.cgi?STORY_

Beckett, I. (1992) 'Conflict management and the police: a policing strategy for public order', in T. Marshall (ed.), *Community Disorders and Policing: Conflict Management in Action*. London: Whiting and Birch.

Benyon, J. (1987) 'Interpretations of civil disorder', in J. Benyon and J. Solomos (eds) *The Roots of Urban Unrest*. Oxford: Pergamon Press.

Benyon, J. and Solomos, J. (eds) (1987) *The Roots of Urban Unrest*. Oxford: Pergamon Press.

Billig, M. (1976) *Social Psychology and Intergroup Relations*. London: Academic Press.

Bishop, H. and Jaworski, A. (2003) '"We beat 'em.": nationalism and the hegemony of homogeneity in the British press reportage of Germany versus England during Euro 2000', *Discourse and Society*, 14 (3): 243–271.

Black, E., Bowditch, G., Brown, A., Chamberlain, G., Gray, L., Harrell, E., Howie, I., Johnston, I., McGinty, S. and Smith, C. (2005) 'Rampage before dawn ignites chaos and confusion', *The Scotsman*, 7 July 2005.

Black, R. (2005) 'G8 to tackle illegal timber trade', *BBC News*, 18 March 2005.
http://news.bbc.co.uk/1/hi/sci/tech/4362505.stm.

Bloom, C. (2003) *Violent London: 2000 Years of Riots, Rebels and Revolts*. London: Sidgwick and Jackson.

Bonelli, L. (2005) 'The control of the enemy within? Police intelligence in the French suburbs (*banlieues*) and its relevance for globalization', in D. Bigo and E. Guild (eds), *Controlling Frontiers: Free Movement into and Within Europe*. Aldershot: Ashgate.

Bonelli, L. (2006) 'The trouble with the banlieues', *Liberty and Security*, 16 January 2006. http://www.libertysecurity.org/article750.html.

Bouteldja, N. (2005) 'Explosion in the suburbs', *The Guardian*, 7 November 2005.

Bradford Commission Report, The (1996) *The Report of an inquiry into the wider implications of the public disorders in Bradford which occurred on 9, 10 and 11 June 1995*. London: The Stationery Office.

Brogden, M., Jefferson, T. and Walklate, S. (1988) *Introducing Policework*. London: Unwin Hyman.

Brooks, D.C. (2004) 'Faction in movement: the impact of inclusivity on the anti-globalization movement', *Social Science Quarterly*, 85 (3): 559–577.

Burke, T. and James, Z. (1998) *Trespass and Protest: Policing Under the Criminal Justice and Public Order Act 1994*. London: HMSO.

Button, M., John, T. and Brierley, N. (2002) 'New challenges in public order policing: the professionalisation of environmental protest and the emergence of the militant environmental activist', *International Journal of the Sociology of Law*, 30: 17–32.

Callinicos, A.T. (1992) 'Meaning of Los Angeles riots', *Economic and Political Weekly*, 25 July: 1603–1606.

Campaign Against Racism and Fascism (CARF) (2001) *The summer of rebellion: CARF special report*. http://www.carf.demon.co.uk/feat54.html.

Campbell, B. (1993) *Goliath: Britain's Dangerous Places*. London: Methuen.

Cannon, L. (1997) *Official Negligence: How Rodney King and the Riots Changed Los Angeles and the LAPD*. New York: Times Books, Random House.

Cantle, T. (2001) *Community Cohesion: A Report of the Independent Review Team*. London: The Home Office.

Carling, A., Davies, D., Fernandes-Bakshi, A., Jarman, N. and Nias, P. (2004) *Fair Justice for All? The Response of the Criminal Justice System to the Bradford Disturbances of July 2001*. Bradford: The Programme for a Peaceful City, University of Bradford.

Castaneda, R. and Henderson, N. (1991) 'Simmering tension between police, Hispanics fed clash', *Washington Post*, 6 May 1991.

Clark, C. and O'Kain, M. (2001) 'Cops riot in Cincinnati', *Socialist Viewpoint*, May: 1(1). http://www.socialistviewpoint.org/may_01/may_01.html.

Clarke, Lord T. (2001) *The Burnley Task Force Report*. Burnley: Burnley Borough Council.

Clennell, A. (2006) 'Cronulla riot report highlights police confusion', The Age Company, 21 October 2006.
http://www.theage.com.au/news/national/cronulla-riot-report-highlights-police-confusion/2006/10/20/1160851138116.html.

Conaway, C. B. (1999) 'Crown Heights: politics and press coverage of the race war that wasn't', *Polity*, 32 (1): 93–118.

Conte, A. (2001) 'Riot began as peaceful protest', *The Cincinnati Post Online Edition*, 11 April, 2001.
http://www.cincypost.com/2001/apr1/11/time041101.html.

Cooper, M. (1992) 'LA's state of siege: City of Angels, cops from hell', in Institute for Alternative Journalism (eds), *Inside the LA Riots: What Really Happened – and Why It Will Happen Again*. New York: Institute for Alternative Journalism.

Cooper, M. and Goldin, G. (1992) 'Some people don't count', in Institute for Alternative Journalism (eds), *Inside the LA Riots: What Really Happened – and Why It Will Happen Again*. New York: Institute for Alternative Journalism.

Cottle, M. (2001) 'Did integration cause the Cincinnati riots?', *The New Republic*, 5 July 2001.

http://www.highbeam.com/library/docFree.asp?docid=1P1:43909594&
key=0C177A56741C1568120A3180569061F7D0C7E78780B0A.

Crabbe, T. (2003) '"The public gets what the public wants": England football fans, "truth" claims and mediated realities', *International Review for the Sociology of Sport*, 38 (4): 413–425.

Critcher, C. (1996) 'On the waterfront: applying the flashpoints model to protests against live animal exports', in C. Critcher and D. Waddington (eds), *Policing Public Order: Theoretical and Practical Issues*. Aldershot: Avebury.

Cronin, P, and Reicher, S. (2006) 'A study of the factors that influence how senior officers police crowd events: on SIDE outside the laboratory', *British Journal of Social Psychology*, 45: 175–196.

Davis, M. (1988) 'Los Angeles: civil liberties between the Hammer and the Rock', *New Left Review*, 1970: 37–60.

Davis, M. (1992a) *City of Quartz: Excavating the Future in Los Angeles*. London: Vintage.

Davis, M. (1992b) 'Burning all illusions in LA', in Institute for Alternative Journalism (eds), *Inside the LA Riots: What Really Happened – and Why It Will Happen Again*. New York: Institute for Alternative Journalism.

Davis, M. (1992c) 'The rebellion that rocked a superpower', *Socialist Review*, June, 152: 8–9.

della Porta, D. (1995) *Social Movements, Political Violence, and the State: A Comparative Analysis of Italy and Germany*. Cambridge: Cambridge University Press.

della Porta, D. (1998) 'Police knowledge and protest policing: some reflections on the Italian case', in D. della Porta and H. Reiter (eds), *Policing Protest: The Control of Mass Demonstrations in Western Democracies*. Minneapolis, Minnesota: University of Minnesota Press.

della Porta, D. and Fillieule, O. (2004) 'Policing social protest', in D. A. Snow, S. A. Soule and H. Kriesi (eds), The *Blackwell Companion to Social Movements*. Oxford: Blackwell.

della Porta, D., Peterson, A. and Reiter, H. (2006) 'Policing transnational protest: an introduction', in D. della Porta, A. Peterson and H. Reiter (eds), *The Policing of Transnational Protest*. Aldershot: Ashgate.

della Porta, D. and Reiter, H. (1998) 'The policing of protest in Western democracies', in D. della Porta and H. Reiter (eds), *Policing Protest: The Control of Mass Demonstrations in Western Democracies*. Minneapolis, Minnesota: University of Minnesota Press.

della Porta, D. and Reiter, R. (2006a) 'The policing of transnational protest: a conclusion', in D. della Porta, A. Peterson and H. Reiter (eds), *The Policing of Transnational Protest*. Aldershot: Ashgate.

della Porta, D. and Reiter, R. (2006b) 'The policing of global protest: the G8 at Genoa and its aftermath', in D. della Porta, A. Peterson and H. Reiter (eds), *The Policing of Transnational Protest*. Aldershot: Ashgate.

Denham, J. (2002) *Building Cohesive Communities: A Report of the Ministerial*

Group on Public Order and Community Cohesion. London: The Home Office.

DiPasquale, D. and Glaeser, E. L. (1998) 'The Los Angeles riot and the economics of urban unrest', *Journal of Urban Economics*, 43: 52–78.

Dodd, V. (2006) 'Police want power to crack down on offensive demo chants and slogans', *The Guardian*, 27 November 2006.

Doherty, B., Paterson, M., Plows, A. and Wall, D. (2003) 'Explaining the fuel protests', *British Journal of Politics and International Relations*, 5 (1): 1–23.

Donson, F., Chesters, G., Welsh, I. and Tickle, A. (2004) 'Rebels with a cause, folk devils without a panic: press jingoism, policing tactics and anti-capitalist protest in London and Prague', *Internet Journal of Criminology.* www.internetjournalofcriminology.com.

Drummond Ayres Jr, B. (1991) 'Street unrest flares again in capital', *New York Times*, 7 May 1991.

Drury, J., Stott, C. and Farsides, T. (2003) 'The role of police perceptions and practices in the development of "public disorder"', *Journal of Applied Social Psychology*, 33 (7): 1480–1500.

Duncan, R. (2005) 'Round one goes to the capital's police', *The Herald*, 4 July 2005.

Dunning, E. (1990) 'Sociological reflections on sport, violence and civilisation', *International Review for the Sociology of Sport*, 25 (1): 65–81.

Dunning, E., Murphy, P. and Waddington, I. (2002) 'Towards a sociological understanding of football hooliganism as a world phenomenon', in E. Dunning *et al.* (eds), *Fighting Fans: Football Hooliganism as a World Phenomenon*. Dublin: University College Dublin Press.

Duvall Smith, A. (2005) 'The week Paris burned', *The Observer*, 6 November 2005.

Earl, J. (2006) 'Introduction: repression and the social control of protest', *Mobilization: An International Journal*, 11 (2): 129–143.

Earl, J. and Soule, S. A. (2006) 'Seeing blue: a police-centered explanation of protest policing', *Mobilization: An International Journal*, 11 (2): 145–164.

Economist, The (1991) 'Riot in Washington: not many hurt', *The Economist*, 11 May 1991, 41 and 44.

Edwards, J. (2001) 'No charges for beanbag rounds', *The Cincinnati Post Online Edition*, 8 November 2001.
http://www.cincypost.com/2001/nov/08/bean110801.html.

Ericson, R. and Doyle, A. (1999) 'Globalisation and the policing of protest: the case of APEC 1997', *British Journal of Sociology*, 50 (4): 589–608.

Farnsworth, K. (2004) 'Anti-globalisation, anti-capitalism and the democratic state', in M. Todd and G. Taylor (eds), *Democracy and Protest*. London: Merlin Press.

Fassin, D. (2006) 'Riots in France and silent anthropologists', *Anthropology Today*, 22 (1): 1–3.

Freedland, J. (2005) 'France is clinging to an ideal that's been pickled into dogma', *The Guardian*, 9 November 2005.

Freer, R. (1994) 'Black–Korean conflict', in M. Baldassare (ed.), *The Los Angeles Riots: Lessons for the Urban Future*. Oxford: Westview Press.

Fukurai, H., Krooth, R. and Butler, E. W. (1994) 'The Rodney King beating verdicts', in M. Baldassare (ed.), *The Los Angeles Riots: Lessons for the Urban Future*. Oxford: Westview Press.

Frosdick, S. (2005) 'Pompey versus Saints: a case study in crowd segregation', *International Journal of Police Science and Management*, 7 (3): 149–159.

Frosdick, S. and Marsh, P. (2005) *Football Hooliganism*. Cullompton: Willan.

Gale, D. E. (1996) *Understanding Urban Unrest: From Reverend King to Rodney King*. London: Sage.

Gillham, P. F. and Marx, G. T. (2000) 'Complexity and irony in policing and protesting: the World Trade Organization in Seattle', *Social Justice*, 27 (2): 212–236.

Gilje, P. A. (1996) *Rioting in America*. Bloomington and Indianapolis: Indiana University Press.

Girgenti, R. H. (1993) *A Report to the Governor On the Disturbance in Crown Heights: Volume 1 – An Assessment of the City's Preparedness and Response to Civil Disorder*. New York: New York State Division of Criminal Justice Services.

Godoy, J. (2005) 'Riots spread into rebellion', *Inter Press Service News Agency*, 6 November 2005. http://www.ipsnews.net/news.asp?idnews=30903.

Gooding-Williams, R. (ed.) (1993) *Reading Rodney King: Reading Urban Uprising*. London: Routledge.

Gordon, T. and Duncan, R. (2005) '"It's just a game they're playing with us": protesters accuse police of adopting underhand tactics', *The Herald*, 7 July 2005.

Gorringe, H. and Rosie, M. (2006) '"Pants to poverty"? Making Poverty History, Edinburgh 2005', *Sociological Research Online*, 11 (1). http://www.socresonline.org.uk/11/1/gorringe.html.

Gray, R., McCulloch, S., Barnes, E., MacLeod, M., Martin, T., MacMillan, A., Brady, B., Lyons, W., Horton, J. and Ghaemi, M. (2005) 'Anarchists riot, but peace wins on the day', *Scotland on Sunday*, 3 July 2005.

Gurr, T. R. (ed.) (1989) *Violence in America, Volume 2: Protest, Rebellion, Reform*. London: Sage.

Harding, J. (2005) 'Diary', *London Review of Books*, 1 December 2005: 34–35.

Hart, O. 'Cincinnati protesters say: "Try the cops for murder"', *The Militant*, 65 (17): 30 April 2001. http://www.themilitant.com/6517/651701.html.

Hartley, J. and Green, J. (2006) 'The public sphere on the beach', *European Journal of Cultural Studies*, 9 (3): 341–362.

Heidensohn, F. (1994) '"We can handle it out here": women officers in Britain and the USA and the policing of public order', *Policing and Society*, 4: 293–303.

Held, D. and McGrew, A. (2002) *Globalization/Anti-Globalization*. London: Polity.

Henley, J. 'The Guardian profile: Nicolas Sarkozy', *The Guardian*, 11 November 2005.

Her Majesty's Inspector of Constabulary (HMIC) (1999) *Keeping the Peace: Policing Disorder*. London: HMIC.

Hevesi, D. (1992) 'Manhattan block erupts after a man is killed in struggle with a policeman', *New York Times*, 5 July 1992.

Hobbs, D. and Robbins, D. (1991) 'The boy done good: football violence, changes and continuities', *The Sociological Review*, 39 (3): 551–579.

Holdaway, S. (1983) *Inside the British Police*. Oxford: Blackwell.

Hundley, J. R. Jnr (1968) 'The dynamics of recent ghetto riots', *Detroit Journal of Urban Law*, 45, 627–39. Reprinted as: Hundley, J. R. Jnr (1975) 'The dynamics of recent ghetto riots', in R. R. Evans (ed.), *Readings in Collective Behavior*. Chicago: Rand McNally.

Hussain, Y. and Bagguley, P. (2005) 'Citizenship, ethnicity and identity: British Pakistanis after the 2001 "riots"', *Sociology*, 39 (3): 407–425.

Indymedia (2005) 'G8 clampdown in Derby', 20 March 2005. http://www.indymedia.org.uk/en/regions/sheffield/2005/o3/307236.html.

Ingle, S. (2006) 'Fan fears grow ahead of England match', Guardian Unlimited, 25 June 2006. http://football.guardian.co.uk/worldcup2006?story/0,,1805689,00.html.

Ireland, D. (2005) 'Why is France burning? The rebellion of a lost generation', *Axis of Logic*, 9 November 2005. http://www.axisoflogic.com/artman/publish/article_19897.shtml.

James, Z. (2006) 'Policing space: managing New Travellers in England', *British Journal of Criminology*, 46 (3): 470–485.

Jan-Kahn, M. (2003) 'The right to riot?', *Community Development Journal*, 38 (1): 32–42.

Janowitz, M. (1969) 'Patterns of collective racial violence', in H. D. Graham and T. R. Gurr (eds), *Violence in America: Historical and Comparative Perspectives, Volume 2*. New York: Praeger.

Jefferson, T. (1987) 'Beyond paramilitarism', *British Journal of Criminology*, 27 (1): 47–53.

Jefferson, T. (1990) *The Case Against Paramilitary Policing*. Milton Keynes: Open University Press.

Jefferson, T. (1993) 'Pondering paramilitarism: a question of standpoints?', *British Journal of Criminology*, 33 (3): 374–388.

Jefferson, T. and Grimshaw, R. (1984) *Controlling the Constable*. London: Frederick Muller.

Jordan, M. (1991) 'Residents differ on where to focus their anger', *Washington Post*, 7 May 1991.

Kabir, N. (2006) 'Muslims in a "white Australia": colour or religion?', *Immigrants and Minorities*, 24 (2): 193–223.

Kalra, V. S. (2002) 'Riots, race and reports: Denham, Cantle, Oldham and Burnley Inquiries', *Sage Race Relations Abstracts*, 27 (4): 20–30.

Kalra, V. S. (2003) 'Police lore and community disorder: diversity in the criminal justice system', in D. Mason (ed.), *Explaining Ethnic Differences: Changing Patterns of Disadvantage in Britain*. Bristol: The Policy Press.

Keith, M. (1993) *Race, Riots and Policing: Lore and Disorder in a Multi-racist Society*. London: UCL Press.

King, A. (1995) 'Outline of a practical theory of football violence', *Sociology*, 29 (4): 635–651.

King, A. (2001) 'Violent pasts: collective memory and football hooliganism', *Sociological Review*, 49 (4): 568–585.

King, M. and Brearley, M. (1996) *Public Order Policing: Contemporary Perspectives on Strategy and Tactics*. Leicester: Perpetuity Press.

King, M. and Waddington, D. (2004) 'Coping with disorder? The changing relationship between police public order strategy and practice – a critical analysis of the Burnley riot', *Policing and Society*, 14 (2): 118–137.

King, M. and Waddington, D. (2005) 'Flashpoints revisited: a critical application to the policing of anti-globalisation protest', *Policing and Society*, 15 (3): 255–282.

King, M. and Waddington, D. (2006) 'The policing of transnational protest in Canada', in D. della Porta, A. Peterson and H. Reiter (eds), *The Policing of Transnational Protest*. Aldershot: Ashgate.

Kinsey, R., Lea, J. and Young, J. (1986) *Losing the Fight Against Crime*. Oxford: Blackwell.

Kundnani, A. (2001) 'From Oldham to Bradford: the violence of the violated', *Race and Class*, 43 (2): 105–131.

Kundnani, A. (2003) 'Nine months for white racist thugs who sparked the Oldham riots', Independent Race and Refugee News Network, 19 June 2003. http://www.irr.org.uk/2003/june/ak000009.html.

Kwong, P. (1992) 'The first multicultural riots', in Institute for Alternative Journalism (eds), *Inside the LA Riots: What Really Happened – and Why It Will Happen Again*. New York: Institute for Alternative Journalism.

Lacey, D. and Bowcott, O. (1995) 'Riot revives football nightmare', *The Guardian*, 16 February 1995.

Lazare, D. (2001) 'Cincinnati and the X-Factor', *Columbia Journalism Review*, July/August (4). www.cjr.org/year/01/4/cincinnati.asp.

Lea, J. (2004) 'From Brixton to Bradford: ideology and discourse on race and urban violence in the United Kingdom', in G. Gilligan and J. Pratt (eds), *Crime, Truth and Justice: Official Inquiry, Discourse, Knowledge*. Cullompton: Willan.

Lea, J. and Young, J. (1982) 'The riots in Britain 1981: urban violence and political marginalisation', in D. Cowell, D. Jones and J. Young (eds), *Policing the Riots*. London: Junction Books.

Lea, J. and Young, J. (1993) *What Is To Be Done About Law And Order?* London: Pluto Press.

Locher, D. A. (2002) *Collective Behavior*. Upper Saddle River, New Jersey: Prentice Hall.

Lo Shiu-hing, S. (2006) 'The politics of policing the anti-WTO protests in Hong Kong', *Asian Journal of Political Science*, 14 (2): 140–162.

Marsh, P., Rosser, E. and Harre, R. (1978) *The Rules of Disorder*. London: Routledge and Kegan Paul.

Marx, G. (1970) 'Civil disorder and the agents of social control', *Journal of Social Issues*, 26 (1): 19–57.

Mawby, R. C. (2002) *Policing Images: Policing, Communication and Legitimacy*. Cullompton: Willan Publishing.

Maynard, R. (2005) 'Battle on beach as mob vows to defend "Aussie way of life"', *The Times*, 12 December 2005.

McDonald, H. (2001) 'What *really* happened in Cincinnati?', *City Journal*, Summer 2001.

http://www.city-journal.org/html/11_3_what_really_happened.html.

McNally, D. (2001) 'Mass protest in Quebec City: from anti-globalization to anti-capitalism', *New Politics*, 8 (3): 76–86.

McPhail, C., Schweingruber, D. and McCarthy, J. (1998) 'Policing protest in the United States: 1960–1995', in D. della Porta and H. Reiter (eds), *Policing Protest: The Control of Mass Demonstrations in Western Democracies*. Minneapolis, Minnesota: University of Minnesota Press.

Miller, A. H. (2001) 'The Los Angeles riots: a study in crisis paralysis', *Journal of Contingencies and Crisis Management*, 9 (4): 189–199.

Mitchell, D. and Staeheli, L. A. (2005) 'Permitting protest: the fine geography of dissent in America', *International Journal of Urban and Regional Research*, 29 (4): 796–813.

Morrison, P. A. and Lowry, I. S. (1994) 'A riot of color: the demographic setting', in M. Baldassare (ed.), *The Los Angeles Riots: Lessons for the Urban Future*. Oxford: Westview Press.

Muir, H. (2006) 'Yard wants ban on flag-burning in crackdown on demos by extremists', *The Guardian*, 30 October 2006.

Murray, G. (2006) 'France: the riots and the republic', *Race and Class*, 47 (4): 26–45.

New York Civil Liberties Union (NCLU) (2003) *Arresting Protest: A Special Report of the New York Civil Liberties Union on New York City's Protest Policies at the February 15, 2003 Antiwar Demonstration in New York City*. New York: NCLU.

Noakes, J.A. and Gillham, P. F. (2006) 'Aspects of the "new penology" in the police response to major political protests in the United States, 1999–2000', in D. della Porta, A, Peterson and H. Reiter (eds), *The Policing of Transnational Protest*. Aldershot: Ashgate.

Noakes, J.A., Klocke, B. and Gillham, P. F. (2005) 'Whose streets? Police and protester struggles over space in Washington, DC, September 2001', *Policing and Society*, 15 (3): 235–54.

Oldham Advertiser (2003) 'Week one of Oldham riots court hearing', *Oldham Advertiser*, 10 April 2003.

Oldham Law Centre (2001) *A Contribution to an 'Oldham Independent Review' – An Inquiry into Racial Viloence in Oldham.* Oldham: Oldham Law Centre.

Oldham Partnership Board (2001) *Building a Shared Future for Oldham: Interim Report to the Home Secretary, June 2001.* Oldham Metropolitan Borough Council and Greater Manchester Police.

Oliver, M. L., Johnson, J. H., Jnr and Farrell, W. C., Jnr (1993) 'Anatomy of a rebellion: a political-economic analysis', in R. Gooding-Williams (ed.), *Reading Rodney King: Reading Urban Uprising.* London: Routledge.

O'Neill, K. (2004) 'Transnational protest: states, circuses and conflict at the frontline of global politics', *International Studies Review*, 6: 233–51.

O'Neill, M. (2005) *Policing Football: Social Interaction and Negotiated Disorder.* London: Palgrave Macmillan.

Otten, M. H. P., Boin, R. A. and van der Torre, E. J. (2001) *Dynamics of Disorder: Lessons from Two Dutch Riots.* The Hague: Crisis Research Center, Leiden University.

Ouseley, H. (2001) *Community Pride Not Prejudice: Making Diversity Work in Bradford.* Bradford: Bradford Vision.

Parry, M. and Malcolm, D. (2004) 'England's Barmy Army: commercialization, masculinity and nationalism', *International Review for the Sociology of Sport*, 39 (1): 74–94.

Pearce, J. and Bujra, J. (2006) 'Young men without a future who brought terror to a city', *Yorkshire Post*, 1 July 2006.

Pennant, C. and Nicholls, A. (2006) *Thirty Years of Hurt: The History of England's Hooligan Army.* Hove: Pennant Books.

Perryman, M. (2002) 'Hooligan wars', in M. Perryman (ed.), *Hooligan Wars: Causes and Effects of Football Violence.* Edinburgh and London: Mainstream Publishing.

Petersilia, J. and Abrahamse, A. (1994) 'A profile of those arrested', in M. Baldassare (ed.), *The Los Angeles Riots: Lessons for the Urban Future.* Oxford: Westview Press.

Porter, B. and Dunn, M. (1984) *The Miami Riot of 1980: Crossing the Bounds.* Massachusetts: Lexington Books.

Post, J. and Younce, D. (1996) 'Protests explode over killing by Florida cop', *The Militant*, 60 (41), 18 November 1996. http://www.themilitant.com/1996/6041/6041_16.html.

Poulton, E. (2005) 'English media representation of football-related disorder: "brutal, short-hand and simplifying?"', *Sport in Society*, 8 (1): 27–47.

Power, A. and Tunstall, R. (1997) *Dangerous Disorder: Riots and Violent Disturbances in Thirteen Areas of Britain, 1991–92.* York: York Publishing Services/Joseph Rowntree Foundation.

Poynting, S. (2006) 'What caused the Cronulla riot?', *Race and Class*, 48 (1): 85–92.

Ray, L. and Smith, D. (2004) 'Racist offending, policing and community conflict', *Sociology*, 38 (4): 681–699.

Reicher, S. D. (1984) 'The St Paul's riot: an exploration of the limits of crowd action in terms of a social identity model', *European Journal of Social Psychology*, 14: 1–24.

Reicher, S. D. (1996) '"The Battle of Westminster": developing the social identity model of crowd behaviour in order to explain the initiation and development of collective conflict', *European Journal of Social Psychology*, 26: 115–134.

Reicher, S., Stott, C., Cronin, P. and Adang, O. (2004) 'An integrated approach to crowd psychology and public order policing', *Policing: An International Journal of Police Strategies and Management*, 17 (4): 558–572.

Reiner, R. (1985) *The Politics of the Police*. Harvester Wheatsheaf.

Ritchie, D. (2001) *Oldham Independent Review Panel Report*. Oldham: Oldham Metropolitan Borough Council and Greater Manchester Police.

Robins, D. and Cohen, P. (1978) *Knuckle Sandwich*. Harmondsworth: Penguin.

Rumsby, B. (2006) 'Barwick salutes England fans', Sporting Life, 4 July 2006. http://worldcup.sportinglife.com/football/teams/story_get.cgi?STORY_NAME=soccer/06/07/04/WORLDCUP_England_Fans.html&TEAMHD=england&PAGE_TYPE=news.

Sage, A. (2005) 'Deaths spark riot of gang youths', *Timesonline*, 31 August 2005. http://www.timesonline.co.uk/article/0,,13509-1850936,00.html.

Schnaubelt, C. M. (1997) 'Lessons in command and control from the Los Angeles riots', *Parameters*, Summer: 88–109. Reprinted at http://www.militarymuseum.org.LAriots1.html.

Schweingruber, D. (2000) 'Mob soociology and escalated force: sociology's contribution to repressive police tactics', *The Sociological Quarterly*, 41 (3): 371–389.

Sears, D. O. (1994) 'Urban rioting in Los Angeles: a comparison of 1965 with 1992', in M. Baldassare (ed.), *The Los Angeles Riots: Lessons for the Urban Future*. Oxford: Westview Press.

Seenan, G. and Vidal, J. (2005) 'Flashpoint feared at today's rally', *The Guardian*, 4 July 2005.

Shapiro, E. S. (2002) 'Interpretations of the Crown Heights riot', *American Jewish History*, 90 (2): 97–122.

Shapiro, E. S. (2006) *Crown Heights: Blacks, Jews and the 1991 Brooklyn Riot*. Walthan, Massachusetts: Brandeis University Press.

Smelser, N. (1962) *Theory of Collective Behaviour*. New York: Free Press.

Smith, D. J. and Gray, J. (1985) *Police and People in London* (The PSI Report). Aldershot: Gower.

Smith, J. (2001) 'Globalizing resistance: the Battle of Seattle and the future of social movements', *Mobilization: An International Journal*, 6 (1): 1–19.

Spiegel, J. P. (1969) 'Hostility, aggression and violence', in A. D. Grimshaw (ed.), *Racial Violence in the United States*. Chicago: Aldine Publishing Co.

Starr, A. (2006) '". . . (Excepting barricades erected to prevent us from peacefully assembling)": so-called "violence" in the global north alterglobalization movement', *Social Movement Studies*, 5 (1): 61–81.

Stol, W. P. and Bervoets, E. J. A. (2002) 'Policing Dutch-Moroccan youth', *Policing and Society*, 12 (3): 191–200.

Stott, C. (2003) 'Police expectations and the control of English soccer fans at "Euro 2000"', *Policing: An International Journal of Police Strategies and Management*, 26 (4): 640–655.

Stott, C., Adang, O., Livingstone, A. and Schreiber, M. (2006) 'Variability in the collective behaviour of England fans at Euro 2004: public order policing, social identity, intergroup dynamics and social change', *European Journal of Social Psychology*, 36: 1–26.

Stott, C. and Drury, J. (2000) 'Crowds, context and identity: dynamic categorization processes in the "poll tax riot"', *Human Relations*, 53 (2): 247–273.

Stott, C., Hutchinson, P. and Drury, J. (2001) '"Hooligans" abroad? Intergroup dynamics, social identity and participation in collective "disorder" at the 1998 World Cup Finals', *British Journal of Social Psychology*, 40: 359–384.

Stott, C. and Pearson, G. (2006) 'Football banning orders, proportionality and public order policing', *The Howard Journal*, 45 (3): 241–254.

Stott, C. and Reicher, S. (1998a) 'Crowd action as intergroup process: introducing the police perspective', *European Journal of Social Psychology*, 28: 509–529.

Stott, C. and Reicher, S. (1998b) 'How conflict escalates: the inter-group dynamics of collective football crowd "violence"', *Sociology*, 32 (2): 353–377.

Taylor, I. (1989) 'Hillsborough, 15 April 1989: some personal contemplations', *New Left Review*, 177: 89–110.

Taylor, S. (1984) 'The Scarman Report and explanations of riots', in J. Benyon (ed.), *Scarman and After: Essays Reflecting on Lord Scarman's Report, the Riots and their Aftermath*. Oxford: Pergamon Press.

Uitermark, J. (2004) 'Looking forward by looking back: May Day protests in London and the strategic significance of the urban', *Antipode*, 36 (4): 706–27.

UK Indymedia (2005) 'What actually happened at Gleneagles yesterday: a personal account', 7 July 2005.
http://www.indymedia.org.uk/en/2005/07/317039.html.

United States Commission on Civil Rights (1993) *Racial and Ethnic Tensions in American Communities: Poverty, Inequality and Discrimination – Volume 1: The Mount Pleasant Report*. Washington, DC: The United States Commission on Civil Rights.

Useem, B. (1997) 'The state and collective disorders: the Los Angeles riot/ protest of April, 1992', *Social Forces*, 76 (2): 357–377.

Vasagar, J. and Ward, D. (2001) 'The five words that baffle Oldham Asians:

"Get out of our area" – That was the warning before the attack. But was it racially motivated?', *The Guardian*, 28 April 2001.

Veno, A. and Veno, E. (1993) 'Situational prevention of public disorder at the Australian Motorcycle Grand Prix', in R. V. Clarke (ed.), *Crime Prevention Studies, Volume 1*. New York: Criminal Justice Press.

Vitale, A. S. (2005a) 'Innovation and institutionalization: factors in the development of "Quality of Life" policing in New York City', *Policing and Society*, 15 (2): 99–124.

Vitale, A. S. (2005b) 'From negotiated management to command and control: how the New York Police Department polices protests', *Policing and Society*, 15 (3): 283–304.

Vulliamy, E. (2005) 'Rumours of a riot', *The Guardian*, 29 November 2005.

Waddington, D. (1987) 'The summer of '81 revisited: an analysis of Sheffield's Haymarket fracas', in A. Cashdan and M. Jordin (eds), *Studies in Communication*. Oxford: Blackwell.

Waddington, D. (1992) *Contemporary Issues in Public Disorder: A Comparative and Historical Approach*. London: Routledge.

Waddington, D. (1996) 'Key issues and controversies', in C. Critcher and D. Waddington (eds), *Policing Public Order: Theoretical and Practical Issues*. Aldershot: Avebury.

Waddington, D. (1998) 'Waddington versus Waddington: public order theory on trial', *Theoretical Criminology*, 2 (3): 373–394.

Waddington, D. (2001) 'Trouble at mill towns', *The Psychologist*, September 2001, 14 (9): 454–55.

Waddington, D. and Critcher, C. (2000) 'Policing pit closures, 1984–1992', in R. Bessel and C. Elmsley (eds), *Patterns of Provocation: Police and Public Disorder*. Oxford: Berghahn Books.

Waddington, D., Jones, K. and Critcher, C. (1987) 'Flashpoints of public disorder', in G. Gaskell and R. Benewick (eds), *The Crowd in Contemporary Britain*. London: Sage.

Waddington, D., Jones, K. and Critcher, C. (1989) *Flashpoints: Studies in Public Disorder*. London: Routledge.

Waddington, D. and King, M. (2005) 'The disorderly crowd: from classical psychological reductionism to socio-contextuel theory – the impact on public order policing strategies', *The Howard Journal*, 44(5): 490–503.

Waddington, P. A. J. (1987) 'Towards paramilitarism? Dilemmas in the policing of public order', *British Journal of Criminology*, 27 (1): 37–46.

Waddington, P. A. J. (1991) *The Strong Arm of the Law: Armed and Public Order Policing*. Oxford: Clarendon.

Waddington, P. A. J. (1993a) 'Dying in a ditch: the use of police powers in public order', *International Journal of the Sociology of Law*, 21: 335–353.

Waddington, P. A. J. (1993b) 'The case against paramilitary policing considered', *British Journal of Criminology*, 33 (3): 353–373.

Waddington, P. A. J. (1994a) 'Coercion and accommodation: policing public order after the Public Order Act', *British Journal of Sociology*, 45 (3): 367–385

Waddington, P. A. J. (1994b) *Liberty and Order: Public Order Policing in a Capital City*. London: UCL Press.

Waddington, P. A. J. (1998) 'Controlling protest in contemporary historical and comparative perspective', in D. della Porta and H. Reiter (eds), *Policing Protest: The Control of Mass Demonstrations in Western Democracies*. Minneapolis, Minnesota: University of Minnesota Press.

Waddington, P. A. J. (2000a) 'Public order policing: citizenship and moral ambiguity', in F. Leishman, B. Loveday and S. Savage (eds), *Core Issues in Policing*. Harlow: Pearson Education. (Second edition.)

Waddington, P. A. J. (2000b) 'Orthodoxy and advocacy in criminology', *Theoretical Criminology*, 4 (1): 93–111.

Waddington, P. A. J. (2003) 'Policing public order and political contention', in T. Newburn (ed.), *Handbook of Policing*. Cullompton: Willan Publishing.

Walsh, D. (2001) 'Three nights of rioting follow police shooting in Cincinnati', *World Socialist Web Site*, 13 April 2001. http://www.wsws.org/articles/2001/apr2001/riot-a13.shtml.

Waple, A. (2005) 'City's Ring of Steel: police launch biggest ever operation as ministers get down to talks', *The Star*, 15 June 2005.

Walton, J. (1987) 'Urban protest and the global political economy: the IMF riots', in M.P. Smith and J. R. Feagin (eds), *The Capitalist City*. Oxford: Blackwell.

Webster, C. (1997) 'The construction of British "Asian" criminality', *International Journal of the Sociology of Law*, 25: 65–86.

Webster, W. (1992) *The City in Crisis: A Report by the Special Advisor to the Board of Police Commissioners on the Civil Disorder in Los Angeles*. Los Angeles: Special Advisor Study.

Weed, M. (2001) 'Ing-ger-land at Euro 2000: how "Handbags at 20 paces" was portrayed as a full-scale riot', *International Review for the Sociology of Sport*, 36 (4): 407–424.

White, J. (2001a) 'Law and order crackdown in aftermath of Cincinnati riots', *World Socialist Web Site*, 26 April 2001. http://wwww.wsws.org/articles/2001/apr2001/cinc-a26.shtml.

White, J. (2001b) 'The Cincinnati riots and the class divide in America – Part 1: gentrification and police repression', *World Socialist Web Site*, 24 May 2001. http://www.wsws.org/articles/2001/may2001/cin1-m24.shtml.

White, J. (2001c) 'The Cincinnati riots: social inequality in the Queen city', *World Socialist Web Site*, 26 June 2001. http://www.wsws.org/articles/2001/jun2001/cinc-j26.shtml.

Williams, J. (2002) 'Who you calling a hooligan?', in M. Perryman (ed.), *Hooligan Wars: Causes and Effects of Football Violence*. Edinburgh and London: Mainstream Publishing.

Williams, J., Dunning, E. and Murphy, P. (1990) *Hooligans Abroad: The Behaviour of English Fans at Continental Matches.* London: Routledge and Kegan Paul. (Second edition.)

Wozniak, J. (2005) 'Winning the Battle of Seattle: state response to perceived crisis', *Illness, Crisis and Loss*, 13 (2): 129–145.

Index

Added to a page number 'f' denotes a figure and 't' denotes a table.

improvement in protective
equipment 11
see also riot development; riot
gear; riot process; riot
promoters

value conflict 44
Vernon, Robert 82
vigilantism 108-9
violence
American urban riots 60, 65, 80
anti-globalisation protests 110,
111, 128
at football matches 167-8, 178, 184
factors conducive to 204-5t
people's willingness to engage in
57
police culture 35, 199
prohibition of demonstrations 33

'wait-and-see' defensive posture 122
Washington, DC
anti-globalisation protests 114t,
115t
anti-war protests 119-21
no-protest zone 111
Washington Heights riots 61, 64
Washington Peace Center (WPC)
121

wastebasket incident 54-5, 206, 207
weak accountability 196
weakness (police), and public
disorder 24-5, 96
weaponry, police 111, 116
Webster Commission 82
Wells, Richard 144
white flight 91
white victim statistics, potential for
rioting 98-9
women, non-involvement, British
riots 89-90
working class activity, football
hooliganism as 170-2, 185
World Cup (1990), Italy 174-7
World Cup (2002), Japan 166, 180
World Cup (2006), Germany 165-6
WPC *see* Washington Peace Center
Wright, Peter 143, 144

Y Basta 3
youth riots, Britain (1991 and 1992)
87-109
youths *see* ethnic-minority youths;
police-youth interactions
yuppification 63

zero tolerance 134-5, 136, 201